ROMANTICISM, REVOLUTION AND LANGUAGE

The repercussions of the French Revolution included erosion of many previously held certainties in Britain, as in the rest of Europe. Even the authority of language as a cornerstone of knowledge was called into question and the founding principles of intellectual disciplines challenged, as Romantic writers developed new ways of expressing their philosophy of the imagination and the human heart. This book traces the impact of revolution on language, from William Blake, Samuel Taylor Coleridge and William Wordsworth, to William Hazlitt, Jane Austen, Elizabeth Gaskell and George Eliot. A leading scholar in Romantic literature and theology, John Beer offers a persuasive new account of post-revolutionary continuities between the major Romantic writers and their Victorian successors.

JOHN BEER is Emeritus Professor of English at the University of Cambridge, and Emeritus Fellow of Peterhouse. He has published widely on Romantic literature, especially on Coleridge, Wordsworth and Blake, as well as on Victorian and modern literature. He was Stanton Lecturer in the Philosophy of Religion at the University of Cambridge for 2006–7.

D1827619

ROMANTICISM, REVOLUTION AND LANGUAGE

The Fate of the Word from Samuel Johnson to George Eliot

JOHN BEER

CAMBRIDGE
UNIVERSITY PRESS

CAMBRIDGE UNIVERSITY PRESS
Cambridge, New York, Melbourne, Madrid, Cape Town,
Singapore, São Paulo, Delhi, Mexico City

Cambridge University Press
The Edinburgh Building, Cambridge CB2 8RU, UK

Published in the United States of America by Cambridge University Press, New York

www.cambridge.org
Information on this title: www.cambridge.org/9781107412620

First published 2009
First paperback edition 2012

A catalogue record for this publication is available from the British Library

Library of Congress Cataloguing in Publication Data
Beer, John B.
Romanticism, revolution and language : the fate of the word from
Samuel Johnson to George Eliot / John Beer.
p. cm.
Includes index.
ISBN 978-0-521-89755-6
1. English literature–18th century–History and criticism.
2. English literature–19th century–History and criticism.
3. France–History–Revolution, 1789–1799–Influence.
4. Literature and revolutions–Great Britain–History–18th century.
5. Literature and revolutions–Great Britain–History–19th century.
6. Politics and literature–Great Britain–History–18th century.
7. Politics and literature–Great Britain–History–19th century.
8. Romanticism–Great Britain. I. Title.
PR447.B38 2009
820.9′145–dc22

2008054303

ISBN 978-0-521-89755-6 Hardback
ISBN 978-1-107-41262-0 Paperback

Contents

Preface and acknowledgments

This volume owes its origins to an invitation to give the Stanton Lectures in the Philosophy of Religion for 2006–7, eight of which were delivered in the Michaelmas term 2006 under the title 'The Crisis of the Word in English Romantic Literature'. I am particularly grateful to the Faculty of Divinity in the University of Cambridge for this opportunity, which provided a basis for most of the chapters gathered here. A small amount of work in the book has been published previously: Chapter 4 is similar to my contribution to the volume *1800: The New Lyrical Ballads*, edited by Nicola Trott and Seamus Perry (London: Palgrave Macmillan, 2001), while a section of Chapter 10 (not among the lectures given in Cambridge) was offered for the Gaskell Centenary conference at Canterbury in July 2007, subsequently to be published in the *Gaskell Society Journal.*

I owe a particular debt of gratitude to Tom Mayberry, whose lecture on Coleridge in Somerset at an early Coleridge Summer Conference first drew my attention to the diary of William Holland and its significance.

The discussions of shifts in British culture during the relevant periods could profitably be complemented by reading recent work on social studies, notably E. P. Thompson's *The Making of the English Working Class* (London: V. Gollancz, 1963).

Abbreviations

AL	*Jane Austen's Letters*, ed. R. W. Chapman (Oxford: Clarendon Press, 1952).
AN	*The Novels of Jane Austen: The Text Based on Collation of the Early Editions*, ed. R. W. Chapman, 6 vols. (Oxford: Clarendon Press, 1923).
BE	*The Poetry and Prose of William Blake*, ed. David V. Erdman; commentary by Harold Bloom (Garden City, N.Y.: Doubleday 1965).
BE ii	*The Complete Poetry and Prose of William Blake*: revised edition of the above (Berkeley: University of California Press, 1982).
BK	*Blake: Complete Writings with Variant Readings*, ed. Geoffrey Keynes (Oxford: Clarendon Press, 1957; repr. with additions and corrections in the Oxford Standard Authors series, 1966).
BQ	*Blake Newsletter: An Illustrated Quarterly*, continued as *Blake: An Illustrated Quarterly* (Albuquerque, N.M.; Berkeley, Calif., 1970–).
CAR	Coleridge, *Aids to Reflection* [1825], ed. John Beer, *CC* 9 (Princeton, N.J. and London, 1993).
CBL	Coleridge, *Biographia Literaria* [1817], ed. James Engell and Walter Jackson Bate, *CC* 7, 2 vols. (Princeton, N.J. and London, 1983).
CC	*The Collected Works of Samuel Taylor Coleridge*, general editor Kathleen Coburn, associate editor Bart Winer, 16 vols. (Princeton, N.J.: Princeton University Press, and London: Routledge and Kegan Paul, 1969–2002).
CET	Coleridge, *Essays on His Times*, ed. D. V. Erdman, *CC* 3, 3 vols. (Princeton, N.J. and London, 1969).

CFriend	Coleridge, *The Friend* [1809–18], ed. Barbara Rooke, *CC* 4, 2 vols. (Princeton, N.J. and London, 1969).
CL	Coleridge, *Collected Letters*, ed. E. L. Griggs, 6 vols. (Oxford: Clarendon Press, 1956–71).
CLects (1795)	Coleridge, *Lectures 1795: On Politics and Religion*, ed. Lewis Patton and Peter Mann, *CC* 1 (Princeton, N.J. and London, 1971).
CLects (1808–19)	Coleridge, *Lectures 1808–1819: On Literature*, ed. R. A. Foakes, *CC* 5, 2 vols. (Princeton, N.J. and London, 1987).
CLects (1818–1819)	Coleridge, *Lectures 1818–1819: On the History of Philosophy*, ed. J. R. De J. Jackson, *CC* 8, 2 vols. (Princeton, N.J. and London, 2000).
CM	Coleridge, *Marginalia*, ed. George Whalley and H. J. Jackson, *CC* 12, 6 vols. (Princeton, N.J. and London, 1980–2001).
CN	Coleridge, *Notebooks*, ed. Kathleen Coburn and Anthony John Harding, 5 vols. in 10 (Princeton, N.J.: Princeton University Press, and London: Routledge and Kegan Paul 1959–2002).
COM	Coleridge, *Opus Maximum*, ed. Thomas McFarland, assisted by Nicholas Halmi, *CC* 15 (Princeton, N.J. and London 2002).
CPL (1949)	*The Philosophical Lectures, hitherto unpublished, of Samuel Taylor Coleridge*, ed. Kathleen Coburn (London: Routledge and Kegan Paul, 1949).
CPW (Beer)	Coleridge, *Poems*, ed. J. B. Beer, new edn, Everyman Library (London: David Campbell Publishers Ltd. and Random House, 2000).
CPW (CC)	Coleridge, *Poetical Works*, ed. J. C. C. Mays, *CC* 16, 6 vols. (Princeton, N.J. and London, 2001).
CPW (EHC)	Coleridge, *Poetical Works*, ed. E. H. Coleridge, 2 vols. (Oxford: Clarendon Press, 1912).
CShC	*Coleridge's Shakespearean Criticism*, [1936], ed. T. M. Raysor; Everymans Library, 2nd edn., 2 vols. (London: J. M. Dent, and New York: E. P. Dutton, 1960).

CSWF	Coleridge, *Shorter Works and Fragments*, ed. H. J. Jackson and J. R. De J. Jackson, *CC* 11, 2 vols. (Princeton, N.J. and London 1995).
CTT	Coleridge, *Table* Talk [1835], ed. Carl Woodring, *CC* 14, 2 vols. (Princeton, N.J. and London 1990).
CWatchman	Coleridge, *The Watchman* [1796], ed. Lewis Patton, *CC* 2 (Princeton, N.J. and London 1970).
DWJ	*Journals of Dorothy Wordsworth*, ed. E. de Selincourt, 2 vols. (Oxford: Clarendon Press, 1941).
GEL	*The George Eliot Letters*, ed. G. S. Haight, 9 vols. (New Haven, Conn.: Yale University Press, 1954–78).
GK	*The Works of Mrs. Gaskell*, with introductions by A. W. Ward, The Knutsford Edition, 8 vols. (London: Smith, Elder and Co., 1906).
GL	*The Letters of Mrs Gaskell*, ed. J. A. V. Chapple and Arthur Pollard (Manchester University Press, 1966).
GL2	*Further Letters of Mrs Gaskell*, ed J. A. V. Chapple and Alan Shelston (Manchester University Press, 2000).
HW	*The Complete Works of William Hazlitt*, ed. P. P. Howe, after the edition of A. R. Waller and Arnold Glover, 21 vols. (London: J. M. Dent, 1930–4).
KL	*The Letters of John Keats, 1814–1821*, ed. Hyder Edward Rollins. 2 vols. (Cambridge, Mass.: Harvard University Press, 1958).
KP	*The Poems of John Keats*, ed. Miriam Allott (London: Longman, 1970).
LL (Marrs)	*The Letters of Charles and Mary Lamb*, ed. Edwin Marrs, 3 vols. only (Ithaca, N.Y. and London: Cornell University Press, 1976).
PMLA	*Publications of the Modern Language Association* (Baltimore: 1889–).
RX	John Livingston Lowes, *The Road to Xanadu* (London: Constable, 1927).
SW	*The Complete Works of Percy Bysshe Shelley*, newly edited by Roger Ingpen and Walter E. Peck, 10 vols. (London: Ernest Benn, and New York: C. Scribner's Sons, 1926–30).

TLS	*Times Literary Supplement.*
WL (1787–1805)	*The Letters of William and Dorothy Wordsworth: The Early Years, 1787–1805*, ed. E. de Selincourt; 2nd edn, rev. C. L. Shaver (Oxford: Clarendon Press, 1967).
WL (1806–11)	*The Letters of William and Dorothy Wordsworth: The Middle Years, 1806–11*, ed. E. de Selincourt; 2nd edn, rev. Mary Moorman (Oxford: Clarendon Press, 1969).
WL (1821–53)	*The Letters of William and Dorothy Wordsworth: The Later Years, 1821–1853*, ed. E. de Selincourt; 2nd edn, rev. A. G. Hill, 4 vols. (Oxford: Clarendon Press, 1978–88).
WPrel	*The Prelude 1799, 1805, 1850*, ed. Jonathan Wordsworth, M. H. Abrams and Stephen Gill (New York and London: W. W. Norton, 1979).
WPrW	Wordsworth, *Prose Works*, ed. W. J. B. Owen and J. W. Smyser, 3 vols. (Oxford: Clarendon Press, 1974).
WPW	Wordsworth, *Poetical Works*, ed. Ernest de Selincourt and Helen Darbishire, 5 vols. (Oxford: Clarendon Press, 1940–9).

CHAPTER I

'Democracy' in Somerset and beyond

The political impact of the French Revolution in England was strangely oblique, even when one remembers that it was largely being experienced at one remove. My concern here is not only with some examples of that oblique reaction but with language generally, and with the manner in which the growing questioning of authority during the period reflected a more profound alteration, taking place over a much longer period – a movement from what might be termed the language of fidelity to the cultivation of dialects that could be regarded as more critically oriented. To put the matter another way, whereas in medieval times writers had been so close to the religion of their surrounding culture that they did not need to think about the possible religious implications of their language, by the middle of the twentieth century, they would have become so self-conscious and self-critical that they could not write anything containing such implications and not be aware of possible commenting voices ranging from the harshly critical to the warmly favourable. The 1790s, I shall maintain, provided a crucial juncture for this development.

In addition, however, attention may be drawn to recent emphases in the writing of history by which the possibility of concentrating on a small and particular detail and expanding one's attention from there can be explored, or, alternately, one may begin by proceeding to the widest possible extreme and moving inward.

To begin with a 'snapshot' approach: on 23 October 1799, the Rector of Over Stowey in Somerset, William Holland, recorded in his diary a visit to the neighbouring parish of Nether Stowey, where, he said, he

. . . Saw that Democratic hoyden Mrs Coleridge who looked so like a friskey girl or something worse that I was not surprised that a Democratic Libertine should choose her for a wife. The husband gone to London suddenly, no one here can tell why. Met the patron of democrats, Mr Thos. Poole who smiled and chatted a little. He was on his gray mare. Satan himself cannot be more false and hypocritical . . .[1]

For a moment a shaft of light falls across a scene in which an old world is confronted by a new. The settled life of Somerset, an agricultural area deeply conservative in its ways, is being entered, perhaps violated, by figures of a different kind: Samuel Taylor Coleridge had already acquired a reputation in nearby Bristol for his advanced views in politics and religion; his wife Sara, a young woman brought up in Bristol, was evidently happy to exhibit her advanced tendencies by not dressing like the other women of the village; nearer home the views of Thomas Poole, well known as the local tanner, were believed to be not entirely patriotic.

What is also notable about this account is not only that it expresses a local immediate suspicion of someone who is known locally as a 'Democrat' but that when Thomas Poole appears a short while afterwards – to be labelled as 'the patron of Democrats' – the immediate description that comes to Holland's mind relates him to Satan. In his traditional universe, where good and evil are polarized, forces identified as 'Democratic' are automatically assumed to be on the side of evil.

Certain reservations must be made here. It would be easy, for example, to assume that Holland must have been a very old man at the time, yet he was still in his early fifties. Tom Poole, towards whom he shows hostility, was respected locally for his championing of local workers and for establishing a book club to help educate them, which survived for many years. Over the years Holland learned to work alongside such people and to live peaceably with them. But at the time he evidently did not at all like these new voices, or what they portended. It was only a few years since news of the French Revolution had reached English shores, with all its distressing possible implications for British politics; already there were fears that French troops might invade England – perhaps even make their way across and inside the Somerset coastline. The prospect of people like Poole and the Coleridges, given their reputation as 'democrats', perverting the minds of pious country folk with their ideas was seen as dangerous and unwelcome.

The fear reflected in some measure the alarm that had overtaken many upholders of conventional values as a result of the Revolution. During the

---

[1] *Paupers and Pig Killers: The Diary of William Holland, a Somerset Parson 1799–1818*, ed. Jack Ayres (Gloucester: Alan Sutton, 1984), p. 15. In addition to the living of Over Stowey, to which he returned in 1798, Holland held that of Monkton Farleigh near Bath, and may have heard there of Coleridge's earlier activities in the areas of Bath and Bristol.

century the very word 'democratic' had been less current, in reaction against the levelling views that had been abroad at the time of the Civil War. The bogey still existed, however: in 1775 Boswell wrote of a contemporary, Dr Joseph Towers, that he was willing to do justice to his merits since, although he abhorred his 'Whiggish democratical notions and propensities' (which, he said, he 'would not call "principles"'), he esteemed him as 'an ingenious, knowing, and very convivial man'.[2]

Holland's hostile account also directs us towards the sense of a fault line that had been developing in British culture for some time. Up till then it had been held together by a kind of loose unity, provided by institutions set up in a series of settlements – sometimes compromise settlements, but still in some sense unified. What had now affected the situation was the growth of a scientific body of work and knowledge that would underlie the new development of industrialism. William Holland and those who thought with him knew little of such developments; but when they saw newcomers in their village such as Mr and Mrs Coleridge they sensed the presence of an alien culture which they instinctively rejected. And once one looks further into the Coleridges' background, one soon senses the further causes for such concern. Sara Coleridge had been brought up in Bristol, by now a thriving commercial centre, and was evidently au fait with the latest fashions and new modes of thinking. Her husband, meanwhile, having been brought up in Ottery St Mary, a more conservative part of the country, had first been sent away to school in London and then from there to Cambridge, another traditionally conservative part of the world, but one which had long been penetrated by the new movements of thought initiated by Newton's theories and where religious ideas were being influenced by liberal-minded thinkers, including a fellow of his college, William Frend.

Holland's hostility evidently owed much also to the response of a neighbour, the Reverend John Poole, who happened to be Tom's cousin, and who lived in Holland's parish of Over Stowey. In general, the Poole family were well regarded. (It is probably no accident that the purpose of Holland's visit to Nether Stowey that day had been to buy a gown for his wife from 'Mr Frank Poole'.)

Tom Poole, on the other hand, had long had a reputation for radicalism. Like other people of the time, he had been able to contemplate with equanimity the deposition of the French king from his position of absolute

---

[2] See the discussion of 21 March 1775 in his *Life of Johnson*.

rule, even if he was now unhappy with the further possibilities that loomed. To a friend in London who was, like himself, a tanner he wrote:

I do execrate as much as any man that unnecessary instance of injustice and cruelty perpetrated in France, and should be happy to see every man who voted for the king's death brought to condign punishment. But 'tis not Louis' death, nor the Scheldt, nor the decree of November that are the causes of the war. It is a desire to suppress the glowing spirit of liberty, which, I thank God, pervades the world, and which, I am persuaded, all the powers on earth cannot destroy . . .

Many thousands of human beings will be sacrificed in the ensuing conflict; and for what? To support three or four individuals, called arbitrary kings, in the situation which they or their ancestors have usurped. I consider every Briton who loses his life in the war as much murdered as the King of France, and every one who approves the war, as signing the death-warrant of each soldier or sailor that falls. But besides these motives, what shall we not suffer in other respects? This country for some time past may be considered as the workshop of France; we have been growing rich by their confusion. And had Government, instead of the measures they have taken, promoted a rational reform according to the spirit of the constitution, we had, indeed, been a happy people. But now, adieu to all reform! There is no alternative between absolute quiescence or the most violent extremities. In the reign of Charles I, France had some shadow of liberty left; but the artful ministers of Louis XIV alarmed the people of that country with the view of the excesses of parties in England, and induced them to make their monarch despotick. I trust in God there is no similarity between the people of this country and of France at that time. The excesses in France are great; but who are the authors of them? The Emperor of Germany, the King of Prussia, and Mr. Burke. Had it not been for their impertinent interference, I firmly believe the King of France would be at this moment a happy monarch, and that people would be enjoying every advantage of political liberty.

The contemplation of this subject gives me great pain, and I think your sentiments will in general coincide with mine. The slave trade, you will see, will not be abolished, because to be humane and honest now is to be a traitor to the constitution, a lover of sedition and licentiousness. But this universal depression of the human mind cannot last long . . .[3]

Earlier in the autumn – it must have been soon after receiving the news of the September massacres – Tom Poole had already expressed to the same friend his grief and anxiety at the bloody turn that events were taking in Paris. Characteristically enough, he begins not with the madness of the people but with the crimes of kings:

Poor Poland, I pity her fate! Is there no vengeance from heaven for the Empress of Russia? Are her gray hairs to go down to the grave in peace? I trust not. I trust

---

[3] Elizabeth Sandford, *Thomas Poole and his Friends*, 2 vols. (London: Macmillan, 1888), I, 40–2.

that mankind will be shown that there is a punishment, even in this world, for such abominable tyranny. Louis XIV succeeded as well as the Empress of Russia, yet he lived to see his power lessened and his pride humbled. But Louis XIV, though he exhausted and desolated his own country, never was guilty of what this woman has done.

Speaking of a French despot we naturally turn to French affairs. What are your sentiments on the present crisis? Are all the horrid excesses and cruelties of which we hear necessary? – There is a something, my dear sir, in the character of the French which I thank God Englishmen do not possess. That savage levity which appeared in this late revolution, and, indeed, on a review of their history, always did appear in their civil wars I must abhor; that entire absence of religion and mockery of justice are detestable; but notwithstanding this, I think they did right in deposing the king, and they have an undoubted right, if they prefer it, to choose a Republican government. But why this disgrace to humanity? – As for Christianity, it is quite out of the question. Had human nature any cause to blush during the glorious Revolution in America?

The philosophers and friends to mankind that formed the first French constitution I admire and revere, and that constitution, the most beautiful fabrick that was ever erected by the human mind, gained ground and admirers every day; but it is fled like a dream, and I tremble lest the present excesses may not give a greater stab to liberty than the Tyrants of the world who are combined against it . . .[4]

This was not just a matter of individual countries such as Poland and France, moreover. The more one looks into the factors involved, the more one recognizes their complicated duality. We are, after all, dealing with various cross-currents, playing across relations between all the nations involved. Even if we simplify matters as far as possible, we have at least four bodies of culture interacting: France, Britain, Germany and the newly constituted United States of America; and in the case of each possible pairing the issues change. Each needs to be considered in turn.

In the case of relations between Britain and France, the Revolution came shortly after 1788, a year in which there had been anniversary celebrations of England's own revolution, the Glorious Revolution of 1688 that, with the end of the Stuarts and the installation of William the Third and his queen, had initiated a regime of toleration. To those with these events foremost in their minds, the coming of the French Revolution seemed to fall into a very natural sequence: the French were simply learning lessons that the British had absorbed a century before, and could now join them on the path of true liberty. The chief feature of the

---

[4] *Ibid.*, 42–3.

English Revolution, however, was that it had been conducted with little or no violence. As the events in France began to descend further and further into murderous excesses, those looking on from the sheltered haven of Britain became more and more uneasy, more fearful that fires were being lighted that would be hard to extinguish if they reached the English side of the Channel. So far as the English reaction was concerned, also, feelings were further complicated by the recent impact of the American War of Independence, which had caused mixed reactions in the Britain from which Americans were separating themselves but a more enthusiastic response in France, where there had long been irritation at the success of the British in occupying considerable areas of the North American territory. As the American War of Independence progressed, the French discovered a number of ways in which they could give quiet assistance to the insurgents.

At the same time, those who had the best interests of France at heart were forced to recognize that to follow British developments in certain respects might not be disadvantageous. They could not ignore the great strides being made by the champions of the Industrial Revolution, particularly in the midland and northern regions of England. There were even some hopes that Matthew Boulton and James Watt might be poached from the English Midlands so that they might settle in France and lend their formidable weight to the speedier industrialization of their new homeland Other engineers did come from England to help things along in northern France, but these particular commanding figures proved resistant to temptation and stayed in England: they indeed visited Paris, but it was simply to join in consultations concerning new steam machines that were to be installed in new pumping engines at Marly.[5] Events like these nevertheless meant that in France the long reliance on agriculture was beginning to give way to a mixed economy, which would inevitably change patterns of wealth and distribution – though as we all know, agriculture would continue to the present day to play a significant part in the French economy.

The result of these various factors was to complicate the relationship between Britain and France. On the one hand, French sympathies with the American insurgents and suspicion of British imperialist aims had led to a certain sourness between the two countries; on the other, if the revolutionary events were read as following the British lead, they could

---

[5] Simon Schama, *Citizens: A Chronicle of the French Revolution* (London: Viking, 1989), p. 232.

be interpreted more kindly in England – and it must not be forgotten that those French radicals who had been aiming to change things in their country had looked to the development of constitutional monarchy in England as a notable example for imitation.

When one considers the precise history leading up to the revolutionary events in France itself, one must also, of course, trace the domestic issues that led to such an outbreak of destructive passion. A harvest failure in 1788, for example, had resulted in extreme hardship. Simon Schama, who has traced such causes in great detail, pinpoints 'Anger and Hunger' as the main driving forces. The hunger became even more real as the price of bread soared beyond the means of ordinary labourers, while the anger arose from various factors, such as the enclosure of land that deprived peasants of their means of livelihood, or practices whittling away at long-established rights.

Although these were the immediate and pressing causes, however, wider and deeper factors made the prospect of a break with established ways possible and even desirable – notably in the larger cities, where intellectual life in France was being affected by what was happening in Britain and in Europe generally. (Nor should it be forgotten that Britain meant particularly Scotland, with its traditionally strong bonding to France.)

Even in Stowey, which may have seemed a little remote from Europe, some inhabitants were well aware of events elsewhere. This was certainly true of Tom Poole, whose remarkably intelligent and thought-out views have already been quoted, and who was well in tune with English writers as they faced the changes brought about in European thought at the time, having been living in London recently and now spending a good deal of his time in study. In 1794 he shocked his cousins, including John Poole, who was training for ordination, by bringing to the house the latest of his friends, Samuel Taylor Coleridge and Robert Southey. John kept a diary in Latin, where he recorded his shocked response:

Each of them was shamefully hot with Democratic rage as regards politics, and both Infidel as to religion. I was extremely indignant.[6]

In recording Coleridge's religious views Tom himself was more punctiliously accurate:

His aberrations from prudence, to use his own expression, have been great; but he now promises to be as sober and rational as his most sober friends could wish.

[6] Sandford, *Thomas Poole*, I, 103.

In religion he is a Unitarian, if not a Deist; in politicks a Democrat, to the utmost extent of the word.

Of Southey, on the other hand, he wrote that he was 'more violent in his principles than even Coldridge [sic] himself. In Religion, shocking to say in a mere Boy as he is, I fear he wavers between Deism and Atheism.'[7]

The visit of the two young men left a vivid impression on the family, where the story persisted of how when John Poole brought the news of Robespierre's death to Stowey, it was to find his cousin Tom with these two young men, who did not show the feelings that right-thinking people might have been expected to manifest at such a piece of intelligence. Instead, one of them – Southey – actually laid his head down upon his arms and exclaimed, 'I had rather have heard of the death of my own father.'[8]

There was a different emphasis in the emotions with which another contemporary greeted the latest developments, however. Wordsworth, who had been following events closely, knew more of Robespierre's reputation and its growing ferocity, so that when he heard the latest news while standing by the Leven estuary, his response was rather one of exultation As he watched a group of travellers who had just been guided along the perilous way across the sands there, he found that one of them was eager to make known the latest development.

> . . . the foremost of the band
> As he approached, no salutation given
> In the familiar language of the day,
> Cried, 'Robespierre is dead!' nor was a doubt,
> After strict question, left within my mind
> That he and his supporters all were fallen.
> Great was my transport, deep my gratitude
> To everlasting Justice, by this fiat
> Made manifest. 'Come now, ye golden times',
> Said I forth-pouring on those open sands
> A hymn of triumph: 'as the morning comes
> From out the bosom of the night, come ye:
> Thus far our trust is verified; behold!
> They who with clumsy desperation brought
> A river of Blood, and preached that nothing else
> Could cleanse the Augean stable, by the might

---

[7] *Ibid.*, 96–7.   [8] *Ibid.*, 101.

Of their own helper have been swept away;
Their madness stands declared and visible . . .'[9]

Opposition to the Revolution had already been wakened, first by horror at news of the 1792 massacres, and then by the change of tack which led to the fate of Robespierre. Southey and Coleridge, who were encountering one another for the first time that summer, were so seized by the possibilities involved that they decided to collaborate on a drama, 'The Fall of Robespierre', which, according to their subsequent accounts, was finished at breakneck speed, and in high spirits. The event had not taken place until the end of July, and Coleridge dated his dedication, when it had been written and finally accepted by a Cambridge bookseller, 22 September. Much of August had been taken up with planning a move to America, and the plan of writing the play as a way of raising funds for it was evidently concocted towards the end of that month; the two men were meanwhile rapt in study of current newspapers, the results being evident from the accuracy of the detailed knowledge displayed.

It is significant that they were drawn by the fast-moving events of 1794 to attempt drama rather than any other literary form. It is also evident that although their prime intent was to celebrate the fall of a tyrant, they felt that Robespierre's qualities had been those of a good man perverted – which left them with a dilemma: how could freedom-lovers now proceed?

By this time, Coleridge, who had not only enjoyed the company of free-thinking undergraduates but spent some time as an ordinary soldier, was keenly aware of what had also become evident in France: that the business of government could not readily be undertaken by the common people as such, so that the idea of democracy needed to pass through various filters before there was any chance of its succeeding. Meanwhile, the debates in the country had polarized into the division between those who could be said to side with the 'Aristocrats', and those with the 'democrats', each using the word associated with the other as a term of abuse. The *Annual Register* for 1794 spoke of them as 'those two odious appellations . . . The former, bestowed on those who opposed all changes in the constitution; the latter on those who demanded these, together with an immediate peace with France, and an acknowledgment of the French republic'.[10] Those who sided most firmly with the French were of course proud to go further and adopt the term 'republican'. Thus Wordsworth,

[9] *WPrel* (1850) x. 570–87.   [10] Quoted in a footnote to *CLects* (1795), p. 8n.

drafting in 1793 the 'Letter to the Bishop of Llandaff', which he did not in fact publish, gave the author as 'A Republican'; in a letter to Mathews some months later, he wrote, 'You know perhaps already that I am of that odious class of men called democrats, and of that class I shall for ever continue.'[11] (Twenty-five years later he would be warning the Freeholders of Westmorland against seeking 'a remedy for aristocratic oppression by throwing yourselves into the arms of a flaming democracy'.[12]) As John Poole saw, both Coleridge and Southey were caught up in the current vehemence, so that Coleridge, asserting his demotic sympathies by undertaking a tour on foot that summer, wrote his 'Perspiration, a Travelling Eclogue', which began

> The Dust flies smothering, as on clattering Wheels
> Loath'd aristocracy careers along.

Returning to university, however, he already showed himself more circumspect, writing the second letter of 'democratic' as a Greek character.[13] In subsequent years, as we have seen, the word could be used as a term of abuse by a Tory such as Holland, though even then its double face meant that it was best reinforced by some further epithet if it were to strike home – hence Holland's 'Democratic Libertine'. Coleridge, defending his political principles to his brother George in 1798, adopted a similar duality: although he acknowledged that despite his rash statements in the past he had now come to a more mature attitude, he still maintained that he could not altogether regret the full process through which he had passed, even if the acquired opprobrium had continued to stick: 'I therefore consent to be deemed a Democrat & a Seditionist.'[14] It was no doubt a similar unwillingness to devote himself unreservedly to the people's cause that had caused him to refuse the term 'democracy' for the scheme he and Southey promoted for their planned settlement in America, developing instead the Greek verbal model, first to 'Pantocracy', then 'Pantisocracy'.[15] Despite its mannered appearance, the term avoided setting up an opposition between 'the people' and 'the aristocrats' by stressing the universality of its offering – to everyone, on equal terms. But the detail of the scheme also made it clear that this was a concept

[11] *WL* (1787–1805), p. 119.
[12] *WPrW* III, 183. Fifteen years later, he wrote, still more apprehensively, at Lowther, 'Hourly the democratic torrent swells . . .' *WPW* IV, 48.
[13] *CL* I, 119.   [14] *CL* I, 397.   [15] *CL* I, 84, 103.

that could make its way only by acting as a leavening; it must be adopted by a few enlightened participants before being offered for universal acceptance.

Coleridge's own subsequent account will bear repetition, since it suggests the extent of the dilemma produced by current vicissitudes:

From my earliest manhood . . . I perceived, that if the People at large were neither ignorant nor immoral, there could be no motive for a sudden and violent change of Government; and if they were, there could be no hope but a change for the worse . . . My feelings, however, and imagination did not remain unkindled in this general conflagration; and I confess I should be more inclined to be ashamed than proud of myself, if they had! I was a sharer in the general vortex, though my little World described the path of its Revolution in an orbit of its own. What I dared not expect from constitutions of Government and whole Nations, I hoped from Religion and a small Company of chosen Individuals, and formed a plan, as harmless as it was extravagant, of trying the experiment of human perfectibility on the banks of the *Susquehannah*; where our little Society, in its second Generation, was to have combined the innocence of the patriarchal Age with the knowledge and genuine refinements of European culture: and where I dreamt of beholding, in the sober evening of my life, the Cottages of Independence in the *undivided* Dale of Industry . . .[16]

One might suspect that this version had gained a little from the shift of events by the time it was written for *The Friend*, but as it happens it can be compared with a disinterested account produced by Tom Poole that September, which began,

Twelve gentlemen of good education and liberal principles are to embark with twelve ladies in April next . . .

Coleridge and Southey's opinion was, he said, that they should settle in a delightful part of the new back settlements:

each man would labor two or three hours in a day, the produce of which labor would, they imagine, be more than sufficient to support the colony . . . The produce of their industry is to be paid up in common for the use of all; and a good library is to be collected, and their leisure hours are to be spent in study, liberal discussions, and the education of their children . . . The regulations relating to the females strike them as the most difficult; whether the marriage contract shall be dissolved if agreeable to one or both parties, and many other circumstances, are not yet determined. The employments of the women are to be the care of infant children, and other occupations suited to their strength;

---

[16] *CFriend* (1809) II, 146.

at the same time the greatest attention is to be paid to the cultivation of their minds . . .'[17]

So far we have focused on a small and highly conservative part of the country and the impact on it of one or two people who had been touched by the new radicalism as it began to spread through one or two English centres. If we turn now to the much broader picture, both in Europe and America, and range more widely, recent developments in historiography may again be drawn upon. I have already produced one opening, the brief cameo provided by William Holland's account of his walk through Nether Stowey and his distaste at what he saw in the main street there; this, I suggested, might suit the method of viewing history by way of snapshot, presenting a single scene and then teasing out its implications. Alternatively, one might turn to the traditional method by which one puts together two or three strands and considers the relations between them, and adopt a broader approach: one might for example think about the French Revolution in terms of what it meant for metropolitan France and put that side by side with its implications for the French colonial developments of the time. A study of this kind would, for instance, dwell on Toussaint L'Ouverture and his ill-fated assumption that if Parisians were breaking their bonds, this must mean that the inhabitants of the French colonies were entitled to think that they too would shortly be emancipated.

Studies of this kind, which have produced notable works of historical generalization, have recently been overtaken by work of an even more generalizing kind that refuses to be bound by any constraints. I am thinking for instance of C. M. Bayly's tome *The Birth of the Modern World*, which responds to recent emphases on movements towards globalization by emphasizing the extent of interconnectedness that characterizes human endeavour across the globe. Once historians begin to think on this scale, the conjunctions spread almost interminably, in harmony with the myriad human activities presented for consideration. Various suppositions that have come to be taken for granted over the years may need to be modified – or even abandoned altogether. One of Bayly's own favourite revisions in this mode is based on an aperçu by Jan de Vries, who pointed out that the common focus on the 'industrial revolution' needed to be complemented by recognition of the fact that there was an 'industrious revolution', across many worldwide cultures, which had

---

[17] Sandford, *Thomas Poole*, I, 97–8.

little to do with the growing reliance on mechanization, more on the discovery of ways of increasing production by simpler means. Such devisings might boost production by way of simple reorganization, leading to an increase in production that had nothing to do with any technological advance.

If a study such as this demonstrates the difficulty of drawing large categories to contain phenomena in economic history that reveal themselves in such a multifarious form once approached in any kind of detail, much the same can be said of the political history of the time. What might seem at first sight to be a fairly monochrome landscape of relations between princely states yields on further study to reveal an intricate pattern of manoeuvring between those states by which they incessantly strove for positions of advantage.

Once the contemporary relations between states are seen to have been in fact so complex, also, the historian feels compelled to correct any misapprehension that statesmen were at that time largely preoccupied by the French Revolution. It was rather the case that Joseph II and the Tsarina Catherine were concentrating their attention then on the East, and in particular on Turkey and Poland. What was going on in Paris could be regarded as simply useful for diverting attention from those areas of concern, leaving the pair free to pursue their own ends without fear of interruption. It was not until the execution of Louis that it became clear that something more might be at stake: sovereigns thus endangered were encouraged to make common cause in their own defence.

The sense that the year 1795 marked a firm turning-point in English attitudes to the events in France can be supported by reference to the sermon which Bishop Horsley had preached on 30 January, the anniversary of the death of Charles I – an appropriate day on which to take stock of an event that had taken place nine days earlier, the execution of Louis XVI. According to Gary Kelly, moreover,[18] the September Massacres in Paris were compared with the St Bartholomew Massacres of August 1572, leading to an atmosphere in which the pleas for toleration that had become growingly frequent in England would be regarded as seditious. One consequence was that the cause of removing the disabilities suffered by Nonconformists was set back by several years.

The violence of recent events meant that discussions between the English and the French were likely to be centred on issues of politics,

---

[18] Gary Kelly, *The English Jacobin Novel 1780–1805* (Oxford: Clarendon Press, 1976), p. 50.

though it should also be remembered that since there was a good deal of intellectual traffic that had to do with the rise of science and the development of industry, it was not always easy to disentangle the current issues. This was particularly the case with intellectual life in the Midlands, where, as is well known, some of the leading figures grouped together to form the Lunar Society (so called because to assist visibility on the roads its members met at times of the full moon). One element in their culture was a devotion to Nonconformist religion. As it happens, both the two major figures involved also were originally ministers of religion: Godwin set out as a Sandemanian; having studied at the Hoxton academy he took some temporary positions and served as a minister for two years at Stowmarket – though incurring the displeasure of some colleagues by his refusal to make the doctrinal commitment that would enable him to be properly ordained. Although he shifted for a time into Unitarianism, he then moved back into his initial belief, before losing much of his faith altogether. In its place, the need for thoroughness of investigation, which had persisted since it was instilled into him at Hoxton, became the hallmark of his method as he embarked on the *Enquiry Concerning Political Justice*. Joseph Priestley, meanwhile, had emerged as a still more distinctive figure with his ministry at the Mill Hill chapel in Leeds, where he came to believe in the teachings of the sixteenth-century writer Socinus, that Christ was a mere man. He later assumed the leadership of English Socinians, expressing the opinion that they were the only body of Christians who were entitled to be called Unitarians.

At Leeds, Priestley clarified some of his beliefs about church organization and the role of the minister. He felt that the church should be governed by a body of elders or trustees who would be elected by vote of the congregation. The minister would have no special authority to run the church nor, indeed, to preside at the worship service. Able laypersons in the congregation were just as well authorized to preside, he believed: later on, in fact, he advocated the establishment of lay-led churches.

In 1773 Priestley gave up his ministry at Leeds to work as librarian and literary companion to the Earl of Shelburne and as tutor to two young boys in the household, after which he moved to Birmingham, where he was asked to become the minister of New Meeting, a congregation with the reputation of being the most liberal in England. This period was marked by the production of his most important works in theology. In 1782 he published his *History of the Corruptions of Christianity*, a work so offensive to the orthodox that in Holland it was officially burnt, while in England he was attacked by members of the orthodox clergy. One of his most vocal critics was Samuel Horsley, Archdeacon of St Albans, whose attacks on Priestley were regarded as successful, and who was made a bishop. During this period it seemed, in fact, that to win preferment in the Church of England, it was no bad thing to achieve a reputation as a Priestley-basher.

Priestley's succession of controversial religious papers included one claiming that, until the Council of Nicaea, where the doctrine of the Trinity was promulgated, the common people thought of Christ as a man and were, therefore, Unitarians. He studied extensively in preparing his books, stating that his search was only for the truth; and that if his investigations proved his beliefs wrong, he would be as happy to give them up as he would be to give up a scientific theory if experiments disproved it.

In the event, however, it was his combined reputation as theologian, scientist and political activist that proved his undoing. On 14 July 1791, when the Constitutional Society in Birmingham held a dinner to commemorate the destruction of the Bastille, feeling against him reached such a peak that a mob was aroused to destroy both the Old Meeting and the New Meeting and to attack his house a mile away at Fairhill, where nearly all his books, papers and scientific apparatus were destroyed. As a result he decided to go to America. (When Coleridge and Southey contemplated a similar move a short time later the knowledge that they had such an illustrious predecessor on whom to model themselves was one of their inspirations; one of the consequences of their failure to follow him was that when he died there was no body of such English followers to keep his views alive there.)

Such a combination of continuous scientific inquiries with insistence on the truth of the Christian faith, however heretically expressed, marks the essential point of divergence between thinkers such as Godwin and Priestley and their counterparts across the Channel, where the quest for freedom of thought tended to lead away from religious affirmations, if not into downright atheism. During the 1790s the implications of these ideas were not lost on the rising number of novelists who dealt with such issues.

At the same time, such novelists were not necessarily unidirectional in their political interests. One of the most interesting studies of them, by Gary Kelly, is entitled *The Jacobin Novel* – perhaps, a misnomer if it suggests a degree of commitment that their authors were far from making. It is important, in fact, to distinguish between the kind of thought that is natural to someone who is trying to produce a piece of connected reasoning and that which comes more naturally to a novelist, for whom an important concern will be to ensure that his audience is entertained. In this respect one might bear in mind an observation by Godwin, as reported by Kelly:

When we met him I had taken no breakfast; and though we had set off from Burton that morning at six, and I spent the whole morning in riding and walking, I felt no inconvenience on waiting for food till our dinner time at two, I was so much interested with Mr Bage's conversation.[19]

Kelly points out that coming from a man who was so familiar with opportunities for intellectual conversation in London, this was high tribute; and that Bage may be claimed to have been in touch with a wider spectrum of eighteenth-century thought than Godwin himself. Certainly he was immersed in the technological interests of the time by reason of his work as a paper manufacturer, and in the intellectual through his membership of the Derby Philosophical Society, where he encountered, among others, Erasmus Darwin and his son Robert, Josiah Wedgwood and his inventor cousin Ralph, William Strutt, eldest son of Jedediah (the mechanical genius who improved the stocking-frame), Joseph Strutt, one of the founders of the Derby Society for Political Information,[20] William Duesbury the china manufacturer and Sir Brooke Boothby.

As one looks at all these figures their lack of commitment to religious dogma is striking. Bage, for instance, began writing fiction in his fifties – his reason, as given to Godwin,[21] being the need for distraction from his recent financial difficulties after the failure of an iron manufactory that he had embarked on with Erasmus Darwin, Samuel Garbett and John Barker, a local banker.[22] His main examples were Fielding and, even more, Smollett, his plots being, as Kelly puts it, 'diffuse, digressive, and cumulative in incident and moral effect, gathering events and characters and conversations around certain ideas, rather than working logically to a conclusion like the plots of Holcroft and Godwin'.[23]

Bage himself, who was, according to Kelly, a materialist, evidently sympathized with Nonconformity, though John H. Sutherland has

[19] C. Kegan Paul, *William Godwin, His Friends and Contemporaries*, 2 vols. (London: H. S. King, 1876), I, 263.

[20] Jenny Uglow, *The Lunar Men: The Friends Who Made the Future, 1730–1810* (London: Faber, 2002), p. 455.

[21] Kegan Paul, *Godwin*, I, 263.

[22] This iron-rolling and slitting mill was set up at Wychnor, north-east of Lichfield, in 1765 and run by Barker till his death in 1781, but was never profitable; Bage lost £1,500. See Uglow, *Lunar Men*, pp. 109–10.

[23] Kelly, *Jacobin Novel*, p. 27.

argued that Scott was mistaken in supposing that he had had a Quaker upbringing.[24] One of his approaches to religious discussion in *Hermsprong* is to be found in the discussion of Dr Blick's behaviour:

'Is this,' Mr Hermsprong asked, 'a general specimen of the English clergy?'

'By no means,' replied Mr Glen; 'except a certain portion of rancour against those who differ from them in religion or politics (an effect probably springing from their *esprit de corps*), they are in general amiable rather than otherwise. But they are men. Sometimes in their too earnest desire of the good things here below, they are apt to forget those above.'[25]

Bage's references in this novel were closely contemporary. He describes with relish one of Dr Blick's more spirited sermons:

It was the 14th of July, an anniversary of the riots at Birmingham; where a quantity of pious makers of buttons, inspired by our Holy Mother, had pulled down the dissenting meeting-houses, together with the dwelling-houses of the most distinguished of that unpopular sect. The Reverend Dr. Blick did not say this was exactly right; he only said, that liberty had grown into licentiousness, and almost into rebellion. Indeed nothing could be more true; for to take the liberty to burn my house, for drinking my neighbour's health (the imputed crime), would be rather rebellious with regard to the laws, and licentious with regard to me.

'If ever the church can be in danger, it is so now,' said the good doctor. 'Now, when the atheistical lawgivers of a neighbouring country have laid their sacrilegious hands upon the sacred property of the church; now, when the whole body of dissenters here have dared to imagine the same thing. These people, to manifest their gratitude for the indulgent, too indulgent toleration, shown them, have been filling the nation with inflammatory complaints against a constitution, the best the world ever saw, or will ever see; against a government, the wisest, mildest, freest from corruption that the purest page of history has ever yet exhibited. Besides this political daring, one of their divines, if any thing divine could be predicated of so abhorred a sect, has absolutely denied the most important tenet of our holy religion, the Trinity in Unity; has endeavoured to take from us the comfortable doctrines of atonement and grace – and indirectly, the immortality of our precious souls; – for, unless they are immaterial, how can they be immortal? But,' said the doctor, rising in energy, 'what can be expected from men who countenance the abominable doctrines of the Rights of Man? Rights contradicted by nature, which has given us an ascending series of inequality, corporeal and mental, and plainly pointed out the way to those wise political

[24] See his 'Bage's Supposed Quaker Upbringing', *Notes and Queries*, 198 (Jan. 1953), 32–3; Kelly, *Jacobin Novel*, p. 21.

[25] Robert Bage, *Hermsprong, or Man as he is not* [1796], ed. V. Wilkins (London: Turnstile Press, 1951), chapter xiii, p. 44.

distinctions created by birth and rank. To this failure of respect to the dignitaries of the nation, and, let me add, to the dignitaries of the church, is to be ascribed the alarming evils which threaten the overthrow of all religion, all government, all that is just and equitable upon earth.'[26]

The allusions to the 'pious maker of buttons' and the 'Holy Mother', as well as the narrator's hostility to violence, strongly suggest the author's distancing of himself at one and the same time from Blick's reactionary stance and from the violence he is deprecating. This is in itself enough to support disparagement of the term 'Jacobin novelist' – a description which the writers themselves would have resisted, and which falls into the trap set by the 'Anti-Jacobins', by accepting the implications with which the latter were anxious to saddle their predecessors. By causing that name to stick, they could avoid terms such as 'ultra-radical' or 'ultra-democratic', and align them with those in France who had supported the excesses in Paris.

It was not only religion that proved controversial in this period, since a radical religious view might well consort with inquiries into science also. At the beginning of 1790, Erasmus Darwin asked his friend James Watt, 'Do you not congratulate your grandchildren on the dawn of universal liberty? I feel myself becoming all french both in chemistry and politics.'[27] Chemistry was of course a major point of contact between the English and French, particularly after the great controversy concerning oxygen. Priestley, after expounding his idea of phlogiston, noticed that a young French student was listening very intently, while saying little. This turned out to be Antoine Laurent Lavoisier, who went on to set forth his own theory of the element, which, after he had entitled it 'oxygen', testing it in new ways, went on to win general acceptance, Despite this, however, there was an unwillingness to adopt the word whole-heartedly, perhaps due to an atavistic leaning towards Priestley's eminence, so that both terms continued to be used for some years.[28]

Once again, however, the interdependence of different modes of discourse is evident, since the quality of oxygen, like that of electricity, linked itself with the idea of liberty. If it was possible to make such striking discoveries in investigating the natural world, was it not possible that similar discoveries awaited those who were willing to venture boldly into

[26] *Ibid.*, chapter xxix, pp. 92–3.
[27] Letter of 19 January 1790: quoted Uglow, *Lunar Men*, p. 436.
[28] See *CSWF* I, 765n. for some account of the position.

the field of morals? Even the most solid-seeming concepts might here prove more slippery and elusive than they seemed at first sight.

In these and many other ways, the questioning attitudes promulgated by the French *philosophes* would infiltrate not only English thought but that of the entire world; in the process the foundations of language itself would become unstable, though, as words themselves came to be seen as lacking in authority, it would also emerge that they could be profitably ambiguous.

All this was important at the intellectual level; in the ordinary world, however, the firmest advance prompted by the events in France was the spread of democracy in the form of government by way of elected representatives. In England the full extent of that reform would take a century to complete and would come largely as a result of pressure from large centres of population. Coleridge's distrust of 'the people' would remain rootedly strong since he relied primarily on 'the Few'. To T. G. Street he wrote in March 1817 that man must be governed 'either by an Aristocracy or a Fool-and-Knave-ocracy'.[29] But in order to produce such an 'Aristocracy', a few chosen spirits must be cultivated; in fact, the ideal democracy must be identified with a religious body – whether it were a church or George Fox's Quakers.[30] In this conviction lay the seeds of Coleridge's later pleas for the education of a 'clerisy' to carry forward the cultivation of wisdom in the professions.

In the meantime, much of the English countryside kept to its usual ways and more conventional attitudes. Reading on through Holland's journal, one sees how close he was in many ways to the kind of clergyman satirized by Bage. In October 1803 he wrote of a 'Mr and Miss Keats' that they could not come to dinner, 'having had a serious Rumpus among the Servants', continuing 'That tribe of beings are much altered of late years, no subordination among them. The Glorious Effects of the French Revolution.' Staunchly devoted to the Anglican Church, he was as firmly opposed to the Anabaptists as he was to movements supporting Roman Catholicism. Of one of his colleagues he wrote that he had been in Holy Orders and in the Church of England 'and Oh Shame, after preaching and doing Duty for half a year, he left the Pure, Sublime Service of the Church of England for the Tawdry Bloated and Overceremonious Worship of the Church of Rome the Scarlet Whore. He pretends from

---

[29] *CL* IV, 714.   [30] *CTT* I, 189, 263, 287.

pure conviction but I say from a disordered turn of the brain, and he has converted, or rather perverted his wife too.'[31]

Holland was anxious about the fate of Somerset and his native Britain in a Europe – and for that matter a world – increasingly dominated by the atheistic French. In that world Napoleon would shortly be assigned Satanic status, while a figure such as Coleridge could be given so subordinate a place that having already been dismissed as a 'Democratic Libertine' he could swiftly be forgotten altogether. This emerged some years later, when Holland met Hartley Coleridge over dinner in the company of Tom Poole. His journal entry on that occasion recorded simply, how he had met 'an odd genius a Mr Coleridge, I think a son of a Mr Coleridge who distinguished himself some time ago as a writer'.

Coleridge himself, who had not been at all perplexed when his father walked with him as a child under the Devonshire stars and vainly tried to invoke in him a sense of cosmic wonder – vainly, because his expansive imagination had already been fully awakened by romantic fictions he had precociously read – had meanwhile moved on to inhabit a world presenting challenges larger than any to be found in a Somerset village, or even from across the Channel.

[31] Ayres (ed.), *Paupers*, pp. 295–6.

CHAPTER 2

Politics, sensibility and the quest for adequacy of language

There are signs that from the time he arrived in Cambridge – and probably well before – Coleridge was thinking intensely about politics. Le Grice's account of his mingling of scholarly interest with what was happening in the world is relevant here:

Ever and anon, a pamphlet issued from the pen of Burke. There was no need of having the book before us. Coleridge had read it in the morning; and in the evening he would repeat whole pages verbatim.[1]

Le Grice's additional reference to the trial of Frend, which took place in May 1793, gives a clear indication of the period in question. By the following year, Coleridge had already run away from Cambridge, served a few months as a dragoon, been discharged and reprimanded by his college, and returned to Cambridge – only to abandon his undergraduate career once more and embark on the enterprise of Pantisocracy. All these events may be seen as responses to the extreme drama that was unfolding across the Channel. where guillotining and counter-guillotining responded to one another in quick succession.

The main impact on Coleridge at this time came from events and activities; yet because he saw himself from the beginning as a literary practitioner, it could not be long before he was responding to the effects on language itself of what was happening across the Channel. In England the movement of change was subtle. The phenomenon that is being presented here as a 'crisis' was in many respects subterranean, its working to be noted only gradually, yet sometimes expressing itself in changes of language. The stability of certain key words would be compromised, for example, one of the most notable being 'honour'. The problem resulting from such a disturbance was available to be sensed by acute readers, particularly in the field of fiction. We might consider, for instance, one

[1] C. V. Le Grice, 'College Reminiscence of Mr Coleridge', *Gentleman's Magazine* (Dec. 1834), 606.

of the most forceful documents of the 1790s: the novel by Godwin entitled *Things as They Are*, now best known under its other title of *Caleb Williams*. The story is a powerful one even for modern readers: a long narrative of flight and pursuit is set in motion when its hero opens a forbidden chest and discovers the villainy of his patron, Lord Falkland. Falkland responds to Williams's attempts to make known the wicked deed he has carried out by recourse to every available device, with the result that in the narrative it is Williams, not Falkland, who is always the fugitive.

To the twenty-first-century reader, the shape of the narrative is not unfamiliar since it corresponds to a recognizably modern theme: the hero who also feels compelled to act as whistle-blower and who faces an unexpected number of obstacles put in his or her way by the powerful interest that is being challenged. What is unexpected in Godwin's tale, however, is not the insight afforded into the problems of achieving justice but the degree of sympathy for Falkland that is eventually evinced by the hero in the final pages of the narrative, suggesting a similar movement in the mind of the author – particularly when he came to revise his text. The original manuscript version concluded with a final beating down of the hero in a trial scene, as Falkland adhered to his version of events and invited the court to consider Caleb's record as a thief, a prison-breaker and 'a consummate adept in every species of disguise' against his own irreproachable record as a 'benevolent and honourable' man. Reviled by the magistrate for his 'villainy', Caleb was cast back into prison, steadily to rigidify there until he was more a stone than a human being.[2] Presumably Godwin came to dislike the unadulterated pessimism of this ending: in the amended version Falkland was confronted not in open court but in the house of the magistrate, where Caleb spoke eloquently of his anguish at having brought things to this crisis, eventually so overcoming Falkland's initial scepticism as to the motives for such behaviour on his part that he confessed his own infamy and flung himself into the hero's arms. The result, however, was to instil a lasting sense of guilt into Caleb's mind as the murderer of his former patron – leading to the eventual statement that he had begun with the aim of vindicating his character and ended with the conviction that he had no character to vindicate. Instead of charging Falkland with evil villainy vindictively, as he had intended, he can now only regret that his patron should have adhered so firmly and for

---

[2] For the original manuscript ending, see the World's Classics edition, ed. David McCracken (Oxford University Press, 1970), Appendix I, pp. 327–34.

so long to a mistaken ancestral code: 'thou imbibedst the poison of chivalry with thy earliest youth . . .'[3]

The effect of the changed ending, however, was to alter the novel's achievement. When it was originally published, Godwin's aim was, he stated, to review 'the modes of domestic and unrecorded despotism by which man becomes the destroyer of man' – a propagandist end which would have been well served by the unrelieved persecution of Williams. But the novel even as it was worked out did not quite have that character, including on occasion fair-minded presentation of the workings of justice in action. The basic plea, as presented in Williams's final remorse, is rather for a large-minded benevolence, with the often-repeated assurance that a plain and honest account of the truth would inevitably have carried conviction: Falkland, if so approached, must have responded. That proposition is open to question, no doubt; but any 'propagandist' effect is restricted to repeated demonstrations of the existing prejudice in favour of the upper classes and against the lower.

The implication, therefore, reinforces the affirmation of honour as a human quality, even if to maintain it at the cost of criminal behaviour represents devotion to a mistaken ideal. And here, by contrast, we glimpse the reason for the support given to Edmund Burke (the *bête noire* of radicals of all ages) as he put the case for old-established honour as a political guide in response to the events in France. In a famous phrase he declared his belief that a thousand swords should have leapt from their scabbards to defend Marie Antoinette, the French queen, before she should have been allowed to be executed. Marie Antoinette was famous of course for her supposed remark that if the people of Paris were complaining of having no bread, they should eat cake (though according to one recent account she was maligned by her enemies in England[4]). But whatever the rights or wrongs of the case so far as her attitude was concerned, Burke was not being callous in condemning her accusers. His argument that one interferes with institutions at one's peril – something that France was to learn during its period of extended violence – was reinforced by the fact that it combined veneration for honour with some homage to the cult of sensibility.

Despite the response that Burke's eloquence was able to evoke, his voice would not be notably felt to be the most valid one during the next

---

[3] *Ibid.*, p. 326.
[4] See Simon Burrows, *Blackmail, Scandal and Revolution: London's French Libellistes, 1758–92* (Manchester University Press, 2006).

century. When in 1796 Ann Radcliffe, writing *The Italian*, was able to set up a situation in which the Marchesa and her confessor, plotting together, could argue themselves into believing the propriety of killing the good and virtuous heroine in order to save her from the sin of permitting herself to marry the Marchese's noble son, and so bringing dishonour to a noble house, every indication to the reader signalled the horror he or she was expected to feel at such a regard for 'honour', evidently regarded by now as unnatural; significantly, it was set against a foreign background. When Coleridge, writing to Wordsworth a few years later, produced his own recipe of ingredients for a popular sensational romance, it began with the words 'a Baron or Baroness ignorant of their Birth . . .'[5] And at the opening of *Persuasion* a decade later, Sir Walter Elliot's complacent regard for his own standing as a baronet makes him a ready butt for the novelist's satire. A century of egalitarian assumptions would follow – exemplified as the delusions of the Durbeyfield family led, in the person of Tess, to a tragic conclusion.

Although simple issues of reverence for the aristocracy might continue to trouble the nineteenth-century mind, then, a term such as 'honour' had been destabilized. Wordsworth, who could never forget that he was originally a republican, would return constantly to worry at its meaning. In the 'Sonnets Dedicated to National Independence and Liberty', he felt bound to look back to traditional emblems:

> In our halls is hung
> Armoury of the invincible Knights of old . . .[6]

When Britain was left alone after the Prussian defeat at Jena in 1806, similarly, he could proudly dismiss the enemies of Britain –

> a servile band,
> Who are to judge of danger which they fear,
> And honour which they do not understand.[7]

A few years later he could actually begin a sonnet on the same subject with the words 'Say, what is honour?', adding the reply,

> 'Tis the finest sense
> Of *justice* which the human mind can frame . . .[8]

---

[5] *CL* III, 294.   [6] *WPW* III, 117.   [7] *Ibid.*, 122.   [8] *Ibid.*, 132.

The very phrasing evidences the difficulty that he found in formulating his meaning satisfactorily. A far more crucial term of the time, prominent in the title of the sonnets just mentioned, was 'liberty'. The essential moral ambiguity of its significance emerged over and over again in the course of contemporary debates, the crucial line of distinction being seen to be that where 'liberty' passed into 'license'.

So far, these questions have involved the higher reaches of polite civilization. In the period under discussion, however, there were growing signs that the nature of culture was itself being redefined. Signs of this are shown by Godwin, who as he describes his efforts towards a new writing does not speak of searching, as a writer in the age of Johnson might have done, to achieve something with 'the stamp of authority'; instead, he recalls his belief that the world would only accept from him a work which had 'the undoubted stamp of originality'. In his reading of fiction, accordingly, he did not look for acceptable models as such but remembered his sense of what most now appealed: 'no works of fiction came amiss to me, provided they were written with energy . . .'

It is hard to think ourselves back into the world of that time, devoid of mass communications such as telephone, radio or television, a world of static forms rather than moving energies. Yet in the field of literature, at least, the scope for developing such new forces was already evident in the very proliferation of available words. In the sphere of newspapers, advances in technology – however primitive by comparison with later ones – were making experimentation freely available. This was one development that could be allowed to invade even Cowper's world of retirement:

> Hark! 'tis the twanging horn! O'er yonder bridge,
> That with its wearisome but needful length
> Bestrides the wintry flood, in which the moon
> Sees her unwrinkled face reflected bright,
> He comes, the herald of a noisy world,
> With spatter'd boots, strapp'd waist, and frozen locks;
> News from all nations lumb'ring at his back.
> True to his charge, the close-pack'd load behind,
> Yet careless what he brings, his one concern
> Is to conduct it to the destin'd inn:
> And, having dropp'd th' expected bag, pass on.
> He whistles as he goes, light-hearted wretch,
> Cold and yet cheerful: messenger of grief
> Perhaps to thousands, and of joy to some
> To him indiff'rent whether grief or joy.

> Houses in ashes, and the fall of stocks,
> Births, deaths, and marriages, epistles wet
> With tears that trickled down the writer's cheeks
> Fast as the periods from his fluent quill,
> Or charg'd with am'rous sighs of absent swains,
> Or nymphs responsive, equally affect
> His horse and him, unconscious of them all.
> But oh th' important budget! usher'd in
> With such heart-shaking music, who can say
> What are its tidings? have our troops awak'd?
> Or do they still, as if with opium drugg'd,
> Snore to the murmurs of th' Atlantic wave?
> Is India free? and does she wear her plum'd
> And jewell'd turban with a smile of peace,
> Or do we grind her still? The grand debate,
> The popular harangue, the tart reply,
> The logic, and the wisdom, and the wit,
> And the loud laugh – I long to know them all . . .[9]

As a picture of the world of journalism this remains surprisingly recognizable; at the time, however, it was immediately available only to the literate, who in many communities would be limited to a few on whom the rest would rely to know what was happening in the world.

Some years later Coleridge would write more admonishingly of the familiarity – amounting to a deadening of sensitivity – engendered by such a newspaper world:

> We send our mandates for the certain death
> Of thousands and ten thousands! Boys and girls,
> And women, that would groan to see a child
> Pull off an insect's leg, all read of war,
> The best amusement for our morning-meal![10]

This is a world drowning in words – words copious and fluently at the writer's command, yet threatening to deaden sensibility. In the streets of the cities, where printed information would later be produced by even more sweeping technological developments, the word of information was still basically that of rumour, passed from mouth to mouth. In such an atmosphere incitements to violence could swiftly spread: the Gordon Riots during the summer of 1780 were still comparatively fresh in the memory.

---

[9] William Cowper, *The Task*, iv. 1–33: *Poems by William Cowper*, 3rd edn, 2 vols. (London: J. Johnson, 1787).
[10] 'Fears in Solitude', 1798, lines 103–7: *CPW* (EHC) I, 259–60.

The emerging struggle involved two conceptions of civilization, the one based in the maintenance of ancient form and relying on institutions such as the Church and the monarchy, the other springing from the culture and customs of the people at large, close to the life of every day.

Julia Swindells has shown how this struggle could be very neatly focused in a small, enclosed community. In Cambridge, where for a long time it had been the custom for undergraduates to put on Latin plays as part of their classical education, the famous Stourbridge Fair also attracted various theatrical performers. Parliament's enactment of the Stage Licensing Act in 1737 has sometimes been put down to spite on Walpole's part against the plays of writers such as Henry Fielding: in other words, against theatrical satires on him and his government. Swindells argues, however, that the purpose of the Act was rather different: that coming very shortly after one concerning Oxford and Cambridge, the aim was to reinforce the universities in their attempts to guard their students against ready association with the common people and their language. In other words, they remained bastions of the teaching of Latin, the magic key for gaining such things as preferment in the Church or membership of Parliament and the government, and regarded as the language of authority.

According to this more established pattern, the situation that was taking shape presupposed a final state of settlement. It seemed as if language itself might soon be regarded as finally fixed – in which light Johnson's enterprise in constructing his Dictionary would be not only a natural development but the one most needed at the time. Johnson's own grasp was broader, however:

Those who have been persuaded to think well of my design, require that it should fix our language, and put a stop to those alterations which time and chance have hitherto been suffered to make in it without opposition. With this consequence I will confess that I flattered myself for a while; but now begin to fear that I have indulged expectation which neither reason nor experience can justify.

He holds up for derision the lexicographer who

being able to produce no example of a nation that has preserved their words and phrases from mutability, shall imagine that his dictionary can embalm his language, and secure it from corruption and decay, that it is in his power to change sublunary nature, or clear the world at once from folly, vanity, and affectation.[11]

---

[11] From the Preface to Samuel Johnson's *A Dictionary of the English Language*, 2 vols. (London: W. Stratham for J. and P. Knapton, etc., 1755), p. [ix].

In the debate after Johnson, two firm attitudes crystallized, asserted by powerful men who were both Whigs but whose assumptions led to diametrically opposed conclusions. Edmund Burke, who had already achieved fame as a writer on various subjects, was, wholly in the tradition of his time, classically educated and deeply read in the Roman writers – able to quote passages of Latin effortlessly, with evident expectation that readers would have no difficulty in reading and understanding them. His belief in the wisdom of existing arrangements has already been mentioned: since they would all have been achieved after considerable experience and thought, change would be reckless, undertaken at one's own peril.

Tom Paine, by contrast, free-thinker and son of a Quaker – a religious persuasion in which the study of Latin was not encouraged – lacked Burke's access to the classical tradition, being more ready to trust his own judgment.

Burke's attitude can be viewed as a direct response to Rousseau. As Charles Parkin pointed out in his brief study,[12] the latter's influential views were constructed round the assumption that human beings could be arbiters of their own fate by living according to the illumination of each one's individual conscience. Burke, by contrast, believed that to adopt this belief was to assume that created human beings could stand in judgment on the nature of their creator. This profoundly mistaken attitude, in his view, involved a setting up of the individual in private judgment. Paine, by contrast, leaping into print shortly afterwards with his short book *The Rights of Man*, and coming at things from a quite different angle, had no difficulty in combating Burke's grounding in a strong sense of the way things were and wariness of disturbing their ordering, given that one never knew what fine balance might be upset by even a small change. Having lived in America for some years, Paine was familiar with the ways that independence and the devising of forms based on simple and rational principles had progressed there. He had seen, in other words, a society constituting itself without the kind of apprehension displayed by Burke.

Reading the two critiques together now, it is hard to resist the conclusion that Paine had the better of the argument. In particular, he showed himself a more accurate recorder of recent events in France. In the event, however, it was Burke, rather than Paine, who swayed opinion in

---

[12] Charles Parkin, *The Moral Basis of Burke's Political Thought* (Cambridge University Press, 1956).

England, where those who were looking on at France were necessarily horrified by hearing of the events of the Terror.

One of the most knowledgeable of the onlookers was William Wordsworth, who, having seen some of the events at first hand, must have felt himself qualified to judge between diverging attitudes. He would evidently have known, for instance, that Paine, with better first-hand knowledge of events in France, was displaying a more informed judgment. The complex and entangled demands of contemporary political thinking are brought out by a long statement in the summer of 1794, when he presented his political views in an ordered form to his friend Mathews, expressing both apprehensiveness and an awareness of the need for restraint.

I disapprove of monarchical and aristocratical governments, however modified. Hereditary distinctions and privileged orders of every species I think must necessarily counteract the progress of human improvement: hence it follows that I am not amongst the admirers of the British constitution. Now, there are two causes which appear to me to be accomplishing the subversion of this constitution; first, the infatuation profligacy and extravagance of men in power, and secondly, the changes of opinion respecting matters of Government which within these few years have rapidly taken place in the minds of speculative men. The operation of the former of these causes I would spare no exertion to diminish, to the latter I would give every additional energy in my power. I conceive that a more excellent system of civil policy might be established amongst us yet in my ardour to attain the goal, I do not forget the nature of the ground where the race is to be run. The destruction of those institutions which I condemn appears to me to be hastening on too rapidly. I recoil from the bare idea of a revolution; yet, if our conduct with reference both to foreign and domestic policy continues such as it has been for the last two years how is that dreadful event to be averted? Aware of the difficulty of this it seems to me that a writer who has the welfare of mankind at heart should call forth his best exertions to convince the people that they can only be preserved from a convulsion by economy in the administration of the public purse and a gradual and constant reform of those abuses which, if left to themselves, may grow to such a height as to render, even a revolution desirable. There is a further duty incumbent upon every enlightened friend of mankind; he should let slip no opportunity of explaining and enforcing those general principles of the social order which are applicable to all times and to all places; he should diffuse by every method a knowledge of those rules of political justice,[13] from which the farther any government deviates the more effectually must it defeat the object for which government was ordained. A knowledge of these rules cannot but lead to good; they include an entire preservative from

---

[13] Possibly a reference to William Godwin's *Political Justice*, published in February 1793.

despotism, they will guide the hand of reform, and if a revolution must afflict us, they alone can mitigate its horrors and establish freedom with tranquillity. After this need I add that I am a determined enemy to every species of violence? I see no connection, but what the obstinacy of pride and ignorance renders necessary, between justice and the sword, between reason and bonds. I deplore the miserable situation of the French;[14] and think we can only be guarded from the same scourge by the undaunted efforts of good men in propagating with unremitting activity those doctrines which long and severe meditation has taught them are essential to the welfare of mankind. Freedom of inquiry is all that I wish for; let nothing be deemed too sacred for investigation; rather than restrain the liberty of the press I would suffer the most atrocious doctrines to be recommended: let the field be open and unencumbered, and truth must be victorious. On this subject I think I have said enough, if it be not necessary to add that, when I observe the people should be enlightened upon the subject of politics, I severely condemn all inflammatory addresses to the passions of men, even when it is intended to direct those passions to a good purpose. I know that the multitude walk in darkness.[15] I would put into each man's hand a lantern to guide him and not have him to set out upon his journey depending for illumination on abortive flashes of lightning, or the coruscations of transitory meteors.[16]

Wordsworth's hope that he might act as a guide to his fellow-men shines out from a passage such as this, and it should not be forgotten that he came from a devout Anglican family: his brother Christopher, who was ordained deacon at Norwich on 12 May 1799, went on to become master of Trinity College, Cambridge, while his grandson would become bishop of Lincoln. Dorothy Wordsworth constantly nursed the anticipation that her brothers would take advantage of their eligibility for ordination. As late as May 1792, William was still expecting to take orders during the next winter or spring,[17] though by February 1794 he wrote to Mathews, 'What is to become of me I know not: I cannot bow down my mind to take orders, and as for the law I have neither strength of mind purse or constitution, to engage in that pursuit.'[18] The period between had evidently convinced him of a change in his own opinions, which is not surprising when one recalls how in the summer of 1793, following the outbreak of hostilities between France and England in February, he had

---

[14] Between March 1793 and 10 June 1794 more than 1,200 persons were executed in Paris. *WL* (1787–1805), p. 124n.
[15] Isaiah ix: 2.   [16] *WL* (1787–1805), pp. 123–5.
[17] *Ibid.*, p. 76.   [18] *Ibid.*, p. 112.

been writing his 'Letter to the Bishop of Llandaff', where he found himself – temporarily at least – defending the French Revolution.

In the months following, his disillusionment led to a long period of depression, in which, he said, he 'yielded up moral questions in despair'. He was succumbing to what may be called, in a special sense, a contemporary 'crisis of the word', increasingly feeling the impossibility of undertaking a vocation in which he would have to administer not only word but sacraments also yet at the same time unable to abandon the conviction that he was in some respect a person set apart: that he had a special vocation, a task to fulfil – even if he was not quite sure what it would be.

For Dorothy there was no question where his special gift lay: it was, to her mind, his extraordinary ability to combine the natural violence of his temperament with an unusually highly developed sensibility. In a letter of February 1792, comparing her two brothers, she wrote:

Christopher is steady and sincere in his attachments. William has both these Virtues in an eminent degree; and a sort of violence of Affection, if I may so Term it which demonstrates itself every moment of the Day when the Objects of his affection are present with him, in a thousand almost imperceptible attentions to their wishes, in a sort of restless watchfulness which I know not how to describe, a Tenderness that never sleeps, and at the same Time such a Delicacy of Manners as I have observed in few Men.[19]

Wordsworth's own early literary efforts were eloquent of this sensibility. Looking for a literary language, he was drawn to the contemporary feeling for the Gothic, writing lyrics about betrayed maidens and setting them in churchyard scenes. But the most original pieces that he wrote were those in which he could display his sensitive reaction to nature. *An Evening Walk* enabled him to describe the subtlety of evening sounds:

> The sound of mountain-streams, unheard by day,
> Now hardly heard, beguiles my homeward way.
> Air listens, like the sleeping water, still,
> List'ning th'aerial music of the hill . . .

Dozens of sounds like these are seized on in the poem's four hundred or so lines, while the companion poem, *Descriptive Sketches*, aiming to catch the sublimity of Alpine mountain scenery, is nearly twice as long. For the most part, following the central tradition of long poems of the time, Wordsworth falls easily into the quiet inevitability of iambic couplets.

---

[19] *Ibid.*, p. 87.

William's absorption in the beauty of nature was something that Dorothy not only registered but longed to share. Writing to Jane Pollard in July 1793, she looked forward to the prospect of their all being together 'with health and strength equal to our vivacity and youthful ardour of mind':

> think of our moonlight walks attended by my own dear William, think of our morning rambles when we shall – after having passed the night together and talked over the pleasures of the previous evening, steal from our lodging-room, perhaps before William rises, and walk alone enjoying all the sweets of female friendship.[20]

For Dorothy, both the appreciation of Nature and the cultivation of sensibility cut across gender: her desire for friendship embraced not only her brothers but Jane, who, with William, was especially favoured. It also affected her religious view, where she could feel a particular delight and sense of the sacred in the presence of the sublime and the beautiful, withWilliam's ideas once again foremost. He in turn owed much to the influence of Rousseau, explored to the full in his own early poetry; he was particularly responsive to the role of women – already a matter of growing contention. For some years now the term 'sensibility' was most readily used in connection with their perceived function of cultivating the side of human nature that could complement the age's devotion to reason. The movement among women in the direction of emancipation had provoked a fierce polemic from anti-Jacobins as violating 'sexual morality and generic decorum as well as national political loyalty'. A typical text in this reaction was Richard Polwhele's poem of 1798, 'The Unsex'd Females'.[21] Those who resisted such forwardness felt that what had been a pleasing development in the opening up of human possibilities was in danger of being taken to an extreme. Women who supplemented their gentler expressions by demands for freedoms of their own might be opening the way to libertinisms of other kinds.

The injustice of treating women as inferior beings was already being questioned, however. Mary Wollstonecraft had achieved notoriety in Britain, largely through her association with other well-known English free-thinkers; moving to Paris brought her into direct contact with the

---

[20] *Ibid.*, p. 102.
[21] Richard Polwhele, *The Unsex'd Females; a Poem, Addressed to the Author of* The Pursuits of Literature [T. J. Mathias] (London: Cadell and Davies, 1798).

new thinking there. As Claire Tomalin has pointed out, Condorcet's writing on the subject had already been published in which he argued that

Either no member of the human race has real rights, or else all have the same; he who votes against the rights of another, whatever his religion, colour, or sex, thereby abjures his own.[22]

Whatever her knowledge of Condorcet's writing, Mary could hardly have avoided that of Diderot, who, in his *Supplément au voyage de Bougainville* wrote vehemently against traditional Christian attitudes to sexual behaviour, arguing for an approach involving nothing but simple enjoyment: 'since the act was both natural and pleasurable, why should it not be enjoyed without scruple?' Mary's future lover and husband, William Godwin, was writing on similar lines, except that his Dissenting heritage did not allow him to dispense with guilt so readily.

While Mary Wollstonecraft was slowly developing her ideas, Helen Maria Williams was gaining a notoriety of her own through her accounts of events in the Revolution, often witnessed at first hand. Devoted to liberty, she acquired the adverse reputation in England of being a suspect Jacobin and sexually licentious. There is little evidence for either charge, but the slur stuck for the rest of the century: when the first *Dictionary of National Biography* was published nearly a hundred years later, the entry on her, by a noted naval historian, ran, in part,

She freely wrote her impressions of the events which she witnessed or heard of, impressions frequently formed on very imperfect, onesided, and garbled information, travestied by the enthusiasm of a clever, badly educated woman.

After drawing attention to the number of enemies she made – who did not scruple to denounce her writing or accuse her of detesting all restraint, legal or social – the account continued:

in fact her writings are very much what might be expected of a warm-hearted and ignorant woman. The honesty with which she wrote carried conviction to many of her readers; and there can be little doubt that her works were the source of many erroneous opinions[23]

Wordsworth was evidently familiar with her writing: one of his early poems was entitled 'Sonnet, on Seeing Miss Helen Maria Williams Weep

---

[22] Claire Tomalin, *The Life and Death of Mary Wollstonecraft* (London: Weidenfeld and Nicolson, 1974), p. 104, quoting from his essay *Sur l'admission des femmes au droit de cité* [1790].

[23] *The Dictionary of National Biography*, ed. Leslie Stephen and Sidney Lee, 72 vols. (London: Smith, Elder, 1885–1913).

at a Tale of Distress'.[24] There is no hard evidence that he ever actually saw Helen Maria Williams at this time, still less saw her weeping, but the title shows what he valued in her at a time when 'sensibility' had become the fashionable word.

Her novel *Julia* is particularly interesting as combining contemporary sensibility with social satire in a manner to be perfected by Jane Austen. The plot, a not infrequent one in the late eighteenth and nineteenth centuries, involves a triangular relationship within a closely knit family environment. When Julia Clifford, the heroine, meets the intended bridegroom of her sister Charlotte, he immediately falls in love with her, realizing that she is the woman whom he should be marrying instead. Being a man of honour, however, he represses this impulse and goes through with his marriage to Charlotte – though without being able to suppress his love as far as the future is concerned. The indication throughout, nevertheless, is that a young man who allows his passion to run away with him in this manner, instead of subduing his inclination once it is clear to him that there can be no outcome which would enable him to indulge it, is at fault.

In her handling of the action and her commentary on it, the author shows herself to be fully in tune with current fashions of sensibility. Julia Clifford's behaviour constantly exhibits a link between her appreciation of nature and her impulse to show benevolence to others, this connection being traced to her cultivation of sympathy:

she bestowed her alms with that gentleness and sympathy by which the value of her donations was increased, and her pity was almost as dear to the poor as her charity.[25]

In her handling of Julia's state of mind, at the same time, Williams displays with strict accuracy the internal conflict:

reflection was at cruel variance with repose; since, whenever the idea of Seymour recurred to her mind, she was imperceptibly led into a comparison between him and others; and the decision which her heart involuntarily made, was by no means conducive to its tranquillity.

'But', she continues,

though she had not the merit of insensibility, the purity of her mind corrected the softness of her heart.[26]

---

[24] *WPW* I, 269. For his reading of Williams, see Duncan Wu, *Wordsworth's Reading 1770–1799* (Cambridge University Press, 1993). A review of her work in the *European Magazine* in 1786 may have prompted him to send his poem there.
[25] Helen Maria Williams, *Julia: A Novel* [1790] (London: Routledge/Thoemmas Press, 1995), I, 90.
[26] *Ibid.*, II, 2–3.

This is the constant burden of the story; it also gives the clearest indication of where she might have been led if she had listened to the promptings of her heart, which were unthinkable to her:

Her ideas of rectitude were of the most exalted kind; and no pain would have been so insufferable to her pure and feeling bosom, as the consciousness of having in the smallest degree deviated from those principles of delicacy, truth, integrity and honour, which were not only the inviolable sentiments of her soul, but the stedfast rules of her actions.[27]

Williams's principles, in other words, were always supportive of traditional conventions. Several of her comments return to the danger involved in allowing one's passions free play; in this respect her final words on Frederick Seymour are eloquent of her convictions:

Such was the fate of this unfortunate young man, who fell the victim of that fatal passion, which he at first unhappily indulged, and which he was at length unable to subdue. The conflicts of his mind, by insensibly weakening his frame, gave greater power to his disorder, and thus probably shortened the life they had embittered.[28]

Once again, the language of nature is brought in to reinforce a sense of the dangers of allowing oneself to indulge passion, even on the smallest scale:

We might as soon arrest the winds in their violence, or stop the torrent in its course.

Nor was Williams in revolt against the canons of the time. When she wrote her novel, she was still very much an Augustan writer, as one can see from her lasting love of balanced antitheses – particularly when marshalled in the direction of satire. Consider, for instance, her account of Charles Seymour:

If the rule of his conduct had been somewhat more noble, nothing could have been more praise-worthy than his adherence to it, which was uniform, and undeviating; neither relaxed by tenderness, or moved by admiration. Politeness, in him, was the offspring, not of benevolence, but of selfishness; and though he laboured to conceal its hereditary likeness, under the mask of ostentatious

[27] *Ibid.*, I, 128–9.   [28] *Ibid.*, II, 237–8.

urbanity, and studied candor, yet some lurking meanness, or insolent neglect, occasionally betrayed, to persons of penetration, its ignoble origin.[29]

While being primarily a novel of sensibility (and its dangers), *Julia* is also notable as displaying another early reaction to the sense of current injustice in France as manifested in the Bastille, the subject of one of the poems with which she intersperses her text: published as a 'prophetic vision', it might have been written several years earlier in line with current passages in such writings as Sterne's *Sentimental Journey* or Cowper's *Task*. The novel's date, however, makes it likely that when it was written the Bastille had already been destroyed; if so, Williams may have been employing it towards the end as a way of acknowledging what was happening in France, without presenting too open an endorsement, while still allowing herself to join in the general enthusiasm for what seemed a rebirth of the human spirit.

The immediate effect of this time of political rapture was also, apparently, to encourage a sense of sexual liberation. Both Williams and Wollstonecraft became attached to men while in France: Williams to the already married (though apparently unhappy) John Hurford Stone and Wollstonecraft to the Gilbert Imlay by whom she bore two children. Whatever the rights and wrongs of these situations, popular gossip read them as examples of sexual licence: apologists for the French Revolution had little fault to find, while more traditionally minded Englishwomen, such as Johnson's friends Mrs Piozzi and Anna Seward, were swift in condemnation. In the case of Williams, no clear evidence exists. The author of the recent *Oxford Dictionary of National Biography* article on John Hurford Stone takes it for granted that he was her lifelong lover, while the author of that on Williams draws attention to Williams's own declaration, cited by Oswald Knapp (editor of letters from Mrs Piozzi), that he was always a member of her family's household, which also included her mother and cousin, and that she had never been alone with him except during her flight to Switzerland after she was released from prison.[30]

At the time, however, women's attitudes were complicated by further considerations. In particular, they were aware of their physical vulnerability and troubled by the importance of preserving respectability. Richardson's *Clarissa* provided an important background text to all this,

---

[29] *Ibid.*, II, 59–60.
[30] See the entries for both women in the *Oxford Dictionary of National Biography* (Oxford University Press, 2000).

but the idea of physical rape, prominent there, could extend much more widely – even to the invasion of women's right to privacy. Thus a key incident in the Revolution, the assault on Versailles, and in particular the invasion of Marie Antoinette's private apartment, was denounced by Mary Wollstonecraft:

The sanctuary of repose, the asylum of care and fatigue, the chaste temple of a woman, I consider the queen only as one, the apartment where she consigns her senses to the bosom of sleep, folded in it's arms forgetful of the world, was violated with murderous fury.[31]

The text on which Wollstonecraft and others were drawing at this time was one that concentrated less on *mores* than on politics: Rousseau's *Discourse on Inequality*. Yet one could not consider raising the status of English middle-class women, a legitimate issue, and ignore the apparent viciousness of lower-class Parisian women.

The most important complication, the question of preserving female chastity, had a practical and political element, raising the question not only of adultery but of property rights for any children produced. The fact that methods of birth control were notoriously inefficient added to the complexity.

Behind this lay a further dilemma. One of the most appealing arguments for sensibility, the contention that it would be morally beneficial to the person cultivating it, has already been mentioned. It was the dear hope of the person most associated with the rise of the cult, the third Earl of Shaftesbury, a disciple of Locke, as propounded in the volume of 1711 to which he gave the title *Characteristicks*. Shaftesbury differed from Locke's unwillingness to entertain the concept of innate ideas and his willingness to see the mind as originally a tabula rasa, arguing that such a doctrine 'threw all Order and Virtue out of the World'.[32] It was impossible moreover, he argued, to be good and not simultaneously see the beauty of virtue:

No sooner does the eye open upon figures, the ear to sounds, than straight the Beautiful results, and grace and harmony are known and acknowledged. No sooner are actions viewed, no sooner the human affections and passions discerned

---

[31] *Vindication of The Rights of Woman* [1790], in *The Works of Mary Wollstonecraft*, ed. Janet Todd and Marilyn Butler; assistant editor: Emma Rees-Mogg (London: Pickering, 1989), VI, 209.

[32] *The Life, Unpublished Letters, and Philosophical Regimen of Anthony, Earl of Shaftesbury*, ed. Benjamin Rand (London: S. Sonnenschein & Co., New York: Macmillan & Co., 1900), p. 403 (cited by Janet Todd, *Sensibility: An Introduction* (London: Methuen, 1986), p. 25).

(and they are most of them as soon discerned as felt), than straight an inward eye distinguishes and sees the fair and shapely, the amiable and admirable, apart from the deformed, the foul, the odious, or the despicable.[33]

This note was to re-echo throughout the century. When Wordsworth wrote in a famous passage that one of the chief effects of exposure to harmonizing scenes in nature like that at Tintern might be traceable subsequently in

> That best portion of a good man's life,
> His little, nameless, unremembered acts
> Of kindness and of love

he was demonstrating how fully the assumption that appreciation of beauty in nature and moral worth were firmly linked had entered contemporary presuppositions.

The last major contribution to development of the debate between the moral and the aesthetic was in Adam Smith's 1759 *Theory of Moral Sentiments*, where the significance of sympathy, as the ability to place oneself in the position of another, was stressed once again – but without the ascription of moral worth. No longer the chief key word, 'sensibility' was giving place to 'imagination'.

If the central figure was still ineluctably that of Rousseau, however, moral questions did not thereby disappear. In one sense they were sharpened, for Rousseau's celebrated insistence on total truth-telling foregrounded such questions in confessional writing. In fiction, on the other hand, they could be side-stepped if the writer chose not to enter that territory. Some female writers followed such a course, dwelling on feelings of their characters that did not involve their engaging directly with moral issues.

Wordsworth, once again, provides notable examples. The 'Lines Composed . . . above Tintern Abbey' have already been touched on, along with their assertion of the praiseworthy moral effect to be anticipated for someone who approaches a scene such as the one he is describing with a sufficiently receptive mind. His faith in the beneficence of Nature was powerful enough for him to believe, at least during the early events in France, that Nature exercised such a controlling presence in human affairs that ultimate issues could safely be left to her. While he was still under the spell of the Revolution, he could boldly resort to natural metaphor to

---

[33] Shaftesbury *Characteristicks of Men, Manners, Opinions and Times* (quoted in Todd, *Sensibility*, p. 25).

enforce his conviction that if violent events such as those which had recently been taking place were viewed in a larger natural perspective, monitory implications would disappear. So in 1793, when Richard Watson, Bishop of Llandaff, expressed his indignation at the course of events in Paris by issuing an Appendix to a sermon he had published several years before, lamenting the decline there, Wordsworth's 'Letter' in reply, defending the republican principles he had recently re-embraced, included at least one such argument from Nature:

The animal just released from its stall will exhaust the overflow of its spirits in a round of wanton vagaries, but it will soon return to itself and enjoy its freedom in moderate and regular delight.[34]

The main problem for Wordsworth, nevertheless, was to know just how to interpret such events. Eugene Stelzig, in a thoughtful essay on the subject, sees the main spectrum of his thought as having ranged between alternative interpretations of human behaviour, an optimistic one, based on the Rousseauian doctrines common at the time, being set against the more cynical view to be found in Shakespearean plays such as *Lear*:

> Humanity must perforce prey on itself
> Like monsters of the deep.

Stelzig quotes Freud's support of the second view: 'Homo homini lupus. Who, in the face of all his experience of life and of history, will have the courage to dispute this assertion?'[35] He continues,

The assumption that man is naturally not good leads readily to an essentially negative and repressive view of government, as it does for Burke, who in his conservative polemic against the French Revolution insists that 'government is not made in virtue of natural rights,' but is rather 'a contrivance of human wisdom to provide for human wants . . . Among these wants is to be reckoned the want, out of civil society, of a sufficient restraint upon their passions.' The well-being of society requires that 'the inclinations of men should frequently be thwarted, their will controlled, and their passions brought into subjection'. As one reads *The Prelude*, particularly Book Ten, one becomes increasingly aware that the opposition was not clearly present to his mind as such, since both poles were so deeply embedded that a constant play between was inevitable. For some the logical end to acceptance of the Burkean view would be the restoration of the Bourbons that eventually took place; and Wordsworth's lasting opposition to

---

[34] *WPrW* I, 33–4, 38.
[35] Freud, *Civilization and Its Discontents* [1930], ed. James Strachey (London: Hogarth Press and the Institute of Psychoanalysis, 1969), p. 58.

Napoleon might have entailed such a view. Pitched against it however was the legacy of his Lakeland upbringing, and his conviction that the equality of human beings had deep roots in human nature.[36]

As an event at the very heart of Europe's most civilized country, the French Revolution marked a turning-point in the long story of the change in world civilization from a settled, ordered state, existing in shared life based on shared beliefs, to one which would be regarded as characterized primarily by relativity and persisting flux.

While questioning every concept of their civilization, thinkers of the time were also willing to propose equally radical changes. A good example can be found in the new calendar which was proposed, as created by a commission under Romme's direction.[37] These, however, did not find immediate acceptance in England, where a readier audience existed for a programme based on human values that made more allowance for sensibility. The classic statement of this project was again Wordsworth's attestation, in 'Lines Composed . . . above Tintern Abbey', to the healing effect of recalling the Wye scenery in times of stress:

> . . . oft, in lonely rooms, and 'mid the din
> Of towns and cities, I have owed to them,
> In hours of weariness, sensations sweet,
> Felt in the blood, and felt along the heart;
> And passing even into my purer mind,
> With tranquil restoration: – feelings too
> Of unremembered pleasure: such, perhaps,
> As have no slight or trivial influence
> On that best portion of a good man's life,
> His little, nameless, unremembered, acts
> Of kindness and of love. Nor less, I trust,
> To them I may have owed another gift,
> Of aspect more sublime; that blessed mood,
> In which the burthen of the mystery,
> In which the heavy and the weary weight
> Of all this unintelligible world,
> Is lightened: – that serene and blessed mood,
> In which the affections gently lead us on, –
> Until, the breath of this corporeal frame
> And even the motion of our human blood

---

[36] Eugene Stelzig, '"The Shield of Human Nature": Wordsworth's Reflections on the Revolution in France', *Nineteenth-Century Literature* 45, 4 (1991), 415–31.

[37] The New Calendar, renumbering the twelve months with thirty days each, came to an end on 1 January 1806.

> Almost suspended, we are laid asleep
> In body, and become a living soul:
> While with an eye made quiet by the power
> Of harmony, and the deep power of joy,
> We see into the life of things.[38]

Cultivation of the affections could, in other words, initiate one into a state of enlightenment.

The continuing power in succeeding years of such faith in words of sensibility is shown by the popularity of the translations of Ossian by James Macpherson – though denounced by Johnson as forgeries in a manner that carried conviction to many readers. The backwash of feeling that had accompanied their appearance was sufficiently powerful for some Romantic writers to declare that the question of their authenticity or otherwise did not really count. In his 1819 essay 'On Poetry in General', Hazlitt would write of Ossian as 'a feeling and a name that can never be destroyed in the minds of his readers'. If he was nothing, he declared, this would be 'another void left in the heart'.[39]

Wordsworth's adherence to this programme suggests that at some level he had evidently retained the faith in Nature that had caused him, even when he first lived in London, to view its panorama with a sardonic eye. But when the initial euphoria of the Revolution was followed by the appalling events of the Terror, his major mood turned to despondency and the loss of hope for human improvement mentioned above. Basic to it, at the same time, was a sense of the need to examine the fundamental nature of what it was to be human and what could be thought of as the basic element of communication in words. What was it, for that matter, that made some words and phrases more significant than others, and how could this sense of their significance be expressed? In *The Prelude* he would recall crucial moments in his experience, such as his moment of vision when he saw in a blind beggar a fitting emblem of the human condition:

> And once, far-travelled in such mood, beyond
> The reach of common indications, lost
> Amid the moving pageant, 'twas my chance
> Abruptly to be smitten with the view
> Of a blind beggar, who, with upright face,
> Stood propped against a wall, upon his chest
> Wearing a written paper, to explain

---

[38] 'Lines Composed . . . above Tintern Abbey', lines 25–49: *WPW* II, 260.
[39] *HW* V, 18.

> The story of the man, and who he was.
> My mind did at this spectacle turn round
> As with the might of waters, and it seemed
> To me that in this label was a type
> Or emblem of the utmost that we know,
> Both of ourselves and of the universe,
> And on the shape of this unmoving man,
> His fixèd face and sightless eyes, I looked,
> As if admonished from another world.[40]

There is much in his early writing which shows his proneness to see in lonely beggars or outcasts such emblems of the human condition – rather in the fashion of Lear's crucial discovery of 'unaccommodated man'. It is also noteworthy, however, that the sightless beggar was accompanied by the label that he wore to communicate to the passer-by the story of his life. Belief in the status of the word was if anything enhanced by such a sight. In other manuscripts of the period, gesturing towards *The Prelude*, the reader can see him trying over and over again to convey how important a person's words might be when evoked in a lonely setting. The supreme example is the episode, worked over repeatedly in the manuscripts, of the Discharged Soldier who ends the night encounter with a speech sounding the ring of the gnomic:

> Assured that now my comrade would repose
> In comfort, I entreated that henceforth
> He would not linger in the public ways,
> But ask for timely furtherance, and help
> Such as his state required. At this reproof,
> With the same ghastly mildness in his look,
> He said, 'My trust is in the God of Heaven,
> And in the eye of him that passes me.'[41]

It is as if, while recalling his sense of significance in what the man finally said, Wordsworth yet finds it hard to convey adequately his sense of its profundity. In working similarly on another manuscript, he describes a woman who looks at a cart delivering bread and in her poverty projects a human personality on to it: 'That wagon does not care for us.'[42] Again, there is a strong sense of words actually heard and left lingering in the mind,

---

[40] *WPrel* (1805), iv. 608–23.   [41] *Ibid.*, iv. 488–95.

[42] *WPW* I, 316; cited by Jonathan Wordsworth, *The Music of Humanity: A Critical Study of Wordsworth's 'Ruined Cottage', Incorporating Texts from a Manuscript of 1799–1800* (London: Nelson, 1969), p. 6.

with the sense that they penetrated to the core of the human condition: in the manuscript the poet's immediate comment was 'The words were simple but her look and voice / Made up their meaning.'

In each case mentioned, it is a particular word, 'eye', 'care', that resonates with particular force, recalling Coleridge's dictum 'Wordsworth's words always *mean* the whole of their possible Meaning.'[43] The most searching of his discussions of encounters with words comes in the eighth book of *The Prelude*, where he tries to sum up some of his findings 'in retrospect', employing the image of a traveller entering a cave who

> looks and sees the cavern spread and grow
> Widening itself on all sides; sees, or thinks
> He sees, erelong, the roof above his head,
> Which instantly unsettles and recedes –
> Substance and shadow, light and darkness, all
> Commingled, making up a canopy
> Of shapes and forms and tendencies to shape
> That shift and vanish, change and interchange
> Like spectres – ferment quiet and sublime,
> Which, after a short space, works less and less
> Till, every effort, every motion gone,
> The scene before him lies in perfect view
> Exposed, and lifeless, as a written book.
> But let him pause awhile and look again,
> And a new quickening shall succeed, at first
> Beginning timidly, then creeping fast
> Through all which he beholds: the senseless mass,
> In its projections, wrinkles, cavities,
> Through all its surface, with all colours streaming,
> Like a magician's airy pageant, parts,
> Unites, embodying everywhere some pressure
> Or image . . .[44]

This last stage of the process is the one at which, according to Wordsworth, the creative work of imagination can most surely be glimpsed, as it creates figures such as warrior, pilgrim or devotee of a religious order. It marks the extreme of his discussion of language and its power, elsewhere expressed in heightened imagery:

> Visionary Power
> Attends upon the motions of the winds

---

[43] Letter to Southey, 14 August 1803: *CL* II, 976.
[44] *WPrel* (1805), viii. 715–36.

Embodied in the mystery of words;
There darkness makes abode, and all the host
Of shadowy things do work their changes there,
As in a mansion like their proper home.
Even forms and substances are circumfused
By that transparent veil with light divine,
And through the turnings intricate of verse
Present themselves as objects recognized
In flashes, and with a glory scarce their own.[45]

This is a long way from the language of authority which Johnson had tried – and largely failed – to help establish. It was rather a dialect of exploration, aimed at discovering the moments of illumination that might lie veiled by the mystery of words, yet which could be approached – if ever – only obliquely.

---

[45] *Ibid.*, v. 619–29.

CHAPTER 3

The heart of Lyrical Ballads

One of the most surprising things that has ever been said about the *Lyrical Ballads* collection was also one of the earliest. Writing to their publisher, Joseph Cottle, in May 1798, Coleridge said:

We deem that the volumes offered to you are to a certain degree *one work*, in *kind tho' not in degree*, as an Ode is one work – & that our different poems are as stanzas, good relatively rather than absolutely: – Mark you, I say in kind tho' not in degree.[1]

To the general reader who is familiar with the finished volume, this must appear an extraordinary statement. We are presented with a collection that begins with a long ballad, ends with a long meditative poem and in the interspace comprises a range of various shorter works in different modes, some written in the poet's own voice, one or two not: and yet the authors can apparently agree in regarding it as 'one work, in kind tho' not in degree'.

One reason why this must seem strange is that readers of the 1798 volume, then as now, tended to approach new work in terms of what was familiar. An early reviewer commented, for instance, that *The Ancient Mariner* did not read like any ballad in the English tradition. He was evidently unaware of the new German ballads that were currently being translated into English – though the one or two reviewers who were did not treat the poem much better, regarding it as a failed attempt to imitate a currently fashionable mode.

Some years ago, however, an important article appeared, entitled 'The Contemporaneity of Lyrical Ballads', written by Robert Mayo, who had made a special study of the magazines of the 1790s.[2] Many of these periodicals made a habit of publishing a few poems in each number.

[1] *CL* I, 412.   [2] *PMLA* 69 (1954), 486–522.

What he found, rather to his surprise, was that many of the poems that might strike the present-day reader as unusual turned out not to seem out of the ordinary once one turned the pages of the contemporary magazines.

He quoted surveys from respected critics and scholars, each asserting that Wordsworth had broken new ground by being the first to write about the real outcasts of society such as beggars, convicts and forsaken women. As he pointed out, however, this was simply a received opinion, passed from one critic to the next: for each of these categories, he showed, there were at least twenty poems that could be cited from the magazines of the time. If one thought of the *Lyrical Ballads* poem title 'The Mad Mother' as unusual in its choice of subject, one might turn to the contemporary magazines and find 'Crazy Kate', 'Mad Peg', 'Crazy Luke', 'Bess of Bedlam', 'Ellen, or the Fair Insane' or 'Moll Pot, the Mad Woman of Gloucester-Street'. If readers thought Coleridge's poem on the nightingale was distinctive in its subject, similarly, Robert Mayo could disillusion them with the titles of a dozen poems on nightingales in the 1790s and the assurance that there were many more. And it was not only the subjects that could be duplicated over and over again. If one was intrigued by the way in which the ballads sometimes reply to one another, one might consider 'The Wish, by a Bachelor' in the *Weekly Magazine*, followed by 'The Reply to the Bachelor's Wish, by a Husband'. And if the title 'Lines written at a small distance from my House, and sent by my little Boy to the Person to whom they are addressed' seemed a little verbose, one might turn to the *Universal Magazine* in 1796 and find 'Lines, Written by Sir Richard Hill, Bart, at Hawkestone, his Elegant Seat in Shropshire, When Contemplating the Scenes around Him in his own Park, and to be Seen in a Natural Cavern of a Vast Rock, from the Top of which is a Very Diversified and Romantic Prospect'. Many of the titles contained terms that were also common – 'Complaints', 'Sketches', 'Inscriptions' and 'Verses' (which latter might be verses 'found under a Yew-Tree', 'Made at Sea during a Heavy Gale' or 'Left in a Summer-house'). Most striking, in view of what has come to be said about this Romantic mode, is the very large number of 'Fragments'.

Not only would the first readers of *Lyrical Ballads* have been conversant with all these features of the collection, but editors had a similar sense of familiarity: fifteen out of the twenty shorter items were reprinted within a year or so of publication in these very same magazines.

By the time one has finished looking at all the features of the *Ballads* that were common to the magazines of the time, indeed, one is left asking what exactly *was* original about them. Mayo insists on their superiority but does not say very much about wherein it consists. Even the forms adopted for the ballads, he points out, are not particularly original, apart from 'Goody Blake and Harry Gill'. He also reminds the reader that Wordsworth and Coleridge never claimed to be addressing new subjects; they simply spoke of experiments in language. And even these claims are not altogether convincing. They do not apply to *The Rime of the Ancient Mariner*, for example, nor for that matter to the 'Lines Composed a Few Miles above Tintern Abbey . . .', a poem which was simply developing the meditative mode in terms already familiar from the work of writers such as Cowper. Both poems, in any case, stand away from the nature of some shorter pieces.

So where is the 'unity' of the collection to be found? The assumption that such a unity existed was always a somewhat fragile one, certainly: so fragile that by 1800 Wordsworth had changed the order of the poems, claiming that *The Ancient Mariner* had been an injury to the volume. He also wanted to change the title, preferring that it should be called simply *Poems* – which suggests that he thought the very conception of the original volume unsatisfactory. In the event, his publishers would not allow him to change it, presumably thinking that the earlier one had proved more saleable (and also perhaps that it might confuse readers to find that they were getting much of the same work under a new title), so the two-volume edition, also, bore it. As Kenneth Johnston has pointed out, this was rather a pity in view of the characteristic direction exhibited by Wordsworth's poetry in the second edition.[3] For when one looks at what he was adding, one finds that the second volume was dominated by poems such as the third one, 'The Brothers', and the last, 'Michael' – each of which demonstrates the new way in which his poetry was developing, to produce poems, often extended, about the pathos of the tragedies that can beset ordinary human beings. Johnston also remarks on the facility with which Wordsworth was producing new short poems in the 1798 period, by comparison with his struggles to produce anything at all during his time at Racedown.[4]

It is nevertheless clear that many of the early readers and reviewers, taken aback by the disparate nature of the collection when it first appeared, did not know what to make of it; Wordsworth may well have been justified in feeling that it in some way affronted the reader more than

---

[3] See Kenneth R. Johnston, 'Wordsworth's Self-Creation and the 1800 *Lyrical Ballads*', in *1800: The New Lyrical Ballads*, ed. Trott and Perry (London: Palgrave, 2001), p. 98.
[4] *Ibid.*, p. 95.

was necessary. Yet it should also be borne in mind that for some readers the collection, whether in its 1798 or 1800 form, had all the excitement of a new departure. John Wilson, writing to Wordsworth in 1802 at the age of seventeen, claimed that *Lyrical Ballads* was 'the book which I value next to my Bible',[5] and the following year de Quincey, who was also seventeen, wrote saying, 'from the wreck of all earthly things which belong to me, I should endeavour to save that work by an impulse second to none but that of self-preservation'.[6] Young men who could say that were evidently responding to something they found important in the collection as a whole; indeed, they seem to have detected immediately some kind of unity there.

In pursuing this puzzle, it is natural to turn for enlightenment, as many later readers have done, to the Preface which Wordsworth wrote for the 1800 edition. The statement there about the language chosen for the poems is the one that has aroused most interest, since it raises important questions about its social basis:

Low and rustic life was generally chosen because in that situation the essential passions of the heart find a better soil in which they can attain their maturity, are less under restraint, and speak a plainer and more emphatic language; because in that situation our elementary feelings exist in a state of greater simplicity and consequently may be more accurately contemplated and more forcibly communicated; because the manners of rural life germinate from those elementary feelings; and from the necessary character of rural occupations are more easily comprehended; and are more durable; and lastly, because in that situation the passions of men are incorporated with the beautiful and permanent forms of nature.[7]

Such statements have received particular attention because they suggest in Wordsworth a view of language that anticipates the Marxist one. Yet as soon as one turns back to the poems themselves, it is clear that their achievement is a long way from realizing any hopes that they might embody such a sharp social critique. Many of them contain no new departures in language or (in the case of *The Ancient Mariner*) experiments of a quite different kind, while those that do are often using language in a way that half-smiles at its own usage: 'To go to sleep for very cold and then not sleep a wink', or the notorious 'his poor old ancles

[5] Letter of 24 May 1802, in Mary Wilson Gordon, *Memoir of Christopher North*, 2 vols. (Edinburgh: Edmonston and Douglas, 1862), I, 38–48.

[6] Letter of 1803, printed in J. E.Jordan, *De Quincey to Wordsworth: A Biography of a Relationship* (Berkeley and Los Angeles: University of California Press, 1962).

[7] *WPrW* I, 124.

swell'. The radical claims of the Preface do not seem well supported by such examples.

In directing his readers specifically to points such as the diction of 'low and rustic life', Wordsworth was in any case not necessarily doing these poems a service, since for a full understanding they require a kind of double reading, which will at one and the same time attend to the line of the verse and maintain an awareness of undercurrents in the authors' minds. Hazlitt is a good guide here: of Wordsworth's achievement in *Lyrical Ballads* he wrote:

Fools have laughed at, wise men scarcely understand them. He takes a subject or a story merely as pegs or loops to hang thought and feeling on; the incidents are trifling, in proportion to his contempt for imposing appearances; the reflections are profound, according to the gravity and the aspiring pretensions of his mind.[8]

We have to see the texts of these poems as complex, in other words, and be ready to give them a double reading before they will make sense – attending to both what is being said directly, and the underlying meditation or questioning.

Another point should be made, again surprising in terms of Hazlitt's assertion. Wordsworth himself claimed almost immediately afterwards that the poems had been written simply to make money and should not have been criticised so sharply by friends such as Southey who knew that; and after Coleridge criticised the theory of poetic language many years later, he said, 'I never cared a straw about the theory – and the Preface was written at the request of Coleridge out of sheer good nature.'[9] Again, this seems at first sight to go against Hazlitt's sensing of a profundity in the poems. If they were simply being written fast, to make money, is the whole issue not being taken too seriously?

I believe, however, that this is only a part of the truth. Although the ballads were clearly written fast, over a few months, there is evidence to suggest that it was a time of considerable intellectual excitement on the part of both poets; there is also an important difference between the successive collections. In the 1800 volume the Wordsworthian profundity that plays an increasing part provides a corresponding unity; in 1798 the situation had been different. A range of ideas had come to the surface in their minds at once, simultaneously, and were fermenting together – ideas which they were ready to explore further. In due course they hoped to

---

[8] Para. 2 of his essay 'Mr Wordsworth', in *The Spirit of the Age* [1825]: *HW* XI.
[9] Annotation to Barron Field's memoir of Wordsworth, quoted *WPrW* I, 167.

produce from them more ambitious works of poetry; in the meantime, however, whether presented in a raw form or, more often, working just behind the presented text, the ideas could occasion poem after poem.

One reason why the 1798 volume of *Lyrical Ballads* should have taken the form it did, and why the authors should have seen a continuous thread running through them, has to do with the political situation of the time. These were, after all, men who had seen the extraordinary excitement accompanying the French Revolution and had lived for the previous five years under the weight of contending emotions. On the one hand, they felt a growing disillusionment concerning the course of the Revolution itself: whatever their feelings about the aspirations involved they could not wish to see the bloodshed and mass executions replicated in England. On the other hand, they were forced to recognize the great wave of idealism that had been released among young men by those same events. Was that all now to be discounted and forgotten? Did it have no significance at all?[10] They could hardly believe that, either. What they were looking for was a line of inquiry and prospect that they could cling to and transmit to their fellows: an explanation of what had happened and a promise of hope for the future. Such a line was to be found in their growing conviction that the world was not simply, as often assumed in contemporary thinking, a great machine, pursuing its way without regard for human beings. Against such a view they could find evidence to suggest that, in ordinary life, charities and bonds of affection between human beings existed that were not called for if human behaviour was dictated simply by mechanical and impersonal factors.

This was in no way equivalent to a sentimental belief that the universe was always working for the benefit of humanity: on the contrary, they were all too aware of the current argument that the universe was *not* on the side of human beings, whose natural behaviour was to fight one another rather than work co-operatively. Shortly after concluding the first edition of the collection, Wordsworth was to write a number of poems now commonly grouped together as the 'Lucy' poems, where, in the face of any sense that nature was benevolent, he explored the implications of the fact of human death. But in the year or two immediately before, they had been searching rather for evidences that might provide a relief from current despair.

---

[10] Compare Hazlitt's similar questions in his essay 'William Godwin', in *The Spirit of the Age* [1825]: *HW* XI.

We do not properly understand *Lyrical Ballads*, then, unless we see that the starting point of the whole enterprise had been a previous state of disillusionment and hopelessness, the poems in the collection representing successive attempts to build away from that hopelessness and towards some kind of positive stance. This helps to explain why *The Rime of the Ancient Mariner* should in the first edition have been chosen to open the volume: it can be regarded as initiating the reader into the state of mind in which the poems that follow had been written. For these are poems written by poets who, like the Mariner, have entered upon an experience of despair and desolation in the world, and yet who – like him again – pass through it, into an appreciation of the blessings of ordinary existence that reflect the positive forces at work. And these are supplemented by poems in which nature itself is seen at times to radiate a simpler and more happy sense – as if the birds and the flowers on a spring morning are acting and growing out of a joy that is far from mechanical, being interwoven at some level with all the processes of life. In just the same way, the Mariner's utterance is at times blessed with images from the pleasures of the natural world: the jargoning of the birds, the melody of the hidden brook.

Approaching the collection from this point of view, one can begin to trace a thread which begins from the Mariner's bewildered appreciation of ordinary life – passing from place to place as a haunted and tormented being, yet also celebrating its simple ceremonies – and moves through other poems that look at human life and find special virtues in its ordinariness. Simple incidents are presented for the reader's contemplation: an old man has lost the strength to perform a straightforward operation on a tree-root; a shepherd is carrying his last surviving sheep. Most tellingly of all, perhaps, a mother is not repelled by the behaviour of her idiot son but appreciates and even enjoys it. And side by side with these are poems which celebrate the pleasures of nature: Coleridge's 'The Nightingale', Wordsworth's 'Lines Written at a Small Distance from my House', 'Expostulation and Reply' and 'The Tables Turned'.

The two threads – enjoyment of the beauty of Nature and appreciation of ordinary human life – which both spring from an appreciation, like the Mariner's, of the interdependence and linking of all life, can eventually be seen to come together and interweave in the last poem, the 'Lines Composed . . . above Tintern Abbey', which opens with appreciation of a quiet, unusually harmonic scene in nature and then proceeds into a meditation on the relationship between appreciation of such scenes and an apprehension of the links that draw all beings together.

'Lines left upon a Seat in a Yew-Tree' is a 'scene-setting' poem of the same kind, suggesting what is lost to a man who is so disillusioned by civilization that he decides simply to live alone in nature. (The motif develops, of course, the tradition of the melancholy hermit in eighteenth-century literature.[11]) Yet this appeal to the link between a sympathetic view of nature and a similar regard for the needs of humanity is hardly enough to explain the extraordinary *diversity* of themes in the collection. That suggests a wider exploration by the poets than my simple summary might suggest. If the ultimate concerns of Wordsworth and Coleridge ran together at this time, with extraordinarily creative results, they were concerns that found their main centre in different areas of their human experience. From this point of view, it is worth looking at the opening of the passage quoted from earlier – an opening which is often overlooked:

The principal object . . . which I proposed to myself in these Poems was to make the incidents of common life interesting, by tracing in them, truly, though not ostentatiously, the primary laws of our nature: chiefly as far as regards the manner in which we associate ideas in a state of excitement.[12]

The ending of this sentence points in a different direction from that involved in the question of language. It suggests some kind of psy-chological exploration – and therefore the dominant presence not of Wordsworth but of Coleridge, who had recently been giving thought to matters of mental process, with the aim of complementing the theories of David Hartley. Hartley, as may be recalled, viewed all mental process as consisting of association between ideas based on sense experience. Such sense experiences, once imprinted on the human body, would persist as vibrations in the memory, which allowed them to associate this way and that, making up the various patterns to be thought of as ideas. Despite his early attraction to this system, Coleridge had come to see that its account of mental process was simplistic. For one thing, it suggested the existence of 'simple sensations', a doubtful concept; for another, it made mental process seem in itself blind and purposeless. In particular, it paid little attention to major currents in the mind that might be thought to dominate associations and at times control them. Having thought at first that it might be possible to direct the associative process by educational methods, so that in the end it would move irresistibly in the direction

---

[11] See Mary Jacobus, *Tradition and Experiment in Wordsworth's* Lyrical Ballads *(1798)* (Oxford: Clarendon Press, 1976).
[12] *WPrW* I, 122–4.

of the divine, Coleridge was faced with the question – if *all* our thought processes were associative, how could they ever truly be changed in this way?

Wordsworth's simple statement suggests that they had envisaged a clue as to how these processes might operate. If the human mind, when in a state of excitement, made associations of a different kind from those which occurred in a passive state of quiet meditation, then the account offered by Locke and Hartley called for modification. The world offered by their work was one of necessity, our only hope lying in learning to manipulate social relationships in such a way that the patterns of association in the minds of all the members of society would be improved. But if there were other powers at work in the human mind, they pointed towards a more complicated view. One might make an analogy with the physical universe: the ideas of Locke and Hartley were sometimes thought of as psychologically complementing the laws of Newton that had simplified our view of the workings of the planetary universe; now, in the same way, a simple basic idea behind the working of complex factors might be proposed. Just as the fact of gravitation cannot explain other things in the universe, such as the existence of light, or for that matter the workings of life, so, it could be argued, Locke and Hartley had provided one straightforward mechanism to explain the workings of the human mind, but had not explained the *life* of that mind, or for that matter its occasional experiences of 'illumination'. Coleridge, by contrast, continually thought of the mind in ways that allowed for such a possibility. There was always a touch of enthusiasm in everything he brushed with this idea, infecting Wordsworth's writing also. In *The Ancient Mariner* its controlling power is to be traced, as the Mariner is stripped of the normal conventional ways of thinking, or non-thinking, that allow him to shoot an albatross casually and without any real consideration of what he is doing. He is thus exposed to a more primitive state of mind, in which he experiences both the depth of human suffering (that of his shipmates even more than his own) and, in due course, a sense of the link between all living things. He cannot understand the full significance of what has happened to him, nor indeed does the poet try to explain it, but as he returns to the world he is haunted by a sense that things are not what they are conventionally made to seem, coupled with a new feeling for the simple charities of human existence represented by such events as weddings and assemblies of human beings to pray together.

If we think of the collection in these terms, our attention is directed to different matters – to those poems that show the human mind in unusual states. Poems such as 'The Thorn', 'The Mad Mother' or 'The Complaint of a Forsaken Indian Woman' present human beings in extremity, suggesting how in such states the human being might seem to be acting according to a quite different sense of the world: the bereaved mother clings simply to the spot where her baby's grave is, the mad mother rests everything on her relationship to her child, the Indian Woman finds it easier to relate herself to the Northern Lights than to the companions who have abandoned her. The constant suggestion is that in such extreme states human beings discover a magnetism revealing the true bonding of their existence.

When Wordsworth comes to write about the last poem, he describes it as one of his attempts to 'follow the fluxes and refluxes of the mind when agitated by the great and simple affections of our nature'. The phrase 'fluxes and refluxes' is again significant, suggesting as it does the mystery involved in the gravitational influence of the moon on the tides. And although, as Wordsworth says, the poem is a picture of the mind in extremity, 'the last struggles of a human being, at the approach of death, cleaving in solitude to life and society', there is something more to it than this. The woman's factual sense of her own weakness is dominated by primary yearnings that are not simply directed towards her companions. It might be truer to say that her condition has set up alternating magnetisms. Alone in the snowy wastes, devoid of all normal contact with the world, her basic magnetization is to the energies of the universe, as manifested in the cracklings of the *aurora borealis*: it is as real in her dreams as in her waking perceptions, so that when she wakes she is surprised by her very survival:

> In sleep I heard the northern gleams;
> The stars they were among my dreams;
> In sleep did I behold the skies,
> I saw the crackling flashes drive;
> And yet they are upon my eyes,
> And yet I am alive.

Her first wish, therefore, is to die: in this magnetized solitude she has no fear of death, which will simply confirm her, in the waste under the stars, as a part of the living universe at large. Yet the thought of fellow human beings, initiated by a feeling of reproach towards the companions who refused to take her further, attracts her back to her child – and this reminds her of the moment when they were separated:

> Through his whole body something ran,
> A most strange something did I see;

– As if he strove to be a man,
That he might pull the sledge for me.
And then he stretched his arms, how wild!
Oh mercy! like a little child.

There is here a suggestion that at the moment when the filial bond was being severed, the child's primal consciousness was not only excited into action but stirred to operate at its extremes: first expanding with its own growth-impulse, trying to assume manhood in a moment in order to help her, before contracting to the helplessness of the baby in its plight and its separation. Her own adult consciousness extends the process. The urge to be with her child relapses towards a more general impulse to be with her people, and then to recognition that she cannot even lift a limb, giving place to a final yearning that she might have her child with her at the moment of death and so die happily, the two great magnetisms in her consciousness finally reconciled.

The same sense of a kind of double magnetism is to be found in the preceding poem – at least as it existed before Wordsworth excised its ending. In 'Animal Tranquillity and Decay, a Sketch', he depicts an old man who has in his old age become so much a part of nature that even the birds do not notice him. Yet when the man speaks, it is to reveal the undertaking of a journey dominated by a quite different kind of attraction: the need to visit his dying son, if at all possible, while he is still alive.

The poem 'Goody Blake and Harry Gill' seems in turn to reflect with a very particular intensity and directness the excitement of Wordsworth's exposure to Coleridge's ideas, since it stands very close to Coleridge's belief in a connection between the primary consciousness of human beings and the warmth-sense of the body. The story from which it is derived appeared in Erasmus Darwin's *Zoonomia*, a work which (I have elsewhere argued[13]) stimulated Coleridge strongly. Wordsworth's anxiety to obtain it is evident from a note in the early spring of 1798 in the course of which he says,

I write merely to request (which I have very particular reasons for doing) that you would contrive to send me Dr Darwin's Zoönomia *by the first carrier*.[14]

The urgency of the underlining suggests that Coleridge had already told him of the story and made him eager to read the original. It earned its particular Wordsworthian significance, in turn, both by its support for

[13] See my *Coleridge's Poetic Intelligence* (London: Macmillan, 1977), esp. pp. 50–7, 74–7.
[14] Letter to Cottle of 1798: *WL* (1787–1805), p. 199 (underlining added).

his sense that the common link between human beings was recognised best by those in a village community and by Darwin's firm claim that it was factually true. Harry Gill, by his mean attitude to his neighbour, depriving her of the fuel which was vital to her life but of little use to himself, had broken the bond of natural affection; it was therefore appropriate (and in this instance, it seemed, an established physical fact) that the coldness of his heart should have become physically manifest in the uncontrollable coldness of his body. Wordsworth himself commented on the peculiar significance of the story in view of Darwin's assertion:

I wished to draw attention to the truth that the power of the human imagination is sufficient to produce such changes even in our physical nature as might almost appear miraculous. The truth is an important one; the fact (for it is a *fact*) is a valuable illustration of it.[15]

The emphasis, characteristically, is on the factual nature of the episode.

Wordsworth, I have suggested, was strongly affected by Coleridge's ideas in the writing of such poems and also those which display his quite unusual enthusiasm for nature – though he also guards his position continually with elements of scepticism: 'And I must think, do all I can', 'If I these thoughts may not prevent', 'For such loss I would believe abundant recompense.' And when we look at the direction in which his mind had been moving before this time, we find that although it had recently been lightened by the presence of Coleridge and Dorothy, his chief poetic preoccupation had previously been not with the undercurrent of life and pleasure in nature but the facts of solitude and suffering. In various poetic drafts of that time, he returns again and again to the same conception: a single figure, often in a landscape, who is eloquent of the disparate human condition – the discharged soldier, the old man travelling, the woman of 'The Ruined Cottage'. There is even a suggestion that such individuals may be gifted with special insight. One of his most characteristic observations, assigned to a character in *The Borderers* and used again later more directly as epigraph for *The White Doe of Rylstone*, occurs in the lines:

> Action is transitory – a step, a blow,
> The motion of a muscle – this way or that –
> 'Tis done. And in the after-vacancy
> We wonder at ourselves like men betray'd.

---

[15] *WPW* II, 401n (underlining added).

Suffering is permanent, obscure and dark,
And shares the nature of infinity.[16]

It is evidently a crucial statement, enshrining his belief that more is sometimes disclosed in suffering than in action, and that what is revealed may be closer to the central truth of things. That sense too has its part to play in what Hazlitt thought of as the 'profundity' of these poems.

There are, it must be acknowledged, contradictions in some of them – most notably in *The Ancient Mariner*. Had the two poets given themselves more time to think, they would have wished, no doubt, to remove some of these contradictory patterns and make their work more homogeneous – as Wordsworth did when he abridged 'Old Man Travelling', and as Coleridge did when he wrote the explanatory marginal glosses for his poem nearly twenty years later. But the fact that they allowed some of the contradictorinesses of actual life to be there actually adds to their value as texts to think with and argue about. As we enter into the poets' minds we can re-experience the current excitement that made them explore in a variety of ways the possible links between certain elements in nature and the workings of the human heart, and as we attend more closely to the text itself, it will be found to reflect some of the obliquities, cross-currents and contradictions that we recognize in our own attempts to understand other people and find a proper language to describe our more puzzling human encounters. The very differences between them – Coleridge responding to the signs of life, Wordsworth standing back and contemplating the significance of isolated organisms in the context of those signs – convey to us the varying strands of emotion and reason at work in these poems, with all their possibilities for varying interpretation.

It may be concluded, then, that if there was a unity to the 1798 poems, it was a unity provided by the mutual stimulus at work between Wordsworth and Coleridge – and to some extent Dorothy Wordsworth also – during those months. It was not a unity that would have been evident to the first readers since to appreciate it truly, they would have needed to share in that underlying interplay. In 1798 it would have been far from most people's apprehension: they would not, like the original participants, have been led to it step by step. Hence the bewilderment of many of the first readers, coupled with the excitement of a few young men who sensed that in English poetry something new was afoot.

---

[16] *The Borderers*, line 1544, and epigraph to *The White Doe*: *WPW* I, 188 and III, 283.

If, even now, we have some difficulty in thinking ourselves back into their shared state of mind at the time, that is, I think, because even while the collection was in the process of formation, a difference of emphasis was at work which was to become steadily more pronounced over the succeeding years. Four years later Coleridge remarked,

I rather suspect that somewhere or other there is a radical Difference in our theoretical Opinions respecting poetry – / this I shall endeavour to go to the Bottom of.[17]

– so laying the first foundation for what was to be his extended discussion of their difference in *Biographia Literaria*. But although that later discussion was probing and extensive, it was still not sufficiently deep; the differences of concern went further than a simple disagreement about poetry. I can best indicate what I mean by pointing to the respective formulae which each poet developed in the subsequent period to indicate their fundamental positions. For Coleridge, it crystallized into the saying that 'every Thing has a Life of its own, and that we are all <u>one Life</u>'.[18] The twin affirmation provided a keynote for his view generally, indicating why he was so deeply interested in mental phenomena – including the way in which we associate ideas in a state of excitement. It also gave him the cue for affirmations and investigations concerning the difference beween saying 'It is' and saying 'I am': a distinction about which Thomas McFarland has written eloquently.[19] And it was the reason for his coming to think that he might, after all, be more of a metaphysician than a poet.

At one level Wordsworth would not have disagreed. After all, in the account of the young boy in the poem of his that became 'The Pedlar' one of the firmest statements was

In all things
He saw one life, and felt that it was joy.[20]

But the most central belief of Wordsworth's lay in his sense not that 'we are all one Life' but that 'we have all of us one human heart', the statement explicitly formulated so in 'The Old Cumberland Beggar' (Line 153). Even while he was composing the lyrics described earlier, in which his awareness of the pathos of the individual figures about whom

---

[17] *CL* II, 830 (cf. 812).   [18] *Ibid.*, 864.
[19] See Thomas McFarland, *Coleridge and the Pantheist Tradition* (Oxford: Clarendon Press, 1969), esp. chapter iv.
[20] 'The Ruined Cottage', lines 251–2: *WPW* V, 385.

they are written is deepened and extended by his contact with Coleridge's psychological speculations, the true weight of his concern lay with what those figures told the reader about the human heart. And this shifting emphasis gained momentum during the years after 1798. It seems as if Wordsworth could no longer see why *The Rime of the Ancient Mariner* had deserved such prominence in the original collection. The Mariner, it now seemed to him, was not a human being with whom readers could readily identify themselves at a human level. He should have had some leading characteristic – a profession, for instance – which would assist their recognition. So he concluded that the poem had been an injury to the volume and resolved that when the next edition came out, it should be downgraded in the order of presentation.[21]

The poems now to be contributed by him would be much more firmly devoted to the theme of the 'one human heart': 'The Brothers', 'Michael', 'Hartleap Well', 'Ruth', 'The Old Cumberland Beggar'. Although he included features of strong psychological interest in some, as, for example, the accounts of the 'calenture' and of somnambulism in 'The Brothers', these were now to be no longer partly speculative but based on firmly attested phenomena. Coleridge's ideas had taken a hard knock during the German trip, when he discovered not only that theories of animal magnetism had lost favour among German intellectuals but that the distinguished physiologist Blumenbach did not even believe in the existence of hypnotic power – prompting, no doubt, the omission from the 1800 version of *The Ancient Mariner* of references to 'that, which comes out of thine eye' – a notable feature of the reworking. The balance of his concern had swung firmly towards development of the philosophy of the mind and heart that would be laid out in much of his future writing.

If this is so, it follows that the kind of unity that has been traced here in the 1798 *Lyrical Ballads* was not matched in the 1800 collection. It had been the effect of an association between Wordsworth's and Coleridge's ideas that flourished during their conversations together, particularly during the year 1798–9, when Coleridge's psychological speculations, working together with Dorothy Wordsworth's sensitive observations and William's reflections on the solitary human condition had combined to produce a state of excitement and mutual stimulus highly favourable to the creative process. That excitement had already begun to diminish by 1800, with the visit to Germany and the scepticism concerning 'magnetic'

[21] See, e.g., the account by Stephen Gill: *William Wordsworth: A Life* (Oxford: Clarendon Press, 1989), pp. 186–8.

phenomena among intellectuals there. Previously it had seemed for a time as if their views were more or less identical. Coleridge's vision of the beautiful interweaving energies of the water-snakes as an emblem of the dynamic harmony at the heart of the 'one Life', and so of all living things, being matched by that which prompted Wordsworth's less active, more meditative account of the mood in which

> with an eye made quiet by the power
> Of harmony, and the deep power of joy
> We see into the life of things.

It was the production of lines such as those that convinced Coleridge that he was in the presence of a great poet whom he could never hope to emulate: he was still quoting from the poem a quarter of a century later.[22] Wordsworth, meanwhile, who was to affirm after Coleridge's death that despite their lack of recent contact Coleridge's mind had been constantly present to him during the intervening period, had developed strong reservations, nevertheless, concerning his vitalist assertions and the fuller implications of his speculations about the unconscious.

The further staking out of his own territory of the human heart for the 1800 collection and the concomitant downplaying of Coleridge's offerings may not have been intended as a personal slight, but they certainly marked the end to a concordat that seemed at times more like the adoption of a dual identity. It would gradually become evident that the differences between them involved more than their theoretical opinions respecting poetry. For a short period, however, they had been so successful in believing that the heart of life and the life of the heart were one and the same that they had been able to regard their respective contributions to the 1798 volume as more like stanzas of a common ode to joy. In that sense, as in others, Hazlitt's assertion proves to have been strictly correct: fools have laughed at them, while wise men scarcely understand them.

---

[22] See *CAR*, p. 404 and n.

CHAPTER 4

The Prelude: *a poem in process*

For many readers, the most distinctive feature of *The Prelude* is its status as one of the first English autobiographies. There had been predecessors, of course, often owing their existence to the religious fashion for telling the story of one's career before one had in some way received enlightenment; but there was an increasing interest in the possibility of achieving the aim expressed memorably by Rousseau in his *Confessions*:

I have begun on a work which is without precedent, whose accomplishment will have no imitator. I propose to set before my fellow-mortals a man in all the truth of nature; and this man shall be myself.

In the decades following, it was probably difficult to embark on any similar enterprise without thinking of Rousseau's words: certainly they often provided a criterion by which subsequent attempts of the kind might be judged. But by the same token, they furnished a stick with which to beat a writer such as Wordsworth if it was suspected that he had been less than open in his account, as when Émile Legouis's book *The Early Life of William Wordsworth, 1770–1798*, which appeared in English translation in 1897, revealed that while in France Wordsworth had fathered an illegitimate daughter by Annette Vallon. This discovery caused scholars to look again at the whole corpus of his work and to note the existence of the tale 'Vaudracour and Julia', first published in 1820 and evidently written as part of the 1805 *Prelude*. Since in its *Prelude* setting it fell into a natural sequence with the French Revolution matter contained there, it was all too easy to suppose not only that the exclusion of the story from *The Prelude* had been part of a deliberate attempt on his part to keep the relationship hidden from the public but that readers would now be justified in searching the poem for clues to other hidden facts of his autobiography. David V. Erdman pointed out that the name Vaudracour need only be changed to Vaudracoeur to emerge as a play on the name

'Heartsworth.'[1] Harold Bloom, similarly, equated Wordsworth with his protagonist, arguing,

Nowhere else in his poetry does Wordsworth say of himself, viewing a woman and not Nature, that

> his present mind
> Was under fascination; he beheld
> A vision, and he lov'd the thing he saw.[2]

Whatever conclusion one reaches about the nature of Wordsworth's early love life, however, one must attend to Brenda Banks's insistence that *The Prelude* is less about personal love than about the French Revolution – though the question still forces itself on us whether the Revolution, either, is really the central concern. It was certainly the case that both Wordsworth and Coleridge were deeply concerned at its fate: Wordsworth's aim in planning a great poem to follow it was to address the anxieties of young men who might have become dispirited by the course of recent events. Coleridge, indeed, put the point even more explicitly, writing in 1799 that he wanted his friend to write a long poem

addressed to those, who, in consequence of the complete failure of the French Revolution, have thrown up all hopes of the amelioration of mankind, and are sinking into an almost epicurean selfishness disguising the same under the soft titles of domestic attachment and contempt for visionary *philosophes . . .*[3]

There is little sign, however, that in his early stages of planning his autobiographical work, Wordsworth saw it as filling this particular bill. There are many references to the Revolution in the poem as it develops, as we shall see, but in those early stages Wordsworth seems rather to have been concerned with the topic that he often associated with it: the development of his own mind. Inasmuch as he wrote verses that might answer to Coleridge's plea, in fact, they are to be found rather in *The Excursion,* in lines devoted to the experiences of the Solitary, as he was

---

[1] See David V. Erdman, 'Wordsworth as Heartsworth; or, Was Regicide the Prophetic Ground of Those "Moral Questions"?', in *The Evidence of the Imagination: Studies of Interactions between Life and Art in English Romantic Fiction,* ed. Donald H. Reiman, Michael C. Jaye and Betty B. Bennett (New York University Press, 1978), pp. 12–41.

[2] Harold Bloom, *The Visionary Company,* rev. edn (Ithaca, N.Y.: Cornell University Press, 1971), p. 157. Brenda Banks, quoting this article and Erdman's in '"Vaudracour and Julia": Wordsworth's Melodrama of Protest', *Nineteenth-Century Literature* 47 (1992), 275–302, cites others taking a similar view.

[3] Letter of 1799: *CL* I, 527.

made to describe them in the third book of that poem. Transposed to Wordsworth himself, they might be thought to describe his awakening to the political possibilities of the time as a result of the events in France:

> From that abstraction I was roused, – and how?
> Even as a thoughtful shepherd by a flash
> Of lightning startled in a gloomy cave
> Of these wild hills. For, lo! the dread Bastille,
> With all the chambers in its horrid towers,
> Fell to the ground: – by violence overthrown
> Of indignation; and with shouts that drowned
> The crash it made in falling! From the wreck
> A golden palace rose, or seemed to rise,
> The appointed seat of equitable law
> And mild paternal sway. The potent shock
> I felt: the transformation I perceived,
> As marvellously seized as in that moment
> When, from the blind mist issuing, I beheld
> Glory – beyond all glory ever seen,
> Confusion infinite of heaven and earth,
> Dazzling the soul. Meanwhile, prophetic harps
> In every grove were ringing, 'War shall cease;
> Did ye not hear that conquest is abjured?
> Bring garlands, bring forth choicest flowers, to deck
> The tree of Liberty.' – My heart rebounded;
> My melancholy voice the chorus joined;
> – 'Be joyful all ye nations; in all lands,
> Ye that are capable of joy be glad!
> Henceforth, whate'er is wanting to yourselves
> In others ye shall promptly find; – and all,
> Enriched by mutual and reflected wealth,
> Shall with one heart honour their common kind.'[4]

If this account corresponds to Wordsworth's feelings of elation at the time, he is true also to his subsequent sense of disillusionment, when the growing confusion of events brought home to him the treacherous results of trusting in society and so enlisted him forcefully among 'the more faithful' who

> were compelled to exclaim,
> As Brutus did to Virtue, 'Liberty,
> I worshipped thee, and find thee but a Shade!'[5]

---

[4] *The Excursion*, iii. 706–33: *WPW* V, 100–1.   [5] *Ibid.*, lines 775–7.

We have already seen how Wordsworth fulfilled the conditions available to a young poet by subscribing to the fashion for writing poetry about nature; now, in his immediate reaction to political developments, he had a chance to go further. Dorothy described how he constantly reminded her of Edmund, the narrator of Beattie's 'The Minstrel';[6] and her brother was happy to accept the characterization, quoting readily from Beattie's text. Now he could demonstrate that devotion to nature need not be confined to English scenery. During his continental tour of 1790 he wrote of his delight in the Alpine parts of Switzerland:

I am a perfect Enthusiast in my admiration of Nature in all her various forms; and I have looked upon and as it were conversed with the objects which this country has presented to my view so long, and with such encreasing pleasure, that the idea of parting from them oppresses me with a sadness similar to what I have always felt in quitting a beloved friend.[7]

So far as religion is concerned, there was a certain obfuscation here, as the relationship between Nature and Nature's God was left – deliberately perhaps – unclear. But the poetic work produced after the tour gives some suggestion of his view. The best indication is to be found in 'Descriptive Sketches', where, with no hint of doctrinaire intent, the two words normally appear in some form of conjunction. In the very first lines he writes,

> Were there, below, a spot of holy ground
> Where from distress a refuge might be found,
> And solitude prepare the soul for heaven;
> Sure, nature's God that spot to man had given . . .[8]

After this the word 'nature' is increasingly associated with scenes of the sublime, as when he invokes the legend of a Golden Age in the Alpine country and follows it with the reflection:

> But human vices have provok'd the rod
> Of angry Nature to avenge her God.[9]

This is soon succeeded by the sense that only in this country of the sublime could the relationship with Nature and God be properly achieved:

---

[6] See Mary Moorman, *William Wordsworth: A Biography, The Early Years, 1770–1803* (Oxford: Clarendon Press, 1957), pp. 60–1.
[7] *WL* (1787–1805), p. 35.
[8] *Descriptive Sketches*, lines 1–4: *WPW* I, 42.
[9] *Ibid.*, lines 486–7: *WPW* I, 72.

> Once, Man entirely free, alone and wild,
> Was blest as free – for he was Nature's child.
> He, all superior but his God disdain'd,
> Walk'd none restraining, and by none restrain'd,
> Confess'd no law but what his reason taught,
> Did all he wish'd, and wish'd but what he ought.[10]

Finally, therefore, the sense of the sublime becomes itself knowledge of the divine:

> For images of other worlds are there;
> Awful the light, and holy is the air.
> Uncertain thro' his fierce uncultur'd soul,
> Like lighted tempests troubled transports roll;
> To viewless realms his Spirit towers amain,
> Beyond the senses and their little reign.
> And oft, when pass'd that solemn vision by,
> He holds with God himself communion high . . .[11]

This invites the reader to examine further the opening lines of the 1793 version of *Descriptive Sketches*:

> Were there, below, a spot of holy ground
> Where from distress a refuge might be found,
> And solitude prepare the soul for heaven;
> Sure, nature's God that spot to man had given
> Where falls the purple morning far and wide
> In flakes of light upon the mountain side;
> Where with loud voice the power of water shakes
> The leafy wood, or sleeps in quiet lakes.

Here the description of such a moment combines unusual beauty with the loud noise of a waterfall, as if Wordsworth finds the sense of the divine to subsist in a dialectic between the beauty of light and the impress of roaring sound. The feeling for quiet sensibility that had characterized *An Evening Walk* has given place to a more complex awareness.

By the time that Wordsworth embarked on the autobiographical venture that would become *The Prelude*, however, a certain amount of further clarification was necessarily required, though the exact nature of his metaphysical beliefs still remained bafflingly obscure.

---

[10] *Ibid.*, lines 520–5: *WPW* I, 72.   [11] *Ibid.*, lines 544–51: *WPW* I, 74.

The position becomes clearer once one gives up the illusion that one can understand *The Prelude* by reading it back from the finished product; the poem is better appreciated, instead, by being thought about from the beginnings out of which it grew, as a poem of process. Wordsworth's early career as a young man of sensibility will take the reader some way towards a sense of his development towards maturity, but the most striking feature of the first drafts is that they show him concerned with the side of his emotional memory that took him away from ordered and rational response, reminding him rather of feelings that had been touched by fear or the workings of extreme energy. Manuscript JJ in the Dove Cottage collection is one of the earliest manifestations of what was happening to him at this time.[12] The great virtue of this early draft is that it enables one to trace the workings of his poetic mind as he begins putting together reconstructions of what now impresses him most among his earliest memories, which are then put together in a slightly more orderly fashion as he weaves the two Parts that comprise his first version – not yet entitled *The Prelude*, of course; in fact not yet given a title at all. As time goes by, it is evidently to be thought of as the 'Poem to Coleridge', or as he put it more wordily when he began a rather more elaborate version, and inscribed its title page, with many ornamentations and curlicues,

Poem
Title not yet fixed upon by
William Wordsworth
Addressed to
S. T. Coleridge

As one reads the poem in the form in which he produced it in five books in 1804, it becomes clear that although it begins boldly enough as a celebration of the occasion on which it is written, its emerging theme is his inability to embark on the truly great poem that he wants to write. And when one turns back to the 1799 two-part *Prelude*, one discovers that it does not open, like most long poems, with some such matter as an invocation of the Muse, or even an inquiry into 'man's first disobedience', but with a simple question: 'Was it for this . . .?' A good deal of ink has been spilt over the question of Wordsworth's point of reference here, but the most likely answer is found in Milton's *Samson Agonistes*: when Samson's father Manoah comes to visit him where he remains in prison, he questions the justice of God in first answering his prayers for the child

---

[12] See the published version at the end of the Clarendon *Prelude* (Oxford: Clarendon Press, 1926).

that has so far been denied to his wife with 'such a Son as all Men haild me happy . . .' and then allowing him to be overcome by his enemies, exclaiming

> For this did th'Angel twice descend? for this
> Ordaind thy nurture holy, as of a Plant?   (lines 361–2)

If it is right to assume that Wordsworth echoes Milton here, the implication is that he thinks of himself as a failed Samson. He had felt himself to be a devoted figure, intended to be a great poet, yet finds himself impotent to produce the great work he envisaged. And if one turns back again to the two-part *Prelude*, one finds that it begins with the relating of a sequence of memorable early moments, in which he felt his uniqueness as a human being. He begins, for example, with the reminiscence of trapping woodcocks – and the strange fearfulness provoked when he occasionally snatched the prey from someone else's snare. The second, associated, experience is of birds' nesting and the 'strange utterance' of the wind on such vertiginous occasions; while soon he is remembering other experiences that contribute to the sequence of what he has come to think of as 'spots of time'. The term itself is curious because of the sense it conveys of seeing time as a great landscape. It is as if an immense panorama were being suggested, primarily shadowed by clouds to the extent of seeming matter of fact and rather dull; yet as one looks, because of breaks in the clouds, some parts of the scenery looked at are illuminated by sunlight.

The revisions undertaken to the growing body of *The Prelude* included, as mentioned earlier, a first version consisting of two books in which he reflected largely on his earliest memories. If one looks at these two in isolation, one does not find mention of the French Revolution; even if thought of as an autobiography, it proves somewhat selective. Over the next few years he added three more books, so as to present a more considered account of his early life, devoting his next book to his first year at Cambridge, the following one to his return to the Lakes for the summer vacation and a fifth to a consideration of books and their effect on him. This fifth book might well have acted as a rounding-off chapter, which would have turned the whole into a consideration of 'the making of a poet'. Such a five-book poem, completed by 1804 and devoted not only to his earliest years but to his education as a whole, would have been a very satisfactory middle-sized poem in its own right on a fascinating subject: the education of a poet. There had still been very little reference to the French Revolution, however, and indeed when he looked back on what he had achieved, he evidently felt the whole set-up he had devised somewhat unsatisfactory since in his five books he had so far said nothing, either, about important topics such as love and domestic affairs. During the next few months, he added several more books, in which he dealt with his response to the Alps, his first years in London, his sense of France as experienced in the years immediately following the French Revolution, and his subsequent growing awareness of the relationship between nature and humanity. Even when we look at this fuller poem, we find that France is not mentioned until halfway through, when Wordsworth traces the course of his career after Cambridge and writes of the walking tour during which he came across current events – almost, it might seem, by accident. 'Nature then was sovereign in my heart', he writes, but this time there was a special impulse –

> . . . 'twas a time when Europe was rejoiced,
> France standing on the top of golden hours,
> And human nature seeming born again.[13]

If we now look to Books 9 and 10 for a detailed account of his reactions to contemporary events, it will be seen that what was happening during these years contributed to the current 'crisis of the word'. In experiencing post-revolutionary France, Wordsworth was trying to come to terms with a civilization from which its traditional underpinning of Christian philosophy had apparently been removed. Particularly important in the midst of this were his conversations with Michel Beaupuy, a man not notable for religious leanings but unmistakably upright in his moral behaviour:

> A meeker man
> Than this lived never, nor a more benign,
> Meek though enthusiastic. Injuries
> Made *him* more gracious, and his nature then
> Did breathe its sweetness out most sensibly,
> As aromatic flowers on Alpine turf,
> When foot hath crushed them.[14]

These conversations gave Wordsworth an unusually forceful understanding of current events:

> And when we chanced
> One day to meet a hunger-bitten Girl,
> Who crept along fitting her languid self

---

[13] *WPrel* (1805), vi. 352–4.   [14] *Ibid.*, ix. 289–305.

> Unto a heifer's motion – by a cord
> Tied to her arm, and picking thus from the lane
> Its sustenance, while the girl with her two hands
> Was busy knitting in a heartless mood
> Of solitude – and at the sight my friend
> In agitation said, ''Tis against that
> Which we are fighting,' I with him believed
> Devoutly that a spirit was abroad
> Which could not be withstood . . .[15]

Along with this optimistic line of conviction, however, there intervened from time to time a melancholy awareness that human faculties may include a permanent sense of threat – best represented, perhaps, in the nightmares that beset him when, fully conscious of the events that had taken place during his absence, he returned to Paris in the following year and found himself haunted –

> And in this way I wrought upon myself,
> Until I seemed to hear a voice that cried,
> To the whole city, 'Sleep no more!' To this
> Add comments of a calmer mind – from which
> I could not gather full security –
> But at the best it seemed a place of fear,
> Appeared unfit for the repose of night,
> Defenceless as a wood where tigers roam.[16]

This dramatic enactment of the terrors that might underlie disappearance of a religious basis to human behaviour brings out what may be seen as the most important layer of all among the considerations underlying the creation of the poem.

Some further questions concerning the poem, such as that of its quality as it proceeded through its varying versions, may also be considered. It is sometimes questioned, for example, whether the 1805 version of the poem is not preferable to that of 1850 (or the reverse). This question has the virtue of involving texts readily comparable with one another; indeed, some years back it offered the occasion for a whole debate at the Wordsworth Summer Conference.[17]

Although the 1805 versus 1850 version of the debate offers clear-cut issues, they also include unfortunate complexities. Ever since de Selincourt

---

[15] *Ibid.*, lines 511–22.   [16] *Ibid.*, x. 75–82.
[17] The proceedings were later recorded in detail in *The Wordsworth Circle*.

edited the major versions together for the Oxford edition, his conclusion that the changes for the 1850 version falsified the 'authentic' Wordsworth, introducing touches of Christian piety untrue to the poet of the 1805 version, his view has tended to dominate attitudes to the poem. Yet Robert Barth was able to show a few years ago that it represented a gross oversimplification, as he demonstrated decisively, over and over again, that if one looks dispassionately at the relevant revisions over the poem as a whole, they cannot be said to follow such a uniform pattern; rather, they seem to move in both directions, sometimes playing up an orthodox Christian interpretation, sometimes playing it down.[18]

Although Barth certainly made a convincing case here, an important qualification is called for. While many of Wordsworth's shifts of attitude were already present when he completed the 1805 version, most of the crucial changes, in either direction, had occurred in work previous to it. The first two books, in other words, have a pantheistic feel; and this is even more the case when they are read in their original seedbed, the 1799 version, where references tends to be to 'spirits', to 'powers' and to 'beings', rather than to Nature. The implication is that in childhood and youth, as he recalled them, his attention was more commonly arrested by the presence of Nature, or at best 'Nature's God', than it ever was by the Christian God as presented in the Bible – though a point of contact might be found in the urge felt by Jesus to retire into the wilderness.

What I am suggesting here is that discussion of *The Prelude* is often distorted through the tendency of scholars and critics to assume a view of the poem as a whole and then to read individual passages in the light of that initial view, whereas it can be more profitable to begin by taking the two-book version of 1799 as one's 'founding text'. One of the prominent points in that version is the attention to his early visionary experiences, the first two of which provide some of the most memorable lines not only in these two parts, but eventually in the poem as a whole. I am thinking, of course, of moments such as that when, in the reaction from the exalted energy produced by skating, he would stop, feeling as if around him the earth were conveying a sense of its whole movement. In the light of such moments, constituting the sequence that he came to term 'spots of time',[19] it can be suggested that in the two-part version he was above all

---

[18] See 'Visions and Revisions: The Journey to the 1850 *Prelude*', in J. Robert Barth, S.J., *Romanticism and Transcendence* (Columbia, Mo. and London: Columbia University Press, 2003), pp. 15–29.

[19] See above, p. 67.

attempting to answer the question: how did I come to be the figure I now am – a highly ambitious poet who finds it hard to write my great poem? And in his answer he constantly returns to the matter of language, including what I have termed 'the crisis of the word'. We might consider, for example, this passage about his early experiences:

> The seasons came,
> And every season brought a countless store
> Of modes and temporary qualities
> Which but for this most watchful power of love
> Had been neglected, left a register
> Of permanent relations else unknown.
> Hence life, and change, and beauty, solitude
> More active even than 'best society',
> Society made sweet as solitude
> By silent inobtrusive sympathies,
> And gentle agitations of the mind
> From manifold distinctions, difference
> Perceived in things where to the common eye
> No difference is, and hence, from the same source
> Sublimer joy. For I would walk alone
> In storm and tempest, or in starlight nights
> Beneath the quiet heavens, and, at that time
> Would feel whate'er there is of power in sound
> To breathe an elevated mood, by form
> Or image unprofaned; and I would stand,
> Beneath some rock, listening to sounds that are
> The ghostly language of the ancient earth,
> Or make their dim abode in distant winds.
> Thence did I drink the visionary power.
> I deem not profitless those fleeting moods
> Of shadowy exultation; not for this,
> That they are kindred to our purer mind
> And intellectual life; but that the soul –
> Remembering how she felt, but what she felt
> Remembering not – retains an obscure sense
> Of possible sublimity, to which
> With growing faculties she doth aspire,
> With faculties still growing, feeling still
> That whatsoever point they gain they still
> Have something to pursue.[20]

---

[20] *WPrel* (1799), ii. 337–71 (cf. *WPrel* (1805), ii. 307–41).

The most striking feature of this long passage lies in its affirmation that the sources and roots of language lie well behind the language of every day. So as he wanders alone at night, hearing the 'strange utterance' of the 'loud dry wind', or stands

>   listening to sounds that are
>   The ghostly language of the ancient earth . . .[21]

he is conscious of a strange alternative, unearthly, universe, where he can sometimes hear 'low breathings' coming after him, or where even the cheerful ringing sounds of skating may resemble an unusual language, verging on the sublime:

>   . . . With the din
>   Meanwhile, the precipices rang aloud;
>   The leafless trees and every icy crag
>   Tinkled like iron; while the distant hills
>   Into the tumult sent an alien sound
>   Of melancholy, not unnoticed, while the stars,
>   Eastward, were sparkling clear, and in the west
>   The orange sky of evening died away.[22]

As one reads the two-part version of *The Prelude*, this sense that the sources of language may lie far below the language that we normally use seems one of the major forces at work, but still more important is the fact that the poetry is built upon such visionary experiences, with their variety of valuable reminiscences. In the end, these were to provide one of the broadest structures for the poem as a whole – stretched out not just over two books but over the full thirteen.

In the process of expansion required for this, the inquiry into the nature of language that had given the poem much of its coherence was swallowed up into the longer inquiry increasingly preoccupying him, concerning the significance of his own career.

In the previous chapter the fuller version was mentioned, along with the important discussions there that help continue the question of language and its effects, such as the very striking section in Book 8 where the act of reading an unfamiliar text is likened to the experience of a traveller entering a cavern, followed by the three stages of his interpreting what he sees. In addition to this, however, although the visionary moments are

---

[21] *WPrel* (1799), i. 64, ii. 357–8 (cf. *WPrel* (1805), i. 348, ii. 327–8).
[22] *WPrel* (1799), i. 47, 162–9 (cf. *WPrel* (1805), i. 330, 466–73).

still arranged to extend over the first books, there are some exceptions, where the poet draws other important lessons. Two important examples are the incident, eventually found in Book 5, of his finding a pile of clothes that turn out to be those of a man who has drowned, and the account in Book 11, of his waiting impatiently for horses to fetch him from school – which then take him to the desolate home where his father is shortly to die. In both cases the theme is mortality: the effect of seeing the drowned man is lightened by the fact that it so resembled the woodcuts with which he had become familiar; while memory of waiting for the horses acts as an admonition of the lasting presence of death, with its potentially unexpected imminence – the paradox being that his memory of the second is curiously comforting. Two other interesting examples of such visionary reminiscences, despite their haunting quality, formed no part of the original two-part poem: they are the crossing of the Alps in Book 6 and the memory, which dominates the final book, of his night ascent of Snowdon. These two culminating 'spots of time' show the broadening view that had come to characterize his extended version of the poem, the dominating theme being now Imagination. Reflection on the working of inspiration was prompted by the strange fact that the moment of revelation accompanying the fact of his crossing the Alps came not at the point of transition – which, paradoxically, caught them unawares – but during the descent through the valley afterwards. Likewise, the revelation on Snowdon came not, as he had hoped and expected, from seeing the sunrise there, but during the night ascent, through the unexpected view of the moon in the strange moment of its rising above the clouds, then to be remembered by him as a better emblem of the human mind than a rising sun could ever be:

> A meditation rose in me that night
> Upon the lonely mountain when the scene
> Had passed away, and it appeared to me
> The perfect image of a mighty mind,
> Of one that feeds upon infinity,
> That is exalted by an under-presence,
> The sense of God, or whatsoe'er is dim
> Or vast in its own being . . .[23]

---

[23] *WPrel* (1805), xiii. 66–73.

If it was an 'image' of the mind, he makes it clear in his later version that it was so in a specific sense:

> a mind sustained
> By recognitions of transcendent power,
> In sense conducting to ideal form . . .[24]

One's initial response is to see this as a supreme example of Wordsworth's egotism – the 'egotistical sublime' of Keats's phrase. But the lasting sense is more complex. Even as Wordsworth, contemplating his stature on Snowdon, projects a possible gigantic intellectual sublime, his figure would be viewed by an external spectator as essentially pathetic – an emblem of vulnerable and necessarily mortal humanity.

The whole of the poem might have concluded at this point, or with further lines to bring out the paradoxically double view of himself, whether as essentially lonely individual or as potential poetic benefactor to the whole of mankind if his gifts could be realized and appreciated. And in one sense he tried to carry on the theme in just such a way, through succeeding paragraphs in which he tries to exalt the belief in love and imagination that sustained him through the vicissitudes of his early life:

> This love more intellectual cannot be
> Without imagination, which in truth
> Is but another name for absolute strength
> And clearest insight, amplitude of mind,
> And reason in her most exalted mood.
> This faculty hath been the moving soul
> Of our long labour: we have traced the stream
> From darkness, and the very place of birth
> In its blind cavern, whence is faintly heard
> The sound of waters; followed it to light
> And open day, accompanied its course
> Among the ways of Nature, afterwards
> Lost sight of it bewildered and engulphed,
> Then given it greeting as it rose once more
> With strength, reflecting in its solemn breast
> The works of man, and face of human life;
> And lastly, from its progress have we drawn
> The feeling of life endless, the one thought
> By which we live, infinity and God.[25]

---

[24] *WPrel* (1850), xiv. 74–6.   [25] *WPrel* (1805), xiii. 166–184.

The poem does not end with this peroration, however. Instead, Wordsworth considers in greater detail the form which it has taken during his own intimate life. First he must pay tribute to Dorothy:

> Child of my parents, sister of my soul,
> Elsewhere have strains of gratitude been breathed
> To thee for all the early tenderness
> Which I from thee imbibed. And true it is
> That later seasons owed to thee no less;
> For, spite of thy sweet influence and the touch
> Of other kindred hands that opened out
> The springs of tender thought in infancy,
> And spite of all which singly I had watched
> Of elegance, and each minuter charm
> In Nature or in life, still to the last –
> Even to the very going-out of youth,
> The period which our story now hath reached –
> I too exclusively esteemed that love,
> And sought that beauty, which as Milton sings
> Hath terror in it. Thou didst soften down
> This over-sternness; but for thee, sweet friend,
> My soul, too reckless of mild grace, had been
> Far longer what by Nature it was framed –
> Longer retained its countenance severe –
> A rock with torrents roaring, with the clouds
> Familiar, and a favorite of the stars:
> But thou didst plant its crevices with flowers,
> Hang it with shrubs that twinkle in the breeze,
> And teach the little birds to build their nests
> And warble in its chambers.[26]

But although by the final version he feels bound to link with her the subsequent intervention of his wife Mary, 'no more a phantom to adorn / A moment, but an inmate of the heart, / And yet a spirit, there for me enshrined / To penetrate the lofty and the low', his more immediate recourse in the 1805 version is to the other intimacy that he recalls from those years:

> With such a theme,
> Coleridge – with this my argument – of thee
> Shall I be silent? O most loving soul,
> Placed on this earth to love and understand,

---

[26] *Ibid.*, xiii. 211–36.

> And from thy presence shed the light of love,
> Shall I be mute ere thou be spoken of?[27]

At this point, however, there occurs one of the most important divergences between the two texts. The 1805 version continues with the words 'Thy gentle spirit to my heart of hearts / Did also find its way', referring also to

> the life
> Of all things and the mighty unity
> In all which we behold, and feel, and are . . .[28]

These lines in turn look back to the earlier tribute, in which (from the two-part version onwards) he wrote, of his friend,

> To thee, unblinded by these outward shews
> The unity of all has been revealed . . .[29]

Coleridge had been obsessed equally by a sense of 'the life of all things' ('the one Life'):

> Thy gentle spirit to my heart of hearts
> Did also find its way; and thus the life
> Of all things and the mighty unity
> In all which we behold, and feel, and are,
> Admitted more habitually a mild
> Interposition, closelier gathering thoughts
> Of man and his concerns, such as become
> A human creature, be he whom he may,
> Poet, or destined to an humbler name . . .[30]

By 1850, these lines are replaced by a slightly longer version. The phrase 'O most loving soul' has become 'O capacious Soul!', and 'gentle spirit' has given place to 'kindred influence'; there is then a long attempt to characterize Coleridge's contribution more fully:

> Thy kindred influence to my heart of hearts
> Did also find its way. Thus fear relaxed
> Her overweening grasp; thus thoughts and things
> In the self-haunting spirit learned to take
> More rational proportions; mystery,

---

[27] *Ibid.*, xiii. 246–51. [28] *Ibid.*, xiii. 253–5.
[29] *WPrel* (1799), ii. 255–6. [30] *WPrel* (1805), xiii. 252–60.

> The incumbent mystery of sense and soul,
> Of life and death, time and eternity,
> Admitted more habitually a mild
> Interposition – a serene delight
> In closelier gathering cares, such as become
> A human creature, howsoe'er endowed,
> Poet, or destined for a humbler name . . .[31]

This repetition of the closing line is followed by lines that Wordsworth evidently valued:

> And so the deep enthusiastic joy,
> The rapture of the hallelujah sent
> From all that breathes and is, was chastened, stemmed,
> And balanced . . .[32]

Here, as often in Wordsworth, a monitory note occurs. In 1805 it runs

> And balanced, by a reason which indeed
> Is reason, duty, and pathetic truth –
> And God and man divided, as they ought,
> Between them the great system of the world,
> Where man is sphered, and which God animates.[33]

By 1850 this becomes

> And balanced by pathetic truth, by trust
> In hopeful reason, leaning on the stay
> Of Providence, and in reverence for duty,
> Here, if need be, struggling with storms, and there
> Strewing in peace life's humblest ground with herbs,
> At every season green, sweet at all hours![34]

Wordsworth has resorted to the more familiar pattern of his art, seeking to come through struggles to a pacific vision of stability, first in time and then in space, with a strong sense of the providential work of the seasons. But although the earlier picture of Coleridge also voices the need for a balanced view, the sense there hovers between the essential unity of the one Life, reflecting God as its great animating principle, and humanity, at once splendid and fragile, ready at one and the same time to mirror the divine or humbly seek its mercy.

---

[31] WPrel (1850), xiv. 281–92.   [32] WPrel (1805), xiii. 261–4.
[33] Ibid., xiii. 264–8.   [34] WPrel (1850), xiv. 296–301.

The earlier view of Wordsworth, which acknowledged both Coleridge's aspirations as a Christian teacher and his pantheistic vision of the nature of life as such, can best be seen at work in some fragments, written probably in Germany in 1799, at the time when he was working on *Peter Bell*, in which he showed himself rapt by the Coleridgean consciousness that could subordinate all eighteenth-century figurings of the rational beneath a sublime sense of the magnetic links between all living things:

> Such consciousness I deem but accidents,
> Relapses from that one interior life
> That lives in all things, sacred from the touch
> Of that false secondary power by which
> In weakness we create distinctions, then
> Believe that all our puny boundaries are things
> Which we perceive, and not which we have made –
> In which all beings live with God, themselves
> Are God, existing in one mighty whole . . .[35]

The Prelude is by no means a simple poem: indeed, it might be better to think of it as a symphony. This kind of symphony is not, however, a harmonizing of different strains, but a mingling of different possible assertions. Coleridge was in one sense perfectly justified in seeing its development as a refining, a single focusing on the consciousness of its creator, and in this sense it is perfectly justifiable to end with Wordsworth's lonely ascent of Snowdon and his meditations concerning the nature of a majestic intellect. In this sense the much earlier recalling of his awareness of the image of Newton when he himself had been at Cambridge is a quiet foreshadowing of what he contemplates at the end of his journey. But because the poem does not end there, it is as if the stream that Wordsworth claims to have been following throughout runs now into a dispersing of various runnels.

Those who have studied the poem most closely have tended to record a suspicion that there is a profound fissure in its structure, corresponding to the duality of theme remarked on earlier – evident even from the titles that Wordsworth gives to the various sections. Revolution may be one of the topics, but if so it must ultimately be to question whether there can be any revolution that does not become the seemingly endless cycle of violence that had been produced in France; whether there may not be an alternative kind of 'revolution' which is an ineluctable sign of growth.

---

[35] See *WPrel*, p. 496.

In this respect it is important to note that when Coleridge used the word in quoting a passage from the poem in *The Friend*, he described it as his 'Poem on the growth and revolutions of an individual mind'.[36] The one hope for mankind might then seem to be the cultivation of Nature as a guide to humanity: in those terms love of nature might truly lead to love of man.

The most important fissure, however, must be that between Coleridge as recalled from the time of their greatest intimacy and the Coleridge who was himself endeavouring to resolve the fractures within the logic of his own thought. This is clear from the very different views of him within the development of the poem itself. When Wordsworth thinks of Coleridge in the 1805 version, it is still in semi-pantheistic terms, as we have seen, but by 1850 he was anxious to stress more fully the role in his thought of 'Providence' and 'duty'.

The tributes to those who have most helped the enterprise thus give a surer clue to what is happening at the end of the poem, manifesting what he had come to believe were his most trustworthy guides, Dorothy's affection and Coleridge's imaginative gifts were the twin supports on which he might hope to rely if the temple of a lasting humanity were ever to be constructed. As he came to find the imagination less and less dependable as a resource, however, the more dominating of the two factors would come to be, correspondingly, affection. Just as the lasting legacy of the collection *Lyrical Ballads* would lie for him less in its dealings with language than in its attempts to foster a new 'language of the heart', Coleridge's attempts in *The Prelude* to investigate the subliminal sources of human behaviour might contribute much to its power but would otherwise be allowed no more than a strictly subordinate role. The subtlety of his friend's investigations into the respective workings of reason and feeling and their sources would nevertheless have provided a vital contribution to the development of the poem as a whole.

[36] *CFriend* (1809) II, 258 (cf. I, 368).

CHAPTER 5

Words or images?
Blake's representation of history

The nature of London as it presented itself to an observer in the 1790s was most memorable for a lack of organization that amounted at times to near-anarchy. Wordsworth, arriving as a young man, noticed this confusion above all:

> All moveables of wonder, from all parts,
> Are here – albinos, painted Indians, dwarfs,
> The horse of knowledge, and the learned pig,
> The stone-eater, the man that swallows fire,
> Giants, ventriloquists, the invisible girl,
> The bust that speaks and moves its goggling eyes,
> The wax-work, clock-work, all the marvellous craft
> Of modern Merlins, wild beasts, puppet-shows,
> All out-of-the-way, far-fetched, perverted things
> All freaks of Nature, all Promethean thoughts
> Of man, his dullness, madness, and their feats
> All jumbled up together to compose
> This parliament of monsters. Tents and booths
> Meanwhile – as if the whole were one vast mill –
> Are vomiting, receiving, on all sides,
> Men, women, three-years' children, babes in arms . . .[1]

To someone who had been brought up in the Lake District – even if he had also been educated in Cambridge – the experience of living in a metropolis where one might not know even the identity of one's next-door neighbour gave an overwhelming sense of human fragmentation.

As a feature of city life, the lapse into dissociation and the rise of individualism had been an increasing phenomenon at least since the seventeenth century. This is something rather separate from the kind of consideration usually given in sociological accounts, which tend to dwell

---

[1] *WPrel* (1805), vii. 680–95.

on the changes brought about when an economy consisting largely of peasant families and tribes moved to an industrialism that herded crowds of people into factories and mills of the new era. This concentration on great sweeps of agricultural land, contrasting that with the rise of great industrial cities that were swallowing segments of the population into an anonymous mass, ignores commercial cities such as London, where the pattern was different. The concern there was primarily with individual tradesmen and small businesses – the very world in which many people found themselves by the end of the eighteenth century. There regulation of employment was virtually non-existent, with labourers at the mercy of their employers. The most glaring example was that of the climbing boys enlisted to sweep the chimneys of premises rarely constructed with any thought to their needs, who often suffered appalling disabilities as a result.

Ranging upwards from this, a swathe of small businesses constituted the commercial backbone of the city and also the core of its conservative politics, resulting in a tension between these small, often family, interests and the forces of popular protest that might receive their impetus from workers of a simpler kind. We might consider, for instance, the case of John Sheppard, an eighteenth-century criminal, who was not particularly popular with the drapers, jewellers, tailors and instrument-makers whom he robbed, but gained wide eminence as a result of his remarkable skill in breaking out of the prisons that tried to hold him. By the time he was imprisoned a fourth time, in Newgate Jail, he had become such a culture hero that he was visited by scores of sightseers and well-wishers, each of whom were willing to pay four shillings a time for the chance of seeing him. A journalist of the time wrote that there were 'three great curiosities in Town at present . . . the young Lions stuffed in the Tower, the Ostrich on Ludgate Hill and John Sheppard in Newgate'.[2] Despite his fame, however, Sheppard, having failed to escape again, or even gain a reprieve, was executed on 16 November 1724, amid unusual scenes of grief and anger. In contrast the man who captured him, the notorious thief-taker Jonathan Wild, was reviled for his activities – which culminated in his own execution on charges of corruption the following year. Popular admiration for the ingenious escaper had done nothing to hinder the legal determination to make Sheppard pay the penalty for his crimes; this human contrast, which had many analogues in the culture of the

[2] Quoted by Richard Holmes (ed.), *Defoe on Sheppard and Wild* (London: Harper Perennial, 2004), p. ix.

following years, could be seen as corresponding also to the subterranean yearnings for liberation accompanying the sense of imprisonment felt in the great city.

One is also struck by the effervescence of life in the community as a whole, however. A look at the 1794 directory[3] impresses by the multifarious activities revealed, every imaginable trade being represented, together with a sense of ceaseless energy and striving. One need think only of the fact that William Blake's father was a hosier, with his own business and shop, and that his sons started their own print-selling business, to appreciate the extent of individual enterprise in middle-class society.

The evident purposefulness of all this activity must have acted as a palliative to any doubts that might have risen when these activities were at full stretch, but periods of holiday-making might find a thoughtful observer at more of a loss. The sense of unmanageable confusion that seized the young Wordsworth when he first experienced Bartholomew Fair, one of the culminating festivals of the London year, has already been mentioned: this sight of London, given uncertainty and alienation on his own part, created a 'blank confusion' that seemed a 'true epitome' of the City herself.[4]

Not everyone was so bewildered. London was also the city which, according to Johnson, contained 'all that life can afford'[5] and where Lamb claimed that he would 'often shed tears in the motley Strand from fullness of joy at so much Life'.[6]

Blake's vision of the place, nevertheless, was penetrating, inciting, while he rejoiced in its inherent sense of life, an admonished awareness of the fear to which such a vulnerable community was open. With little in the way of an efficient police force, the response to violence was likely to be both peremptory and implacable. With efficient communications not available, any 'risings' of the London mob, constructed as they might be from causes consisting of little but rumour, could be unpredictable and alarming. In such a case the only resource available to the Lord Mayor was a call-out of the militia, who might in turn feel themselves licensed to use extreme force – as was the case in 1780 after the horrific outburst of violence known as the Gordon Riots (where it was later claimed that the destruction of property had exceeded that in Paris during the French

---

[3] Available online at www.londonancestor.com/kents/kents-menu.htm.
[4] *WPrel* (1805), vii. 696–707.
[5] Boswell's record of his conversation, 20 September 1777.
[6] *LL* (Marrs) I, 267.

Revolution). During this period, as Gilchrist describes, Blake at one point found himself carried along helplessly by the mob:

In this outburst of anarchy, Blake long remembered an involuntary participation of his own. On the third day, Tuesday, 6th of June, 'the Mass-houses' having already been demolished – one, in Blake's near neighbourhood, Warwick Street, Golden Square and various private houses also, the rioters, flushed with gin and victory, were turning their attention to grander schemes of devastation. That evening, the artist happened to be walking in a route chosen by one of the mobs at large, whose course lay from Justice Hyde's house near Leicester Fields, for the destruction of which less than an hour had sufficed, through Long Acre, past the quiet house of Blake's old master, engraver Basire, in Great Queen Street, Lincoln's Inn Fields, and down Holborn, bound for Newgate. Suddenly, he encountered the advancing wave of triumphant Blackguardism, and was forced (for from such a great surging mob there is no disentanglement) to go along in the very front rank, and witness the storm and burning of the fortress-like prison, and release of its three hundred inmates.[7]

In some cases the soldiers refused to fire on people whom they regarded as fellow-citizens. This did not stop the aftermath and ultimate response from being extremely violent: once the forces of authority had resumed control large numbers of the rioters, some of them no more than boys, were hanged at Tyburn.

How were such things to be imaged or described? We might look firstly at a design by James Gillray, one of the most popular artists of the time, who seems never to have been closely aligned with one of the major political groupings, but who enjoyed a considerable success through his satirical cartoons, produced at a prolific rate. His only known education, interestingly, was in early childhood at a Moravian academy in Bedford.[8] Having studied as an artist, he became manically industrious and ended by living above Mrs Hannah Humphrey, a print-seller who showed his works outside her premises in St James's Street. There they proved such an attraction that people often found themselves kept off the pavement by others who were crowding the windows: it suggests something of the cultural starvation of people at this time, and their appetite for sensation, that a coloured satirical print should have had such an effect.

A poster[9] which appeared in 1792 was prompted by a notable case of the time. Richard Brothers, who was a half-pay officer in the Navy, had

---

[7] See G. E. Bentley Jr, *Blake Records* (Oxford: Clarendon Press, 1969), p. 18.

[8] Marilyn Butler, *Romantics, Rebels, and Revolutionaries* (Oxford: Clarendon Press, 1981), p. 53.

[9] Held in collections at the Fitzwilliam Museum, Cambridge, and the British Museum, among others.

forgone his allowance rather than take the Oath of Loyalty and in 1792 began to produce prophecies against the impending war with France, followed in 1794 by a work entitled *A Revealed Knowledge of the Prophecies and Times,* in which he both denounced the war, identified by him with the War prophesied in Revelation xix, and predicted the return of the Jews to Jerusalem. At this the authorities took fright and a warrant for his arrest was issued on grounds of his 'unlawfully, maliciously, and wickedly writing, publishing, and printing various fantastical prophecies, with intent to cause dissension and other disturbances within the Realm, contrary to the Statute'.[10] Examined by the Privy Council, he was judged insane, and confined to a Brighton asylum for the next eleven years. Blake, meanwhile, who was also presenting himself as a prophet, suffered no such penalty – though the fate of Brothers may have curbed his enthusiasm and affected the nature of his subsequent writings.

To someone looking at the print now, the most interesting feature is less the political point than the ready resort to symbolism. For Gillray, however, the symbolism was essentially geared to the political issue: Brothers himself he dressed as a *sans-culotte*; and while surrounding the moon above him with a circle of unreality, he gave the sun a revolutionary red cap and portrayed him leering at a landscape that was being drenched with drops of blood. Meanwhile Brothers, rearing the 'horns of glory' normally assigned to Moses, was shown as urging his followers over the remains of devilish king and priest and past the swallowing up of St Paul's Cathedral and the Monument towards a Promised Land marked by a construction labelled 'Gate of Jerusalem'. Any Londoner who saw that would be likely to have recognized at once its resemblance to a local landmark, the gallows outside Newgate Jail.

Gillray was adept at using recognizable symbolism to make a 'prophetic' political point, whereas the four-square gallows would have been more likely to suggest to his contemporary Blake, who normally used symbolism for its own sake, a resemblance to one of the four-square trilitha at Stonehenge. When Blake shows his own image of the Gate of Jerusalem, it is as a Gothic arch, aspiring to the sublime. In the same way, his imagery of sun and moon, in *Jerusalem*, stresses their provisional nature as emblems of qualities in the divine due to be superseded in the full divine vision.

---

[10]   *Times* report of 6 March 1795: see Morton Paley, 'William Blake, the Prince of the Hebrews, and the Woman Clothed with the Sun', in *William Blake, Essays in Honour of Sir Geoffrey Keynes,* ed. Morton Paley and Michael Phillips (Oxford: Clarendon Press, 1973), p. 261.

Blake's portrayal of the Hebrews is satiric, but kindly. In the address to the Jews which precedes the second section of his *Jerusalem*, he probes Jewish tradition for what he takes to be its permanent value. The Jewish pattern of humility is in itself a characteristic that he can honour; other elements in their worship, such as the stress on sacrifice and following of the Law, seem perversions of what is truly valuable. This last includes even their traditional profession as money-changers, if only because it suggests that they are supporters, however unconscious, of the 'exchanges' that are the mark of true humanity:

> In my Exchanges every Land
> Shall walk, & mine in every Land,
> Mutual shall build Jerusalem:
> Both heart in heart & hand in hand.[11]

Blake's strong visionary powers were further nurtured and chastened by his religious upbringing. Keri Davies's work on his forebears has enquired into the beliefs of his mother, originally Catherine Wright, and established that having come from a small village in Nottinghamshire, she was received into a Moravian congregation in Fetter Lane in London. The Moravians, as episcopal, were in communion with the Church of England, while not discouraged from regarding themselves as dissenters. Nancy Bogen's suggestion some years ago that the Blakes might have attended the Fetter Lane chapel while not ceasing to be Anglicans ('It was possible to be at the time both of and not of the Anglican Church'[12]) has thus been fortified.

The Moravians were notable for strong outpourings of emotion: John Wesley, an important adherent before he became one of the founders of Methodism, dated his conversion to an evening of 24 May 1738, when at a meeting among them in Aldersgate Street he felt his heart 'strangely warmed'.[13] Such manifestations no doubt had some effect on William Blake also: the issue of a possible resemblance between Moravian hymns and some of his early poetry was in fact raised some years ago.[14] The indications are, however, that while his mother aligned herself with her

---

[11] *BE*, p. 172; *BK*, p. 652.
[12] See Nancy Bogen, 'The Problem of William Blake's Early Religion', *The Personalist* 49 (1968), 509–22.
[13] See his diary record for 24 May 1738.
[14] See Margaret Ruth Lowery, *Windows of the Morning: A Critical Study of William Blake's Poetical Sketches, 1783* (New Haven: Yale University Press, 1940). Margaret Lowery was one of the first to discuss William Muir's statement that Blake's parents had worshipped at Fetter Lane.

first husband's allegiance, she found total commitment to the sect difficult. A letter from her to the brethren is extant (presumably following her husband's example), in which she recorded that the Saviour had been pleased to make her 'Suck his wounds and hug the Cross more then Ever'.[15]

Her letter also bears witness to the strong part played by feeling in the Moravian hymns, particularly their extravagant devotion to the detail of Christ's sufferings. It is hard to imagine that her son enjoyed some of their more mawkish expressions, or that he took over much more than their general tone of humane feeling and their philosophy of love: a devotion to Christ's blood and wounds is notably absent from his own work. Imagery in Moravian hymnody such as that of lion and lamb looks forward to his more sophisticated use of such child-like imagery in the *Songs of Innocence*, on the other hand, though his comments on phrases such as the 'lambkins and chickens of Christ' might well have been scathing.

There is some evidence that Blake's father joined the Baptists, at least for a time,[16]while the children, including William, were for the most part baptized in the Grinling Gibbons font at the Anglican St James's Church in Piccadilly – in line again, perhaps, with the Moravian position that made it possible to be at one and the same time both Anglican and 'Dissenting'. As G. E. Bentley has argued, however,[17] the best way of describing Blake's own religious position as he grew up would probably be to speak in terms of 'Enthusiasm', a term to be associated less with a particular religious persuasion than with a widely ranging religious attitude and by no means untrue to a Moravianism which, as Davies points out, was less a sect than a spirituality. One advantage of considering him in this context is that 'enthusiasts' of the time could well feel themselves justified in cultivating extremes which might lead others to label them as mad – a category which they felt they could accept with equanimity: in a letter of 26 November 1800, Blake, for instance, wrote of himself as an 'Enthusiastic, hope-fostered visionary',[18] and shortly before this William Hayley said that he could not even write the word without recalling him.[19]

[15] Transcribed by A. P. K. Davies in his unpublished PhD thesis, 'William Blake in Context' (University of Surrey, 2003), p. 297, and in his article (published with M. K. Schuchard), 'Recovering the Lost Moravian History of William Blake's Family': *BQ* 38 (2004), 36–43.

[16] G. E. Bentley Jr, ed., *Blake Records* (Oxford: Clarendon Press, 1969) p. 8 and n.

[17] G. E. Bentley Jr, *The Stranger from Paradise* (New Haven and London: Yale University Press, 2001), pp. 7–9.

[18] Letter of 26 November 1800: *BE*, p. 707; *BK*, p. 807.

[19] Letter of 11 August 1800: Bentley, *Stranger*, p. 8n.

A few years later he would write to a correspondent, 'Dear Sir, excuse my enthusiasm or rather madness, for I am really drunk with intellectual vision whenever I take a pencil or graver into my hand, even as I used to be in my youth.'[20] To use the word avoids the need to identify his beliefs too narrowly.

It is also worth remembering that when Coleridge was remembering his own enthusiasm for the French Revolution in later years ('it had all my wishes – but none of my expectations'), he also recalled fondly the exculpation offered by one of his brothers: 'It was well said by my brother James once, when someone said I was a Jacobin – "No! Samuel is not a Jacobin – he is a hot-headed Moravian".'[21] As someone who enjoyed Jacob Boehme and his works, he evidently felt an immediate affinity to that enthusiast's religious sect.

Although similar as young men, and working out cognate destinies, Blake and Coleridge probably never encountered one another then, though it would be pleasant to imagine Blake in his twenties as one of those who, as Lamb tells his readers, paused on their way through the yard at Christ's Hospital to stand entranced by the sight and sound of the 'inspired charity school boy' expounding the mysteries of Iamblichus and Plotinus; in the London of their time, meanwhile, the contemporary revolutionary ferment must have evoked a response from everyone.

In his youth Blake explored various modes of expression. His *Poetical Sketches* were, according to accounts from others, accompanied by himself on the harp, with the musical settings transcribed: the text itself was published, to the applause of certain readers. In his manuscript 'An Island in the Moon', his character Quid proposes a form of printing which looks like a scheme he might have been toying with for his own work:

I would have all the writing Engraved instead of Printed & at every other leaf a high finish print all in three Volumes folio, & sell them a hundred pounds a piece. they would Print off two thousand . . .[22]

This was not altogether unlike his early production of poetic etchings with titles such as 'There is no Natural Religion', or the early version of *Songs of Innocence*. His manuscript poem 'Tiriel', also, was accompanied by illustrations roughly related to the text.

---

[20] Letter to Hayley, 23 October 1804: *BK*, p. 852.
[21] *CTT*, 21 July 1832: I, 309–10; II, 178–9.
[22] *BE*, p. 456; *BK*, p. 62.

When he embarked on his long poem 'The French Revolution', however, he simply allowed the first book to reach the proof stage and left it isolated as a fragment, without illustration. Various explanations for his apparent abandonment of it have been offered. It is noticeable, for instance, that later historical figures associated with the events, such as Danton, Marat and Robespierre, had not yet been mentioned, which makes it more likely that the work, bearing on its title page the date 1791, was either never to be completed (in spite of the statement that it was) or was given up once the course of events moved into the period of the Terror. This would certainly square with the tradition that his enthusiasm for the Revolution ended abruptly at the time of the September massacres in 1792, and that he then he tore off his revolutionary cockade, never to wear it again.

The writing of this long poem was raising exacerbated questions of representation, however. As subsequent scholars have recognized, the keeping of an accurate documentary record was not at the forefront of Blake's concerns; he seems rather to have been working towards other effects, the most obvious of which was to achieve sensational impact. His descriptions of the horrors of the Bastille, early in the poem, focus on a series of 'dens' and the victim imprisoned in each. 'In the tower named Bloody', for example,

. . . a skeleton yellow remained in its chains on its couch
Of stone, once a man who refus'd to sign papers of abhorrence; the eternal worm
Crept in the skeleton. In the den nam'd Religion, a loathsome sick woman, bound down
To a bed of straw; the seven diseases of earth, like birds of prey, stood on the couch,
And fed on the body. She refus'd to be whore to the Minister, and with a knife smote him.[23]

Despite its firm pattern of lengthy lines the poem already contained scope for exploring metaphorical content, as when the prisoners glimpse, even from within their confinement, the possibility of an opposite mode of existence:

For the Commons convene in the Hall of the Nation; like spirits of fire in the beautiful
Porches of the Sun, to plant beauty in the desart craving abyss, they gleam
On the anxious city . . .   (lines 54–6)

---

[23] *The French Revolution*, lines 33–7: *BE*, pp. 282–96; *BK*, pp. 134–46.

This visionary use of metaphor begins to indicate an appropriate symbolism, to be developed in other passages.

In his attempt to give poetic expression to his sense of what has been happening in France, Blake also draws on associations between particular areas and their traditional representation. The mention of Burgundy gives him an obvious opportunity to associate that province with both war and wine:

Then the ancientest Peer, Duke of Burgundy, rose from the monarch's right
    hand, red as wines
From his mountains; an odor of war, like a ripe vineyard, rose from his garments,
And the chamber became as a clouded sky; o'er the council he stretch'd his red
    limbs,
Cloth'd in flames of crimson, as a ripe vineyard stretches over sheaves of
    corn . . .   (lines 83–6)

The double imagery of wine and war continues as the Duke is surrounded by 'A bright cloud of infant souls', and 'his words fall like purple autumn on the sheaves'. The set of his mind is in one direction only, however: the threat of instability drives him to opt for war:

'Shall this marble built heaven become a clay cottage, this earth an oak stool, and
    these mowers
From the Atlantic mountains, mow down all this great starry harvest of six
    thousand years?
And shall Necker, the hind of Geneva, stretch out his crook'd sickle o'er fertile
    France,
Till our purple and crimson is faded to russet, and the kingdoms of earth bound
    in sheaves,
And the ancient forests of chivalry hewn, and the joys of the combat burnt for
    fuel;
Till the power and dominion is rent from the pole, sword and sceptre from sun
    and moon,
The law and gospel from fire and air, and eternal reason and science
From the deep and the solid, and man lay his faded head down on the rock
Of eternity, where the eternal lion and eagle remain to devour?'   (lines 89–97)

Blake's satire here works in more than one way. Radical irony is directed against an authoritarianism which cannot bear to regard a marble-built palace as the equal of a human cottage or question the use of resources such as timber for the prosecution of warfare; there is equally a more imaginatively rooted irony, directed against the visionless philosophy that sets its standard according to the apparent permanence of the stars and an adherence to written texts rather than the life that might inform them.

Whereas Burgundy argues forcefully, but from a mistaken view of things, the Archbishop of Paris, who rises 'In the rushing of scales and hissing of flames and rolling of sulphurous smoke', is evidently a more devilish figure, his serpentine energies perverted to a baser level as he hears an aged man, 'hovering in mist', expressing his own fears of what is to come:

'. . . Nobles and Clergy shall fail from before me, and my cloud and vision be no
    more;
The mitre become black, the crown vanish, and the scepter and ivory staff
Of the ruler wither among bones of death; they shall consume from the thistly
    field,
And the sound of the bell, and voice of the sabbath, and singing of the holy choir,
Is turn'd into songs of the harlot in day, and cries of the virgin in night.
They shall drop at the plow and faint at the harrow, unredeem'd, unconfess'd,
    unpardon'd;
The priest rot in his surplice by the lawless lover, the holy beside the accursed,
The King, frowning in purple, beside the grey plowman, and their worms
    embrace together.'   (lines 143–50)

The Archbishop's horror can again be viewed ironically: the priest and the lawless lover are alike human beings, and if worms embrace in consuming both king and ploughman, this does no more than demonstrate the true humanity of the latter and the common life of all.

    The limited vision of such protagonists means, however, that Burgundy, for example, can ultimately envisage only one possible harvest as outcome, the harvest of war, providing through its bloodshed the seed that the earth is calling for:

This to prevent, urg'd by cries in day, and prophetic dreams hovering in night,
To enrich the lean earth that craves, furrow'd with plows, whose seed is departing
    from her,
Thy nobles have gather'd thy starry hosts round this rebellious city,
To rouze up the ancient forests of Europe, with clarions of cloud breathing war,
To hear the horse neigh to the drum and trumpet . . .   (lines 98–102)

His arguments carry the day and the King, despite misgivings, follows the choice between husbandmen and soldiers, or between patient agriculture and the use of force, into the active acceptance of warfare:

'I hear rushing of muskets, and bright'ning of swords, and visages redd'ning with
    war,
Frowning and looking up from brooding villages and every dark'ning city,
Ancient wonders frown over the kingdom, and cries of women and babes are
    heard,

And tempests of doubt roll around me, and fierce sorrows, because of the Nobles
   of France.
Depart, answer not, for the tempest must fall, as in years that are passed
   away.'   (lines 116–20)

The ultimate ideological battle is not, however, between the pastoral and
the military but between the meanness of the reactionary, symbolized here
in the Archbishop, who takes on the characteristics of Milton's Satan
down to his ultimate inability to do more than hiss, and the visionary
magnanimity of Orleans:

Then Orleans generous as mountains arose, and unfolded his robe, and put forth
His benevolent hand, looking on the Archbishop, who, changed as pale as lead,
Would have risen but could not, his voice issued harsh grating; instead of words
   harsh hissings
Shook the chamber; he ceas'd abash'd. Then Orleans spoke, all was silent,
He breath'd on them, and said, 'O princes of fire, whose flames are for growth
   not consuming,
Fear not dreams, fear not visions, nor be you dismay'd with sorrows which flee at
   the morning;
Can the fires of Nobility ever be quench'd, or the stars by a stormy night?
Is the body diseas'd when the members are healthful? can the man be bound in
   sorrow
Whose ev'ry function is fill'd with its fiery desire? can the soul whose brain and
   heart
Cast their rivers in equal tides thro' the great Paradise, languish because the feet
Hands, head, bosom, and parts of love, follow their high breathing joy?'
                                                                    (lines 175–85)

   Blake's vision of humanity at its best is here manifested. In subsequent
lines the army is commanded by the people to retire ten miles, and the book
ends in a situation of stalemate as the King and Nobles are left wondering
what to do next. But it is hard to see how the poem might have proceeded
from here, and indeed Blake may have thought it better to leave it to one
side while pursuing other possibilities. He was clearly moving from a view
of history in which events were rendered through natural description,
supplemented at times by the skilful use of metaphors, to a point where
the patterns within the metaphors could themselves be extrapolated,
emerging in time as a developing set of ideas, with individual elements
playing their part, to provide the dominating structure of a poem.
   As he participated in this transition, Blake was increasingly fascinated by the prophetic role. In his *Lectures* of 1787, Robert Lowth had
written that the obscurity of prophecy could serve a good rhetorical

purpose: 'It whets the understanding, excites an appetite for knowledge, keeps alive the attention, and exercises the genius by the labour of the investigation.'[24] As Jon Mee points out, this relates interestingly to Blake's dictum, 'The wisest of the Ancients considerd what is not too Explicit as the fittest for Instruction, because it rouzes the faculties to act.'[25] It also leads on quite naturally to his other great statement:

Prophets in the modern sense of the word have never existed. Jonah was no prophet in the modern sense for his prophecy of Nineveh failed. Every honest man is a Prophet he utters his opinion both of private & public matters Thus If you go on So the result is So He never says, such a thing Shall happen let you do what you will. a Prophet is a Seer not an Arbitrary Dictator . . .[26]

Even while he was working through his more humanitarian poems, in other words, Blake was becoming increasingly preoccupied by intellectual issues. His belief that it was necessary to explore the political implications of what was happening in the contemporary world was proceeding hand in hand with efforts to work towards the cleansing of human perception in order that human beings might see the infinite in all things.

Leaving aside the opening of 'The French Revolution' as a worthy but limited attempt to express some of his aims, therefore, he set out the first fruits of his 'prophetic' enterprise in the illuminated book *America* of 1793, where he attempted a reading of the events of the recent War of Independence against a larger struggle, involving the deity Urizen, a female whom he called 'the daughter of Urthona' and the rebellious spirit 'red Orc' along with his parents Los and Enitharmon. These appear most prominently at the beginning in a two-page 'Preludium', which sets the events to be described against the larger mythological pattern created by their disordered relationship. Rebellious at his confinement, Orc breaks the bonds imposed on him by his father and seizes the shadowy daughter, who glimpses fufilment in his embrace at the very moment that she feels herself being tormentingly destroyed:

I know thee, I have found thee, & I will not let thee go;
Thou art the image of God who dwells in darkness of Africa;
And thou art fall'n to give me life in regions of dark death.
On my American plains I feel the struggling afflictions

---

[24] *Lectures on the Sacred Poetry of the Hebrews* (London: J. Johnson, 1787), II, 168; Jon Mee, *Dangerous Enthusiasm* (Oxford: Clarendon Press, 1992), p. 27.
[25] *BE*, p. 676; *BK*, p. 793.
[26] Annotation to Richard Watson's *Apology for the Bible* (Cork: A. Edwards, 1796): *BE*, pp. 606–7; *BK*, p. 392.

> Endur'd by roots that writhe their arms into the nether deep:
> I see a serpent in Canada, who courts me to his love;
> In Mexico an Eagle, and a Lion in Peru;
> I see a Whale in the South-sea, drinking my soul away.
> O what limb rending pains I feel. thy fire & my frost
> Mingle in howling pains, in furrows by thy lightnings rent;
> This is eternal death; and this the torment long foretold.[27]

This death-dealing ravishment, in which the very energy expended gives a negative image of what true sexual fulfilment might be like, is not an event preliminary to those which are to happen in the book itself, but an interpretative enactment of their meaning. The revolutionary violence involved in achieving independence is the distorting of an energy that might have made the union between Britain and America a fruitful marriage.

In considering this version of 'prophecy', one should take into account the general dangers accompanying political publication at this time. As mentioned earlier, 'The French Revolution', although set up in proof by Joseph Johnson, had never seen the light of day as a finished publication, which may reflect a fear of possible prosecution. It may have been such fears, similarly, that led to the cancellation of a plate for *America* describing the destruction of the house of the 'council' of 'George the third' – a thin disguise for Parliament. When the 'Prophecy' proper follows, on the other hand, the protagonists are explicitly named as the tyrannical King of England and the American leaders: for the book as a whole, he was taking a wider sweep, linking his view of the break between America and England to his sexual critique. A fragment composed at this time makes the connection evident:

> As when a dream of Thiralatha flies the midnight hour:
> In vain the dreamer grasps the joyful images, they fly
> Seen in obscured traces in the Vale of Leutha, So
> The British Colonies beneath the woful Princes fade . . .
> But tho' obscur'd, this is the form of the Angelic land.[28]

In this little cameo the experience of a fleeting sexual dream that leaves the male dreamer with nothing but a residue of expelled semen parallels the failed relationship between Britain and the American colonies. The same idea of a lapse of powers that might have led to a different result

---

[27] Plate 2, lines 7–17.   [28] Fragment [d] 1–4, 6 (*BE*, p. 58).

informs the opening illustration to the book, showing an angelic figure totally shut up in self-absorption, while the woman he should be cherishing looks on in anxiety, clutching a child who is showing signs of rebellion. Again the implication is that if the English and the Americans had treated each other with the same shared insight that characterizes a good and properly consummated marriage, they might have been spared the outbreak of war and the subsequent political severance.

In pursuance of a similar end, Blake sometimes counterpoints his text with an illustration that comments on it satirically, as in lines that describe the failed and angry angel:

> Albion's Angel wrathful burnt
> Beside the Stone of Night; and, like the Eternal Lion's howl
> In famine and war, reply'd: 'Art thou not Orc, who serpent-form'd
> Stands at the gate of Enitharmon to devour her children?
> Blasphemous Demon, Antichrist, hater of Dignities . . .

These strictures are illustrated ironically by a design showing a paradisal scene, with a male and female figure lying on a sleeping ram, emblematizing sexual fulfilment. Meanwhile the lines devoted to Orc express the visionary energy of his bid for freedom:

> The morning comes, the night decays, the watchmen leave their stations;
> The grave is burst, the spices shed, the linen wrapped up;
> The bones of death, the cov'ring clay, the sinews shrunk & dry'd.
> Reviving shake, inspiring move, breathing! awakening!
> Spring like redeemed captives when their bonds & bars are burst . . .

These are illustrated by a design of Urizen himself, spreading his arms and casting the forbidding presence of his clouds over the fulfilment of any such vision.

The last design in the volume is dominated by a great figure so frozen into rigidity that sheep can graze on his sides and small liberated figures stroll above him, while his beard streams off from him like a great waterfall. At the foot of the plate, meanwhile, the forms of serpent and vegetation are artfully combined so as to suggest vegetable and serpentine energies interweaving harmoniously and peacefully together, threatened horrors having disappeared.

Immediately after *America*, in 1794, came the prophetic book *Europe*, following the same pattern: a two-page section leads into the prophecy itself. In this case the 'Preludium' takes the mythological story beyond the rape of the shadowy female by Orc to record her cries of lamentation in face of the unlimited energy released – an unending succession of 'howling terrors, all devouring fiery kings'. Impregnated by Orc with his infinite energy, she can see no hope of a happy outcome:

> . . . who shall bind the infinite with an eternal band?
> To compass it with swaddling bands? and who shall cherish it
> With milk and honey?
> I see it smile & I roll inward & my voice is past.[29]

The supreme irony here is that even as she poses her question of the impossible, she glimpses a possible reply. Her mention of 'swaddling bands' and 'milk and honey' reminds an alert reader of the coming of the infinite divine being – the Messiah prophesied by Isaiah or the infant Jupiter of classical mythology, both fed on milk (or butter) and honey. The infant Jesus was, of course, wrapped in swaddling bands. The infinite can redeem humanity, in other words, but only through realizing itself in human form – a fact which she glimpses when she sees it *smile.*

Here again the use of visual images is important. For Blake, the birth of the divine (illustrated on the plate in the form of a radiant child) immediately prompts the conventional powers to bind it down with restrictions. According to his own interpretation of European history, this has been achieved by the imposition of a 'Female Will' and by a cult of virginity. The result has been a culture of 'Thou shalt not' and of 'Fear', in which even 'Albion's Angel' is not powerful enough to blow the trump of the Last Judgment.

The drift of the argument in *Europe* is to show how a Christian message that has been veiled, along with cults exalting virginity, have together fostered a so-called 'Enlightenment' philosophy with no place for the visionary. The frontispiece is one of Blake's best-known designs, satirizing the Creator who, in *Paradise Lost,*

> . . . took the Golden Compasses, prepared
> In God's eternal store, to circumscribe
> This Universe, and all created things.[30]

This Urizenic figure is not depicted as a villain, since with his limited vision he is labouring to prevent humanity from being swallowed up by the abyss. And this is evidently how, in terms of his developing mythology, Blake sees the course of events in Europe also: as fear of the destructive energy represented by Orc leads his mother Enitharmon to establish the domination of Woman by proclaiming the sinfulness of

---

[29] Plate 2, 13–16 (*BE*, p. 60).   [30] Milton, *Paradise Lost,* vii. 225–7.

sexual love, cults of chastity arise in the Christian church and a limited philosophy, restricted to what can be perceived by the five senses, is promulgated by European thinkers. The developing tale is one of increasing gloom, in the course of which a passage of intense and intricately intellectual speculation encapsulates much that Blake has come to believe concerning the development of Enlightenment philosophy. Firstly, he describes the fate of the senses once the angels of reason have chosen to abandon their debate and follow the king:

> In thoughts perturb'd, they rose from the bright ruins silent following
> The fiery King, who sought his ancient temple serpent-form'd
> That stretches out its shady length along the Island white.
> Round him roll'd his clouds of war; silent the Angel went,
> Along the infinite shores of Thames to golden Verulam.
> There stand the venerable porches that high-towering rear
> Their oak-surrounded pillars, form'd of massy stones, uncut
> With tool; stones precious; such eternal in the heavens,
> Of colours twelve, few known on earth, give light in the opake,
> Plac'd in the order of the stars, when the five senses whelm'd
> In deluge o'er the earth-born man; then turn'd the fluxile eyes
> Into two stationary orbs, concentrating all things.
> The ever-varying spiral ascents to the heavens of heavens
> Were bended downward; and the nostrils golden gates shut
> Turn'd outward, barr'd and petrify'd against the infinite.[31]

Once the temple of a philosophy inspired by that of Bacon, Lord Verulam, has been established, and any sense of the infinite abolished in consequence, the energies residing in the infinite take their revenge, turning into flaming terrors:

> Thought chang'd the infinite to a serpent; that which pitieth:
> To a devouring flame; and man fled from its face and hid
> In forests of night; then all the eternal forests were divided
> Into earths rolling in circles of space, that like an ocean rush'd
> And overwhelmed all except this finite wall of flesh.
> Then was the serpent temple form'd, image of infinite
> Shut up in finite revolutions, and man became an Angel;
> Heaven a mighty circle turning; God a tyrant crown'd.[32]

The intricacy of the verbal discussion contrasts directly with the straightforward simplicity of the accompanying figure, where the image of the

---

[31] Plate 10, lines 1–15.   [32] *Ibid.*, lines 16–23.

'infinite / Shut up in finite revolutions', a series of descending circles dominating the left-hand side of the page, forms the figure of a serpent constrained. Meanwhile the process by which human beings are confined to the use of their 'angelic' reason is expounded further: the heavens are explained purely in Newtonian terms, while the rule of God is the exact mirror-image of a crowned tyrant – tyrants themselves assuming, by the same token, that they are authorized by divine right to rule. The human head, in turn, is depicted as having lost its true aura:

> Once open to the heavens and elevated on the human neck,
> Now overgrown with hair and coverd with a stony roof,
> Downward 'tis sunk beneath th' attractive north, that round the feet
> A raging whirlpool draws the dizzy enquirer to his grave.[33]

The coiling serpent of *America* into which a human being was seen peering, its vision lost in trying to follow its endless revolutions, has thus been transposed into the vortex that is its analogue, swallowing it into death.

The book now turns to comedy, the 'red-limbed angel' who cannot resolve the situation by blowing the trumpet of the Last Judgment being forced to hand over the task to the 'mighty Spirit', Newton. The immediate result is to call all the children of Enitharmon to the sports of night 'beneath the solemn moon', while Enitharmon herself mourns her lost dominion. Orc glimpses his future in the revolutionary fields of France and Los, in turn, calls 'all his sons to the strife of blood'.

In both *America* and *Europe* the interplay between text and illustration was at its most intense – though, as has been pointed out, Blake would sometimes achieve an effect of counterpoint by putting on one plate a design more clearly relevant to another. The imagery of the serpent works hard – indeed Blake made several attempts to work into the title page of *Europe* a gigantic snake. The history of Europe is thus reinterpreted visually, in terms of misused energies and misunderstood reason.

Blake was now torn in allegiance, divided between word and image. The potentialities of images preoccupied him more and more, allowing him to achieve effects of a new subtlety. Reason, it seemed, must be exercised within the constraints of language, but energies could be expressed more broadly – in, say, flames of fire, or the interworking of vegetative and animal powers.

Repeatedly he returned to the matter of illustration. An image might express things that words did not but could not be relied on alone. It was

---

[33] *Ibid.*, lines 28–31.

not in the energies of the tyger, or the passive stance of the questioner who wondered about its meaning, but in the interplay of both that the magic of the song could consist. This called for the working of an art bringing together the image of Vala within Nature and the drama of the Four Zoas in every human body: not their contradiction but their – barely conceivable – reconciliation. In the achievement of such an end, both words and images would co-operate, playing the fullest roles imaginable; the project remained, nevertheless, enigmatic.

CHAPTER 6

Blake, Coleridge and 'The Riddle of the World'

Although Blake and Coleridge may or may not have set eyes on one another in youth, they were at least united in having literary ambitions. They were both fascinated by Milton's poem 'On the Morning of Christ's Nativity', for instance: while they might be daunted by the prospect of achieving anything to equal *Paradise Lost*, the mannerist mode of Milton's early poetry offered a more manageable and humane model to a young poet. Writing the first version of his *Religious Musings* in 1794, Coleridge assumed the persona of a humble shepherd so as to join his praises at the birth of the 'Meek Man and lowliest of the Sons of Men!' In the same year Blake went so far as to write his own pastiche of Milton at the opening of *Europe*, taking over his use of the Christmas season and the story of the universal peace at the time, and turning them to different effect:

> The deep of winter came;
> What time the secret child,
> Descended thro' the orient gates of the eternal day:
> War ceas'd, & all the troops like shadows fled to their abodes.

In this version of Blake's, the birth is that of Orc, the 'horrent Demon', the light of whose fury appears 'in the vineyards of red France' and in response to whom his father Los calls all his sons 'to the strife of blood'.

As with this subversion of the gospel narrative, Blake believed *Paradise Lost* to embody a profound misreading of the human condition. In his view Milton was writing 'in fetters when he wrote of Angels & God, and at liberty when of devils & Hell'; in his work 'the Father is Destiny, the Son a ratio of the five senses, & the Holy Ghost Vacuum'.[1] For Blake, an epic which might achieve what Milton had falsely attempted would

---

[1] *BK*, p. 150.

need an altogether different mythology for its basis, one built on the supposition not of human inadequacy but of human potentiality. Accordingly, he supplemented the series of Prophetic Books that presented various aspects of the European situation in terms of his own interpretation of human nature by embarking on a more ambitious work, 'Vala', where he tried to present his mythology on an epic scale.

'Vala', later renamed 'The Four Zoas', was an early psychological drama. In it, characters who have already appeared in his Prophetic Books participate in the larger narrative which is to describe their nature more fully as different energies of the Eternal Man who, by becoming himself disordered, has precipitated chaos among each.

This noble and intriguing conception turned out also to be deeply flawed, however. For while the Christian God must be accepted as being ultimately incomprehensible, a Being who by the nature of things cannot be probed beyond himself, it is very natural for a reader to ask, concerning the Eternal Man, against what further pattern he is to be viewed. The lack of such a controlling pattern – or any hint of it – meant that the narrative of 'Vala' must lack ultimate grounding.

This was not the only contradiction that opened itself to an inquiring mind. If one accepted that every living thing was holy, one must also take an indulgent attitude towards the caterpillar that 'chooses the fairest leaves to lay her eggs on'.[2] And how would the Blake who wanted to produce on a large scale his image of Pitt in his 'spiritual form', reconcile this with his previous attitudes to that politician's policies? But in Blake's thought contradictions ran deep. Even when he wrote his early lyrics, an ecstatic poem about love needed to be accompanied by one expressing his rage at a possible rival; for every Song of Innocence there must be one of Experience. What best encouraged the possibility of fruitful dialectic could as easily fall apart into occasions of contempt or scurrilous satire. It is no wonder that a set of verses entitled 'The Everlasting Gospel' could also contain the couplet

> Do what you will, this Life's a Fiction
> And is made up of Contradiction.[3]

Coleridge, meanwhile, did not attempt an epic poem of the same order; of the one he projected on 'The Fall of Jerusalem' no vestige survives. In his view the opportunity for epic writing of a Miltonic kind lay rather

---

[2] *BK*, p. 152.   [3] *BK*, p. 751.

with Wordsworth and his plan for 'The Recluse' – another prospect which was to be only partly completed. What none of these poets grasped was that in the intellectual world now opening up the possibility of large-scale literary work lay rather with autobiography – or, indeed, that Wordsworth had already foreshadowed this adventurous way forward by producing the 'Poem on his Own Mind' that would eventually be published as *The Prelude*.

One could not engage in serious autobiography, however, without acknowledging the extent to which it must be 'made up of contradiction'; and this recognition was likely to militate against commitment to purity of doctrine. In this new world, it had to be recognized, the word was not pure, but fraught with ambiguity.

Coleridge would also give much thought to the paradoxes inherent in the nature of human reason and the consequent need to reinterpret its role, but at the turn of the century was more preoccupied by what had emerged during the writing of *Lyrical Ballads* concerning the nature of life itself. Wordsworth's contributions were the work of a poet who had been thinking about the reawakening of life in spring after winter, or imagining the fate of a man who had watched his flock of sheep die off one after another, or the state of a child who could not imagine what death might be like, or that of an Indian woman who had been left in the wilds to die by the surviving members of her tribe. Other poems of the time suggest how obsessively Wordsworth and Coleridge were at the time thinking about issues of life and death, as in Wordsworth's poem 'A whirlblast from behind the hill', where he describes himself sitting in a holly grove covered by dead leaves during a hailstorm and watching the icy hailstones, which are themselves dead, make the dead leaves dance as if they were alive; or Coleridge's 'Kubla Khan', to be seen as partly about the fantastic works that human beings undertake in order to avoid having to think about the inevitability of death; or his *Christabel*, where a young nature-worshipper is brought up in a castle where everything is dominated by the death-consciousness of her father. This double consciousness was carried on by Wordsworth in work on his autobiographical poem, where he described how he had grown up 'fostered alike by beauty and by fear' and where many of his early experiences had been revelations of the significance of death, and of life, when their manifestations were experienced against a natural landscape.

It is one thing to be obsessed for a time by these issues, however, another to see how they are to be coped with on a permanent basis; although such considerations gave a particular sharpness to Wordsworth's and Coleridge's writings for a time, their considerations in the longer term had to do with how human beings learn to live with these consciousnesses.

For Coleridge, nevertheless, the word 'life' assumed a new importance; although he did not use the exact phrase 'one Life' until later, he used the single word with an emphasis and emotional charge that betrays the depth of his interest. At the end of 'This Lime-tree Bower my Prison', for instance, as he pictures his friend Charles Lamb delighting in a sunset scene not available to himself, his account culminates in the homeward flight of a rook which, he imagines,

> Flew creeking o'er thy head, and had a charm
> For thee, my gentle-hearted Charles, to whom
> No sound is dissonant which tells of Life.

The placing of that last word is telling. And his concern at this time with life and all its manifestations emerges even more clearly at the start of 'Frost at Midnight'. In the common human understanding of silence, it is a sign of death, so that a totally silent landscape would be sinister and deathly; but Coleridge maintains that this may not necessarily be so; silence, however disturbing, may also mask a beneficent work not disclosing itself – at least, not as yet. After the description of the Frost's 'secret ministry' and the sinister cry of the owlet, he continues,

> 'Tis calm indeed! so calm, that it disturbs
> And vexes meditation with its strange
> And extreme silentness. Sea, hill, and wood,
> This populous village! Sea, and hill, and wood,
> With all the numberless goings-on of life,
> Inaudible as dreams!

About the same time, Dorothy Wordsworth, beginning her Alfoxden journal and looking for the first signs of spring, showed herself equally alive to the work of nature and to the difference between the human sense of absence and that of populousness:

After the wet dark days, the country seems more populous. It peoples itself in the sunbeams . . .[4]

Dorothy too was struck by the mystery of the fact that life may continue, and give evidence of its presence, without betraying itself in the form of audible sounds.

---

[4] *DWJ* I, 3.

As it happens, also, the expression 'one Life', not used in Coleridge's early poetry when he was writing about nature, emerged in an interesting context some twenty years later, when he was revising a poem written shortly before he met William and Dorothy. 'The Eolian Harp', where he first showed his talents as a nature poet, contains in its opening lines snatches of description that are vivid, but nearly always modified in some way by the poet's intellect. So his description of the flowers that cover the walls of their cottage, 'white-flower'd Jasmin and the broad-leav'd Myrtle', is followed immediately by the parenthesis '(Meet emblems they of Innocence and Love!)'. As the couple look to the scenes beyond there is a similar tendency to move beyond immediate sense-experience: they

> . . . watch the clouds, that late were rich with light
> Slow sad'ning round, and mark the star of eve
> Serenely brilliant (such should Wisdom be!)
> Shine opposite! How exquisite the scents
> Snatch'd from yon bean-field! And the world *so* hush'd!
> The stilly murmur of the distant Sea
> Tells us of Silence.

The loss of brightness in the clouds causes them to be described as 'saddening'; the sight of the evening star prompts the need to make it an emblem of wisdom; even the sound of the sea – though this is a more subtle point – reminds one of the nature of silence. At this point, however, the use of metaphor has become more complex. As Coleridge turns to the Aeolian harp that he has installed in the opening of his window to make music from the currents of air that pass through – a music that can fairly be described as the music of nature, since made without human intervention – his imagination takes over until it becomes a music from fairyland,

> Where Melodies round honey-dropping flowers,
> Footless and wild, like birds of Paradise,
> Nor pause, nor perch, hovering on untam'd wing.

When Coleridge came to print these lines in his collection *Sibylline Leaves* twenty years later, he was moved to add a new passage, included in the Errata slip, that may reflect his recent reading of some German writing on the relationship between sound and light which, he thought, echoed some of his own early speculations, including those on the nature of life:

> O! the one Life within us and abroad,
> Which meets all motion and becomes its soul,
> A light in sound, a sound-like power in light,

Rhythm in all thought and joyance every where –
Methinks it should have been impossible
Not to love all things in a world so fill'd;
Where the breeze warbles, and the mute still air
Is Music slumbering on her instrument.

Where had all this thinking about life originated in the first place? The Coleridge who went across from Somerset to Dorset two years after writing his first version of 'The Eolian Harp' and met the Wordsworths there in 1797 was a man who had already been thinking seriously about its nature, which was in fact a subject of great interest among educated writers of the time, including John Thelwall, who had published a pamphlet on Animal Vitality, and to whom at the end of 1796 Coleridge wrote a letter in which he boldly broached the subject, retailing the various current views. According to him, Beddoes and Erasmus Darwin thought it inexplicable, Monro believed in a plastic immaterial nature (which Coleridge thought rather like the view outlined in 'The Aeolian Harp'), John Hunter believed that the blood was the life, Ferriar, an orthodox Churchman, believed in a soul, and Plato thought it was harmony – which Coleridge regarded as a part of his 'dear gorgeous nonsense'. As for himself, he wrote,

I do not know what to think about it – on the whole, I have rather made up my mind that I am a mere apparition – a naked spirit! – and that Life is I myself I! Which is a mighty clear account of it.[5]

Coleridge, then, was already thinking hard about a matter that was to concern him all his life – exactly what was involved in saying 'I am' that made it a different kind of statement from the third person 'it is'? – and being intrigued by its mystery. But by 1798, living near the Wordsworths in North Somerset, he was even more concerned with the nature of life as it manifested itself objectively in the scenes about them. I have already mentioned his concern with its presence at the close of the poem 'This Lime-Tree Bower my Prison', but it was also inherent in a more intimate passage towards the beginning. Coleridge's friends are pictured descending into a dell where the signs of life are minimal yet the plants, though deprived of sunshine and receiving little moisture, have a memorable quality:

That still roaring dell of which I told;
The roaring dell, o'erwooded, narrow, deep,

[5] *CL* I, 294–5.

And only speckled by the mid-day sun;
Where its slim trunk the ash from rock to rock
Flings arching like a bridge; – that branchless ash,
Unsunn'd and damp, whose few poor yellow leaves
Ne'er tremble in the gale, yet tremble still
Fann'd by the water-fall! and there my friends
Behold the dark green file of long lank weeds,
That all at once (a most fantastic sight!)
Still nod and drip beneath the dripping edge
Of the blue clay-stone.[6]

This is more than an acutely detailed piece of natural description. It is the work of a man who has looked at nature analytically, considering the powers that make for life and those that make against it. He is writing at a time when his fellows have been asking themselves for the first time about the nature of vital powers, following the discovery of oxygen. It had always been known that sun and water were necessary for the sustenance of vegetable life, but discoveries in the electrical and chemical fields brought such considerations into newly sharpened focus. What Coleridge presents in this scene is a view of life at its lowest ebb, with hardly any sunlight or water. Since the only breeze that reaches the plants is created by the motion of the waterfall, similarly, the supply of oxygen is minimal. Yet their poor yellow leaves, together with the long lank weeds, survive as an epitome of what natural life is like at its nadir.

The Wordsworths' preoccupation with signs of life was also evidently disturbing to Coleridge, however, as his friend continued to produce verse after verse devoted to the human condition that was devoid of religious reference. It hardly relieved the situation when William proposed their collaborating on a narrative ballad that might take its place alongside the Gothic tales in verse and prose that were currently fashionable. As is well known, Wordsworth had been reading in Shelvocke's *Voyages* the account of a sailor who had attacked a sea-bird that attached itself to the vessel in which he was travelling and who as a result was believed to have attracted ill luck. To the Wordsworths such a story offered the possibility of constructing a narrative around the concept of a link of life between all organic beings, while for Coleridge it meant that he need not take a firm line on the religious and moral questions that were currently occupying his mind, using the narrative, rather, to dramatize a story that corresponded to his own position: the role of a man at sea, cut off from any firm

---

[6] *CPW* (EHC) I, 178–91.

guidance to what he should believe, was very like his own amid the intellectual currents of his time.

As some readers have noted, the moral universe of the poem is confusing. The Mariner himself is apparently portrayed as a Christian in an earlier period, when Catholicism would have been the established faith. He comes from a port that has a Kirk standing above it, and in the poem, when he is anxious or troubled, his instinct is to turn to Mary or a saint. There is no evidence that they actually work for his benefit, but he is comforted by believing that they do.

In the same way his first impulse on returning to his own country and a community that he recognizes is to turn to the Hermit, who by good fortune has assisted the pilot and pilot's boy in rescuing him, and to beg for absolution from his responsibility in killing the albatross.

But if one ignores the elements of traditional religion, what sort of universe is it that the Mariner inhabits? Leslie Stephen, many years ago, was caustic on the subject:

The moral, which would apparently be that people who sympathize with a man who shoots an albatross will die in prolonged torture of thirst, is open to obvious objections.[7]

Stephen's logic by no means exhausts the puzzles of the poem, moreover. The various presences who pass through the poem themselves suggest conflicting accounts of what is going on. The two figures who draw near in the spectre-boat are at first even more riddling: the fleshless male resembles Death, though it is not until the 1817 revision that he is actually called by that name, while the female, who at first was nameless, is then for the first time identified as Life-in-Death. These two also show the lack of any moral frame to their activities by playing a game of dice – again without obvious point, though in the later version it is revealed that they have been playing for the Mariner himself. Whether their game has anything to do with his previous actions is never known. The events of the tale are more like those of the Oriental kind that Coleridge thought the whole poem should have resembled:[8] capricious and unpredictable.

Against these creatures, who depart as mysteriously as they came, must be set another pair: the Two Voices, who discuss the Mariner's plight. It seems that one can only ask questions, the other give answers. Who or what they are is never made clear, but evidently in some sense they control

---

[7] Leslie Stephen, *Hours in a Library* (London: Smith, Elder, 1892), III, 359.
[8] See his *Table Talk* of 31 March 1832: *CTT* I, 272–3; cf. *ibid.*, II, 100 and n.

the situation – though the speed of the ship is recognized to be associated with the intensity of the Mariner's trance.

There is evidently an ambiguity in Coleridge's poetic thinking at this time, which is emphasized further once one realizes that even while he was working on *The Rime of the Ancient Mariner,* he produced another poem, 'The Raven', which tells a not dissimilar story of an offence against a bird and its effects, but more briefly, and in a sharper, even cynical tone. It records how a company of swine found the acorns that had fallen from an oak and ate all except one, which was then picked up by a melancholy raven, who buried it by a river. When he returned many years later, the acorn having meantime grown into an oak, the raven, with his mate, were able to rear their family there:

> But soon came a Woodman in leathern guise,
> His brow, like a pent-house, hung over his eyes.
> He'd an axe in his hand, not a word he spoke,
> But with many a hem! and a sturdy stroke,
> At length he brought down the poor Raven's own oak.
> His young ones were killed; for they could not depart,
> And their mother did die of a broken heart.

When the oak was subsequently used to build a fine ship, it went to sea accompanied by the raven, who followed its later career with malicious glee:

> The ship, it was launched; but in sight of the land
> Such a storm there did rise as no ship would withstand.
> It bulged on a rock, and the waves rush'd in fast;
> Round and round flew the Raven, and cawed to the blast.
> He heard the last shriek of the perishing souls –
> See! see! o'er the topmast the mad water rolls!
>
> Right glad was the Raven, and off he went fleet,
> And Death riding home on a cloud he did meet,
> And he thank'd him again and again for this treat:
> They had taken his all; and REVENGE IT WAS SWEET![9]

When Coleridge published this story in the *Morning Post,* he accompanied with it an introduction, in which he assumed the Spenserean pseudonym of 'Cuddy' and satirically discussed whether it might be an unknown work by the author of the *Shepherds Calendar,* whose work includes the emblematic tale of the oak and the briar. The story here is more than the simple fable of Spenser's dialogue between age and youth, however. Some

[9] *CPW* (EHC) I, 169–71.

proposed interpretations read it in political terms, the felling of the oak being seen as the destruction brought about by the French Revolution, and the raven identified with the melancholy Burke prophesying the Revolution's effect. Coleridge may have been uneasy that such an interpretation was possible, though if so one must ask why he made the allegory in the first place. He may, equally, have been worried by the possible effect of a poem with such a tone appearing alongside *The Rime of the Ancient Mariner,* also a tale of a bird that attached itself to human company, but one more benign in its ethos, which was perhaps why he subtitled this one 'A Christmas Tale, Told by a School Boy to his Little Brothers and Sisters' – later introducing an irrelevant footnote about a possible illustration containing a children's roundabout – and in *Sibylline Leaves* set it among his 'Juvenile Poems'. Yet he remained troubled by the presence of this poem among his others from a contrary point of view, also. Republishing it in 1817, he added to the final couplet the lines

> We must not think so; but forget and forgive,
> And what Heaven gives life to, we'll still let it live.

Even this did not satisfy him. Later still, he subjoined a further note:

Added thro' cowardly fear of the Goody! What a Hollow, where the Heart of Faith ought to be, does it not betray – this alarm concerning Christian morality, that will not permit even a Raven to be a Raven, nor a Fox a Fox, but demands conventicular justice to be inflicted on their unchristian conduct, or at least an antidote to be annexed.[10]

The contradiction between the two modes would continue to dog Coleridge. While writing poetry that was aimed at rising above the everyday and setting the affections in right tune,[11] he could devote himself to the quotidian in poems such as 'Parliamentary Oscillators', where the practical joke of an owl tied to the back of a duck is treated with indulgence, or 'Fire, Famine and Slaughter', a polemic directed very pointedly against Pitt, where he felt bound to disclaim malignant intent. In the same manner he could write a comic skit on the supposed ruins of the House that Jack Built even while he was also taking over its prime mode by describing how

> The spirit who bideth by himself
> In the land of mist and snow,

---

[10] *Ibid.,* 171n.
[11] See his letter to George Coleridge of 19 March 1798: *CL* I, 397.

> He lov'd the bird that lov'd the man
> Who shot him with his bow.

The matter of Coleridge's vacillations is certainly complex. Another, associated brief composition of his was also poetic, yet not so much a straightforward poem as a riddle: an epigram of four lines published in the *Morning Post* for 24 January 1800. We would hardly know anything about it, in fact, were it not that he mentioned it himself in a footnote to *Biographia Literaria*, where, having described how he contributed his three Higginbottom sonnets in 1797, he continued with another anecdote recalling how he had heard that an amateur performer wanting to meet him had been hesitant on the ground that he had written a severe epigram on *The Ancient Mariner* that had given its author great pain. Coleridge says that he replied by saying that if the epigram was a good one, he would be delighted to hear it, only to hear from him what he himself had written for the *Morning Post* – recorded as follows:

To the author of the Ancient Mariner

> Your poem must eternal be,
> Dear sir! It cannot fail,
> For 'tis incomprehensible
> And without head or tail.

The little story appears an innocent enough one, introduced no doubt in order to show that Coleridge could not only take a joke against himself but even on occasion produce one. There are strange features, however. The first is that the record is not strictly true.[12] If one turns up the *Morning Post* for 24 January 1800 the poem is there all right, but not addressed to the author of *The Ancient Mariner* at all. It is entitled 'To Mr Pye', the current Poet Laureate. Thomas James Pye is, in fact, the subject of one of the more scathing entries in the original *Dictionary of National Biography*, where he is described as 'poetaster and poet laureate', responsible for poems of uniform dullness. As was the custom at the end of a century, Pye had produced a 'carmen seculare' – literally, a 'century poem'; Coleridge's full title runs 'To Mr Pye on his carmen seculare (a title which has by various persons who have heard it been thus translated, "A poem an age long")'.

The second point worth noting is that the epigram is based on one by Lessing, the title of which has been translated as 'On the eternity of

---

[12] For bibliographical details, see *CPW* (EHC) II, 959 and *CPW (CC)*, where it appears as item 233 in both vols. I and II.

certain poems'. But this is something of a red herring, since a single phrase of the poem ('must be eternal because . . .') is all that Coleridge took. Lessing's verse is different, continuing with the assertion that these poems must be eternal because there will always be poets ready to write such boring stuff.

Thirdly, however, one must ask about the actual point of the epigram. Why does Coleridge lay such stress on the words 'eternal' and 'incomprehensible', words which he actually italicizes in his original *Morning Post* version, and on the phrase 'without head or tail'?

I suggest that it is not so much an epigram as a riddle, in which case an answer to it may be looked for elsewhere in his writing. In his first major poem, 'The Eolian Harp', he embarks on several brilliant intellectual speculations only to recoil –

> For never guiltless may I speak of Him,
> Th' INCOMPREHENSIBLE! Save when with awe
> I praise him, and with Faith that inly *feels* . . .[13]

The word was not idly chosen: within a few months he was writing to John Edwards: 'Has not Dr Priestly forgotten that incomprehensibility is as necessary an attribute of the First Cause, as Love, or Power, or Intelligence?'[14] He was still making a case for the incomprehensibility of the divine thirty years later.[15] And as for his second point, we may turn to one of his most interesting letters, the one to Joseph Cottle on 7 March 1815, where he tried to intimate tactfully that what Cottle had been aiming at was not very easily to be conveyed, continuing,

The common end of all *narrative*, nay of *all* Poems, is to convert a *series* into a *Whole*: to make those events, which in real or imagined History move on in a *strait* Line, assume to our Understandings a *circular* motion – the snake with it's Tail in it's Mouth.[16]

He goes on to relate this to the knowledge possessed by the Divine Being, who sees Present, Past and Future, and whose knowledge is therefore englobed in a manner that human knowledge cannot be. And since the serpent with its tail in its mouth is a well-known image for eternity, a narrative which achieved that status would be the nearest an artist could get, not only to the divine but also to the eternal.

---

[13] *CPW* (Beer), pp. 72–4.
[14] Letter to Revd John Edwards of 20 March 1796: *CL* I, 193.
[15] See *CAR*, pp. 338–9 and n.   [16] *CL* IV, 545.

What I am suggesting, in other words, is that when Coleridge wrote his poem about Mr Pye, the terms he was using did not make very good sense concerning Pye, except in a general way, but they did define the qualities of a truly eternal poem: it would be, like the divine, incomprehensible, yet like the highest form of narrative it would resemble the snake with its tail in its mouth – and so, quite literally, have neither head nor tail.

In 1798, indeed, Coleridge himself had published just such a poem. It was hard to understand and full of contradictions. One never knows just who is in control of the universe in which the Ancient Mariner moves: is it the figures of Death and the woman 'far liker Death than he' who play dice for his fate, or is it the Spirit that 'bideth by himself in the land of mist of snow' and 'who loved the bird who loved the man who shot him with his bow'? And if one is looking for poetic justice, one must face the point that the Mariner, who after all committed the crime, is the only one to survive, while his shipmates, who simply approved his action at one point, die in agonies of thirst. Is the Mariner's unquestioning faith in 'Mary Queen' and his own 'kind saint' enough to account for all that happens?

If one looks at the poem with such questionings in mind, it is truly incomprehensible. And yet it is also a narrative with its tail in its mouth. Following the Mariner's action in extremity, a blessing which came from outside himself, he was, in the strange logic of the poem, restored to the country from which he had set out, seeing it as if for the first time:

> . . . is this indeed
> The light-house top I see?
> Is this the Hill? Is this the Kirk?
> Is this mine own countrée?

If we are justified in regarding Coleridge's poem as a riddle, and if it is here read aright, it can be proposed that the reason why after twenty years he remembered his poem addressed to Mr Pye as a poem addressed to the author of *The Ancient Mariner* was that, at another depth of his mind, he knew it to have been just that. As an attempt to probe the meaning of things, it was incomprehensible, thwarting readers who looked for an Aristotelian beginning, middle and end, yet at the same time giving them a curious sense of provisional satisfaction. The best comparison is with one of the designs by M. C. Escher that incorporate an impossible geometry. The staircase round the building seems to go on and on for ever, yet the apparent rising of each separate flight of steps is thwarted by the overall design. Although the point is worrying when one first notices it, the effect in the long run is aesthetically pleasing: one ceases to be concerned at its impossibility.

Coleridge's considered opinion, many years later, was that the *Rime* was 'a poem of pure imagination'; he also said that it 'might be excelled but could not be imitated'.[17] This is another puzzle, which, John Sterling argued,[18] was hard to make sense of, since it would be only too easy for poets to try their hands at Gothic tales of the kind; he wondered if Coleridge meant simply that it corresponded to his ideal. But he may well have meant something else – that other poets could, and perhaps would, write finer imaginative poems, but that no one would ever be in quite the same position to create the kind of poem that he now saw his to be. His apocalypse, his revelation, had been, like Wordsworth's after crossing the Alps, the realization that a poem could, like a landscape, be at one and the same time fraught with contradictions, crossing all the major lines of one's discourse, yet still possessed of a remarkable unity – in this case the unity of its 'chant'. However incomprehensible it might seem once one began asking questions, it would remain secure in the wholeness of comprising the three qualities he valued most: light, energy and love. In that respect its tail would always be firmly disappearing into its mouth, a lasting tribute to its unity.

Coleridge had to accept – ruefully, perhaps – that his early readers showed no signs of making such connections; yet he could not escape the fact that for him its success was an indication of its own internal apocalypse, the revelation of the power of the imagination itself. And for any reader who was sufficiently seized by the attractions of the poem, the same would in some sense remain true: its positive qualities and its music ensured that, contradictions or no, its appeal would be 'eternal' in the only sense that mattered to its creator:

To find no contradiction in the union of old and new, to contemplate the ANCIENT OF DAYS with feelings as fresh as if all had then sprang forth at his own fiat, this characterizes the minds that feel the Riddle of the World, and may help to unravel it!'[19]

If the word were not to be treated with monumental reverence but kept truly alive, these necessities of its paradoxical existence would need to be continually acknowledged and propitiated.

---

[17] Allsop record, *CTT* II, 359.   [18] *Ibid.*, note.
[19] *CFriend* (1809) II, 73; repeated *verbatim* in chapter 4 of *CBL* I, 80–1.

CHAPTER 7

Challenges from the non-verbal and return to the Word

Wordsworth might absorb himself in the mysteries of the human heart, but by 1799 Coleridge's insight into the nature of genius was leading him further: for him now the whole universe was more mysterious than it might have seemed in the middle of the eighteenth century. After his return from Germany, he was increasingly interested in the work of Humphry Davy, with whom he had become acquainted in Bristol, and – through their common friendship – of Thomas Beddoes at the Pneumatic Institution there. When Davy moved to London and the Royal Institution, Coleridge kept in touch, following some of his experiments eagerly: Davy's reports on his experiments with nitrous oxide actually included statements from Coleridge himself.

At his first inhalation, Coleridge reported, he had experienced 'a highly pleasurable sensation of warmth over my whole frame, resembling that which I remember once to have experienced after returning from a walk in the snow into a warm room'. A further experiment of the kind was still more spectacular in its effects:

I could not avoid, nor indeed felt any wish to avoid, beating the ground with my feet; and after the mouthpiece was removed, I remained for a few seconds motionless, in great extasy.

On Boxing Day 1799, Davy experimented on himself, reporting similar pleasurable sensations – and indeed his loss of all connection with external things and illusion of making discoveries – until,

with the most intense belief and prophetic manner, I exclaimed to Dr Kinglake, 'Nothing exists but thoughts! – the universe is composed of impressions, ideas, pleasures and pains!'[1]

---

[1] *The Collected Works of Sir Humphry Davy*, ed. John Davy, 9 vols. (London: Smith, Elder and Co., 1839–40), III, 306–7.

Coleridge's urge to experiment continued. If one assumes that he was the 'noticeable Man with large grey eyes' of Wordsworth's 'Stanzas Written in My Pocket-copy of Thomson's "Castle of Indolence"', he displayed his delight in natural objects as seen through the microscope:

> Glasses he had, that little things display,
> The beetle, panoplied in gems and gold,
> A mailed angel on a battle-day;
> The mysteries that cups of flowers enfold,
> And all the gorgeous sights which fairies do behold.[2]

In February 1801, certainly, he made plans for the establishment of a small laboratory in Keswick with the help of William Calvert (Wordsworth's friend Raisley Calvert's brother there) and invited Humphry Davy to join them to pursue the subject, together with Wordsworth himself.[3] A month later he wrote to Godwin, explaining how in his illness he had

compelled into hours of Delight many a sleepless, painful hour of Darkness by chasing down metaphysical Game – and since then I have continued the Hunt, till I found myself unaware at the Root of Pure Mathematics – and up that tall, smooth Tree, whose few poor Branches are all at it's very summit, am I climbing by pure adhesive strength of arms and thighs – still slipping down, still renewing my ascent. – You would not know me – ! all sounds of similitude keep at such a distance from each other in my mind that I have forgotten how to make a rhyme. I look at the Mountains (that visible God Almighty that looks in at all my windows), I look at the Mountains only for the Curves of their outlines; the Stars, as I behold them, form themselves into Triangles; and my hands are scarred with scratches from a Cat, whose back I was rubbing in the Dark in order to see whether the sparks in it were refrangible by a Prism.[4]

Coleridge's speculations were becoming ever more wide-ranging, as if he felt that the political stalemate at the end of the old century called for a widening of intellectual horizons in the new.

The fact that the calendar shift had not been marked by an apocalyptic turn in human events can hardly have escaped Blake's attention, either. He may well have reflected also, that his scheme of accounting for human nature in terms of the 'Four Mighty Ones' that 'are in every Man' might be oversimplistic – even, perhaps, Urizenic – if one considered the full complexity of human nature.

---

[2] *WPW* II, 27.   [3] *CL* II, 670–1.   [4] 25 March 1801: *CL* II, 714.

Another element that had entered Blake's thinking during these years was more directly physical: as with Coleridge, it concerned the rising interest in phenomena such as mesmerism and animal magnetism, which had played a prominent part in the intellectual ferment of recent years.[5] Given that virtually no language had as yet been developed for thinking about such matters, it was not easy to gain any factual purchase on what was happening, but, as Robert Rix has pointed out, related interests had already led to the expulsion from the New Jerusalem Church of certain Swedenborgians who wished to explore them.[6] Blake seems to have been in touch with them: it was an area where some of Swedenborg's own followers, at least, could not be said to have 'written all the old falsehoods'.[7]

As Rix also points out, Blake 'cast his support in favour of individual visionary experience, which later came to be considered a heresy in the New Jerusalem Church'.[8] He believes that during his stay in Felpham, his interest drew in addition the sympathy of William Hayley, who had been taking a keen interest in Animal Magnetism;[9] and notes that while there Blake's attribution of the origin of his poetry to spirit communication suggests that he may have cultivated something like a trance-like state, not unlike somnambulism: Blake asserts, for example, that he speaks daily and hourly with his dead brother Robert, who dictates to him,[10] and that he can 'converse with my friends in Eternity. See Visions, Dream Dreams, & Prophecy . . .'[11] He claimed meanwhile to be nothing but a 'Secretary', as the 'Authors' of his poetry were 'in Eternity'.[12]

From a letter of 1804, we know that Blake believed his wife's rheumatism to have been cured with the use of electricity, praising a 'Mr. Birch'

---

[5] See, e.g., my *Coleridge the Visionary* (London: Chatto and Windus, 1959), pp. 51–2.

[6] See especially Robert W. Rix, 'Healing the Spirit: William Blake and Magnetic Religion', *Romanticism on the Net* 25 (www.ron.umontreal.ca) (February 2002), and M. K. Schuchard, 'Blake's Healing Trio: Magnetism, Medicine and Mania', *BQ* 23 (1989), 20–31.

[7] *BK*, p. 157.

[8] Rix, *Romanticism on the Net* 25, para. 17.

[9] Rix points out that Hayley took a keen interest in Animal Magnetism, purchasing an 'electrical machine' that functioned as a healing 'shower bath' (E. Morchard Bishop, *Blake's Hayley* (London: Gollancz, 1951), pp. 95–96). He thinks that Hayley would therefore have understood the connection Blake makes between poetry and electrical Phenomena in a letter: 'My fingers Emit sparks of fire with Expectation of my future labours' (letter to Hayley, 16 September 1800, *BE*, p. 681; *BK*, p. 801). He casts *Jerusalem* in a framework steeped in magnetic-spiritualist metaphors. It could also be mentioned that Blake is likely to have seen such apparatuses with his own eyes when Dr Birch cured his wife Catherine.

[10] Letter to Hayley, 6 May 1800: *BE*, p. 678; *BK*, p. 797.

[11] Letter to Butts, 25 April 1803: *BE*, p. 697; *BK*, p. 822.

[12] Letter to Butts, 6 July 1803: *BE* ii, p. 730; *BK*, p. 825.

for his 'Electrical Magic'.[13] He criticized three contemporary magnetizers, however, Richard Cosway, George Baldwin and an unknown 'Frazer' in a satiric *Notebook* poem of unknown date. The reason for his attack, he claimed, was that they 'Fear to associate with Blake'; he further criticized them for capitalizing on the popular market for Magnetism at the expense of higher spiritual purposes: 'This Life is a Warfare against Evils / They heal the sick he [Blake] casts out Devils'.[14]

From 'The Four Zoas' onwards, moreover, dream visions play an increasingly central role in Blake's poetry. In *Milton*, he returns several times to the poet's sleep and dreams in reference to somnambulistic visions, where his 'Sleeping Body' joins company with the divine 'Spirits of the Seven Angels', 'walking' with them 'as one walks / In sleep'.[15] In fact Rix finds the reference to magnetic therapy in Blake's poetic vocabulary there 'unmistakable'. In the beginning, Blake invokes his 'Muses' to 'Come into my hand / By your mild power; descending down the Nerves of my right arm . . .'[16] Albion's cure is figured in terms of electrical therapy: 'Now Albions sleeping Humanity began to turn upon his Couch; / Feeling the electrical flame of Miltons awful precipitate descent.'[17] In *Jerusalem*, similarly, the introductory address 'To the Public' voices Blake's strongest commitment to the importance of spirit visitations: 'We who dwell on Earth can do nothing of ourselves, everything is conducted by Spirits, no less than Digestion or Sleep.'[18] It certainly seems

---

[13] Letter to Hayley, 18 December 1804: *BE* ii, p. 759; *BK* 854. Dr John Birch was a surgeon of St Thomas's Hospital in London (where de Mainauduc had been a student in 1789); he established there a department for treating patients by means of medical electricity. Birch describes his methods and machines in his *Essay on the Mechanical Application of Electricity*, which was published and sold in 1802 by Joseph Johnson (see Morton D. Paley, *Apocalypse and Millennium in English Romantic Poetry* (Oxford: Clarendon Press, 1999), p. 82). In his letters, Blake refers to Birch in favourable terms (letters to Butts, 11 Sept. 1801, 717; and 25 April 1803, 728). It appears from the correspondence that Birch was a mutual friend of both the Butts family and the Blakes.

[14] *BE*, p. 496; *BK*, p. 545. Of 'Frazer' we know little, but he has been identified by Schuchard ('Blake's Healing Trio', p. 21) as a student of de Mainauduc's. After Cosway set himself up as a popular magnetic entrepreneur, Blake's patron George Cumberland wrote on the verso of a broadsheet entitled 'A Syllabus of Dr de MAINADUC's INSTRUCTIONS', a memorandum criticizing him for his commercial opportunism. In his *Legacy to his Daughter or the Divinity of Truth* (London: W. Bulmer and Co., 1811), George Baldwin refers to the Bible as an authority to prove that divine Vision is an essential part of spiritual life. However, he also admits his hesitation in committing himself to Spiritualism in public, which has delayed the publication of his book, out of the fear 'that I shall be called a Visionary' (p. iii).

[15] *BE*, p. 108; *BK*, p. 496.   [16] *BE*, p. 95; *BK*, p. 481.

[17] *BE*, p. 113; *BK*, p. 502.   [18] *BE*, p. 144; *BK*, p. 621.

as if during these years he developed an original form of self-hypnosis, enabling him to mediate between his subconscious and his powers of writing. (The sense of wide-spread scientific interest picked up from such straws in the wind is reinforced by evidence that in the same years Shelley also was carrying out chemical and electrical experiments.[19])

In addition to his interest in scientific experiments, Coleridge had at this time a more immediate source of stimulation: his own volatile state of health. As Neil Vickers has shown in *Coleridge and the Doctors*, the late eighteenth and early nineteenth centuries were a period of considerable medical interest, involving particularly Erasmus Darwin and Thomas Beddoes. Although these two were never backward in arguing with one another's conclusions, they entertained strong feelings of mutual respect.

The fact that their position in England was somewhat isolated also draws attention to the superiority of other European cities. Edinburgh, for instance, was more notable than any English centre, and one of its chief luminaries, John Brown, pioneered a scheme, subsequently known as Brunonian medicine, which proved immensely influential in Germany. Brown was particularly interested in methods of treatment, one of his important tenets being based on the idea that medical disorder was caused by the existence of too much, or too little, excitement within the patient's nervous system. Since Brown also believed that alcohol was chiefly a stimulant and opium depressive, it followed that his treatments became a simple matter of prescribing alcohol where more stimulation was needed, opium where less.

Among other things, these experiments and speculations emphasized the importance of the non-verbal in human behaviour. Yet at the same time interest in the role of words, though by no means a new phenomenon, became more intense, with wordplay a notable concern. Patricia Parker begins her study *Shakespeare from the Margins: Language, Culture, Context*[20] by seeming to contest Dr Johnson's criticism of Shakespeare's allure, including his dismissal of puns with the statement 'a quibble was to him the fatal Cleopatra for which he lost the world and was content to

---

[19] For Shelley's interest in Davy's *Elements of Chemical Philosophy*, see, e.g., Richard Holmes's *Shelley: The Pursuit* (London: Weidenfeld and Nicolson, 1974), pp. 153 and 347. He would no doubt have been familiar with Joseph Priestley's *History and Present State of Electricity* (London: J. Dodsley, J. Johnson and B. Davenport, and T. Cadell, 1767) and subsequent works.

[20] Patricia Parker, *Shakespeare from the Margins: Language, Culture, Context* (University of Chicago Press, 1996).

lose it'. By contrast, she attempts to reorient the reading of Shakespeare by setting the attractions of this Cleopatra at the centre of her project.

Something of the same fascination haunts early Romanticism generally; indeed, there is sometimes a touch of the neurotic in the cult, as if the making of a pun could be a means of side-tracking serious topics. (It was also a useful rhetorical device for a stammerer such as Charles Lamb, offering a way of delaying the actual articulation of the word and thus increasing its impact.)

Coleridge, like Lamb, was fascinated by wordplay. In verses to Poole he recalled some of the parlour games they had enjoyed at Stowey:

> Conundrum, Rebus, Crambo, and Charade:
> Enigmas that had driven the Theban mad
> And Puns then best when exquisitely bad:
> And I if I of archer vein I hit.
> With my own laughter stifled my own wit![21]

(The closing lines are a reminder of the pervasive presence of erotic undertones and ambiguities in the writing of the time.)

Coleridge's fascination with language became more pressing as he passed into the uncertainty that characterized his state after his return from Germany. We have dwelt on the ambiguous connotations of the word 'liberty' at the time – at what point would it turn into licence? – and of 'nature' – was it always on the side of human beings? The deepest ambiguity of all lay in the concept of 'love'. The German visit was followed by a difficult period in which Coleridge became increasingly conscious that his marriage, undertaken largely at Southey's urging, had not brought him the kind of fulfilment that he felt in the company of the Wordsworths – which was still more fully realized as he fell in love with Wordsworth's sister-in-law, Sara Hutchinson.

The leitmotif of unexpected wordplay involved in discovering that two women in his life, one bringing illusory love and the other genuine, both bore the same name, Sara, focused the matter of naming more vividly. In the course of anguished meditations, he at one point wrote in a notebook the riddling words:

> NAMES do not always meet with LOVE
> And LOVE wants courage without a name.[22]

---

[21] *CPW* (EHC) I, 247. Quoted in letter to Thelwall of 31 December 1796: *CL* I, 295.
[22] *CN* I, 1066.

In another notebook entry, where he thought of comparing the search for the original cause of something with the search for the fountains of the Nile (with all its streams and junctions), he commented

at last, it all comes to a name –.

At the turn of the century, concerned to elucidate the significance of words as such, he was particularly fascinated by the ways in which they might be said to turn into things. This potentiality had intrigued him when he looked back to the making of *Kubla Khan* – which, as he put it, could hardly be called composition since 'all the images rose up before him as things, with a parallel production of the correspondent expressions, without any sensation or consciousness of effort'. It continued to interest him deeply: several years later, he tried to account for the famous incident in which Luther flung an ink-pot at the Devil by supposing that

in some one of those momentary Slumbers, into which the suspension of all Thought in the perplexity of intense thinking so often passes; Luther should have had a full view of the Room in which he was sitting . . . and at the same time a brain-image of the Devil, vivid enough to have acquired apparent *Outness*, and a distance regulated by the proportion of its distinctness to that of the objects really impressed on the outward senses.[23]

It was not only the nature of naming that occupied his mind, then, but this strangely complex nature of language itself. In the phenomenon of the 'bull', humour is produced by the conjunction of two different statements somehow set together, making nonsense which has at the same time a wild kind of sense. Apparent examples among the notebooks of this time: 'The Irishman's heroic cunning – in getting an accomplice hung, lest he should betray (etc.)'; a supposed prayer: 'Let us adore the bounty of God, who placed Death at the end of Life, that we might have time for Repentance.'[24] Another (in *Biographia Literaria*): 'I was a fine child, but they changed me.' In the 1812 *Omniana*, he proposed as his definition that a Bull consisted in 'a mental juxtaposition of incongruous ideas with the sensation, but without the sense, of connection', continuing,

The psychological conditions of the
    possibility of a Bull . . . require a larger space than can
    be afforded in the Omniana . . .[25]

---

[23] *CFriend* (1809) II, 117.   [24] *Ibid.*, 1054, 1053.   [25] *CSWF* I, 308.

One suspects, however, that a reason for not proceeding was his recognition that the enterprise was not so easy. When he came back to the subject in the *Biographia* (characteristically in an extended footnote), it was with an ampler characterization of the Bull –

The psychological condition, or that which constitutes the possibility of this state, being such disproportionate vividness of two distinct thoughts, as extinguishes or obscures the consciousness of the intermediate images or conceptions, or wholly abstracts the attention from them.[26]

How far he ever fully elucidated their nature is open to question, but he was evidently attempting to understand them in terms of association theory; at the same time the inquiry formed another aspect of his lifelong obsession with the phenomenon of ambiguity.

Study of the nature of language, and particularly of the history of its development, was in its infancy during Coleridge's early years. Work on antiquarianism had been undertaken within the confines of a biblical chronology that not only limited the possible timescale involved but weighted opinion in favour of supposing all languages to be descended from one original, changed and distorted by the dispersal of races and of the participating individuals. It could even be suggested that the original language might have consisted not of letters but of hieroglyphics, existing beneath the words. So if one considered the resemblance between the Hebrew aleph and the Greek alpha, and thought of the basic image as that of some kind of fountain or river; or between the Hebrew beth and the Greek beta, both visualized as representing the opening of a cave, one could soon project an original landscape in which Alph the sacred river ran through caverns measureless to man. But if Coleridge's thinking had been on these lines when he projected the landscape of *Kubla Khan*, it could not, however imaginative, be related easily to the history of language as it was being investigated in his time.

Horne Tooke's theory, by contrast, presupposing that all words could be traced back to firm concepts, gradually modified in usage, offered a more promising way forward – particularly if one took the further step of assuming that words themselves had an organic life. Coleridge sent for his book in 1798 before leaving for Germany and dined with him after his return. As happened more than once, however, contact with a person of promising ideas proved subsequently disappointing. Even by 1800, characterizing Tooke to Josiah Wedgwood as 'a clear-headed old man, as every

---

[26] *CBL* I, 72fn.

man needs must be who attends to the real import of words', he added 'there is a sort of charletannery in his manner that did not please me'.[27] Thirty years later he again suspected duality:

Horne Tooke was pre-eminently a ready-witted man. He had that clearness which is founded on shallowness; he doubted nothing, and therefore gave you all he himself meant with great completeness. His voice was very fine and his tones exquisitely discriminating. His mind had no progression.[28]

Much of Coleridge's thinking was now devoted to the exact nature of such a possible 'progression', and how his poetic experience might help it along. In September 1800[29] he urged Godwin to

write a book on the power of words, and the processes by which human feelings form affinities with them – in short I wish you to philosophize Horn Tooke's System, and to solve the great Questions – whether there be reason to hold, that an action bearing all the semblance of pre-designing Consciousness may yet be simply organic, & whether a series of such actions are possible – and close on the heels of this question would follow the old 'Is Logic the essence of Thinking?' – in other words – Is thinking impossible without arbitrary signs? & – how far is the word 'arbitrary' a misnomer? Are not words &c parts & germinations of the Plant? And what is the Law of their Growth? – In something of this order I would endeavor to destroy the old antithesis of Words & Things, elevating, as it were, words into Things, & living Things too. All the nonsense of vibrations etc. you would of course dismiss.

This account shows how far he had progressed from his earlier, more naive views of language – a development also associated with his changing view of James Mackintosh. Among the cases where Coleridge's behaviour could be contradictory – or even appear two-faced – his behaviour towards Mackintosh provides an extreme example, partly to be explained by the fact that it brought together different levels of his experience. Sympathizers with calls for reform were likely to see the Scottish lawyer as the hero of his early rejoinder to Burke's *Reflections on the Late Revolution in France*, entitled *Vindiciae Gallicae*. The book ranked with Godwin's *Political Justice* as a major influence on the young of the time. Like many of his generation, however, he changed his mind as the years went by; and his was one of the most dramatic reversals, eventually announced in public in a lecture of 1800 at which Godwin himself was present. His vehement and comprehensive abjuration of his former principles on that occasion was

[27] *CL* I, 559.   [28] *CTT* I, 117.   [29] *CL* I, 625–6.

taken as a personal attack by Godwin, who wrote demanding an explanation. Mackintosh's reply was both courteous and polished, denying that criticism of Godwin himself could have been intended. Whether or not Coleridge accepted the explanation is not clear, but he was evidently not happy concerning the affair. He would have known Godwin's soreness concerning Mackintosh's attack: as described by Hazlitt:

He laid about him like one inspired; nothing could withstand his envenomed tooth . . . The havoc was amazing, the desolation was complete. As to our visionary sceptics and Utopian philosophers, they stood no chance with our lecturer. Poor Godwin, who had come in the bonhomie and candour of his nature, to hear what new light had broken in upon his old friend, was obliged to quit the field, and slank away after an exulting taunt thrown out at 'such fanciful chimeras as a golden mountain or a perfect man'.[30]

Godwin himself would hardly have accepted the word 'slank', of course; he simply declared that he could no longer bear to attend lectures that seemed to carry references to himself without an opportunity to contradict what was said.[31]

Coleridge, meanwhile, having produced a recantation of his own concerning the French Revolution (though in his case, he maintained, the commitment had never been strong[32]) cannot have been altogether unsympathetic to Mackintosh's changed position. His main charge was rather that by such an open and public avowal, he had aided the anti-Jacobin faction and lent support to their recent slanders of figures such as Southey, Lloyd, Lamb and himself.[33] When Southey's *Wat Tyler* was republished piratically some years later and Southey defended himself against charges of sedition, Coleridge wrote in a letter:

What injudicious advisers must not Southey have had! It vexes me to the quick. Never yet did any human Being gain any thing by self-desertion. I shall never forget the *disgust*, with which Mackintosh's 'bear witness, I *recant, abjure* and *abhor* the principles' – i.e. of his own Vindiciae Gallicae, struck his Auditors in Lincoln's Inn –[34]

---

[30] *HW* XI, 98.

[31] He replied to Mackintosh in his *Thoughts occasioned by the Perusal of Dr Parr's Spital Sermon* (London: Taylor and Wilks, 1801), which Coleridge annotated: *CL* II, 736n; *CM* III, 845–51.

[32] See 'France: An Ode', originally entitled 'The Recantation: An Ode': *CPW* (EHC) I, 243–7; and cf. *CFriend* (1809) II, 146–7.

[33] See E. K. Chambers, *Samuel Taylor Coleridge* (Oxford: Clarendon Press, 1938), p. 93.

[34] Letter to Street, 22 March 1817: *CL* IV, 713. According to the account of Mackintosh in the *Oxford Dictionary of National Biography* (Oxford University Press, 2004), the exact wording he intended to use (and probably did use) was 'I abhor, abjure, and for ever renounce the French Revolution . . .'

This disgust, felt not only by Godwin but by others such as Hazlitt, helps to explain Coleridge's attitude in subsequent years: the distaste was largely political in its basis, and shared with like-minded members of his immediate circle. Lamb wrote a bitter, tasteless epigram on Mackintosh's apostasy for the *Albion*, comparing him, to his disadvantage, with Judas.[35] In May 1800 Coleridge was able to report to Godwin how Humphry Davy 'defends you with a friend's zeal against the Animalcula, who live on the dung of the great Dung-fly Mackintosh'.[36] Another letter to Godwin a little later was still more virulent: he recorded his favourable reaction to two recent visitors and went on to hope that their attitudes would have been altered from those inculcated by the 'Scotch Gentleman':

that Gemman's Lectures & Conversations are but the Steam of an Excrement, & truly animalcular must those Souls be, to whom *this* can form a cloud that hides from them the face of Sun or Star. He is a thing that must make itself known to all noses, sooner or later, but some men's olfactories are quicker than others – / You for instance *smelt* at him & found him out – I & Wordsworth *winded* him at a distance.[37]

These acrid things about Mackintosh were both produced for the eyes of the aggrieved Godwin. Concerning his attitude as a whole, on the other hand, there is need for discrimination. When they first knew each other, Mackintosh had shown him little but kindness, sending him a letter in November 1797[38] full of praise for a young and struggling writer whom he had heard of through Beddoes and 'my amiable Friend Miss Allen'; he reported that he had been able to persuade Daniel Stuart to offer him some money in return for contributions to his paper, the *Morning Post*. Coleridge's reply and his following letter, both of them recently discovered by Edmund Garratt,[39] show delight at Mackintosh's recognition and gratitude for his help in finding journalistic work. By the beginning of the following year, however, as Hazlitt recalled, Coleridge's vein was more critical:

At dinner-time he grew more animated, and dilated in a very edifying manner on Mary Wollstonecraft and Mackintosh. The last, he said, he considered (on my

---

[35] Letter to Manning of August 1801: *LL* (Marrs) II, 113. It has been claimed that the *Albion* had to cease publication as a result of including this poem.

[36] Letter to Godwin, 21 May 1800: *CL* I, 588. He put his views more soberly in a letter of 13 October: *ibid.*, 636.

[37] *CL* II, 737.

[38] *CL* I, 359–60n.

[39] See Garratt's article 'Lime Blossom, Bees and Flies: Three Unpublished Letters of S. T. Coleridge to Sir James Mackintosh', in *Romanticism* 7 (2001), 1–15.

father's speaking of his *Vindiciae Gallicae* as a capital performance) as a clever, scholastic man – a master of the topics – or as the ready warehouseman of letters, who knew exactly where to lay his hand on what he wanted, though the goods were not his own. He thought him no match for Burke, either in style or matter. Burke was a metaphysician, Mackintosh a mere logician.[40]

This conversation took place at the beginning of 1798. Coleridge's new stance may have owed something even at this stage to Mackintosh's opinions concerning Wordsworth, and his failure to appreciate poetry such as that being assembled for *Lyrical Ballads*.[41] In his memoir Clement Carlyon states that in Germany Coleridge was already speaking of the intellectual exchanges between them when they had met at the Wedgwoods' house at Cote – apparently a first encounter, between the November exchange of letters and his departure for the continent in the following autumn; he also mentioned that Coleridge had 'no great liking' for him.[42] Daniel Stuart recorded a memory of Coleridge being there 'during the Christmas holidays', monopolizing the attention of the company, particularly that of Tom Wedgwood:

> several of the party wished him out of the house. I believe the Wedgewoods were at the same time very liberal to him with their purse: he was said to be – his family, at least – starving, and that he had no means of employment. Mackintosh wrote to me, soliciting for him an engagement to write for the *Morning Post* pieces of poetry and such trifles. I agreed; and settled him at a small salary. Mackintosh, at the instance of some of the inmates, attacked Coleridge on all subjects, politics, poetry, religion, ethics, &c. Mackintosh was by far the most dexterous disputer. Coleridge overwhelmed listeners in, as he said, with reference to Madame de Staël, a monologue;[43] but at sharp cut-and-thrust fencing, by a

---

[40] *HW* XVII, III.

[41] In her note to *CN* I, 2468, Kathleen Coburn presents the evidence in favour of Shawcross's suggestion that Mackintosh was the 'Papilianus' addressed in the motto to *Lyrical Ballads*. ('How absolutely *not* after your liking, O learned jurist!'), quoted in this notebook entry about a dream, also in connection with Mackintosh's inability to appreciate subtle psychological thinking (which he would 'prove to be Nonsense by a Scotch Smile'). In a letter to Godwin of June 1801, Coleridge hoped with satisfaction that Sharp and Rogers, who had been visiting the Lakes, would return 'with far other opinion respecting Wordsworth, than the Scotch Gentleman has been solicitous to impress his Listeners with': *CL* II, 737. See also his comment, reported by Hazlitt, to Mackintosh and Tom Wedgwood on their 'indifferent opinions' of Wordsworth: 'He strides on so far before you that he dwindles in the distance': *HW* XVII, III. By 1808, however, Mackintosh was expressing a favourable opinion of Wordsworth's poems: see *WL* (1806–11), p. 265.

[42] Clement Carlyon, *Early Years and Late Reflections*, 4 vols. (London: Whittaker, 1856), I, 68–70. He also reported Coleridge's view, however, that Mackintosh could only appreciate people of superior intellectual qualities, evidently including himself among the number.

[43] For a different account, see Seamus Perry, *S. T. Coleridge: Interviews and Recollections* (London: Palgrave, 2000), pp. 148 and 150, n. 40, reporting that Madame de Staël spoke of Coleridge as excellent in monologue, 'mais il ne savait pas le dialogue'.

master like Mackintosh, he was speedily confused and subdued. He felt himself lowered in the eyes of the Wedgewoods: a salary, though small as it was, was provided for him; and Mackintosh drove him out of the house: an offence which Coleridge never forgave.[44]

Stuart's memory was by then not very accurate, and his account must be treated with caution. That the inhabitants of the house-party should have resented this monopolizing young talker and applauded Mackintosh's debating attacks is quite plausible, but in what sense he 'drove him out' is not clear, and Coleridge's subsequent intimacy with Tom Wedgwood militates against the idea that the object of the pension (which was in fact generous) was to keep him away. Stuart himself reports Coleridge's subsequent comment on Mackintosh's skill in maintaining an argument about Locke but privately confessing afterwards that he had never read him. Stuart's account of their duels recalls rather Lamb's memories of the 'wit-combats' at school between Coleridge and Le Grice, with Coleridge like a Spanish great galleon, slow and solid, against the faster manoeuvres of his opponent's English man of war.[45] It may help to explain why some covert hostility towards Coleridge survived among the rest of the Wedgwood family, but it must also be borne in mind that in 1798 Mackintosh was married for the second time, to Catherine Allen, sister of Josiah Wedgwood's wife, and so secured a permanent connection with them. In 1800 he sent a ticket for his forthcoming lectures to Coleridge, who, according to his account to Poole, was not impressed, thinking them largely plagiarized from Condillac,[46] and taking issue with him on the question of priority in formulating the doctrine of innate ideas[47] – though he acknowledged having learned from him that the association of ideas had not been introduced by Locke until the fourth edition of his work.[48]

A fuller criticism of Mackintosh's style was expressed elsewhere in the same notebook; Coleridge's distaste was clearly based not just on his political behaviour but on what he perceived as a fundamentally different cast of mind:

Mackintosh intertrudes, not introduces his beauties. Nothing grows out of his main argument but much is shoved between – each digression occasions a move

---

[44] Daniel Stuart, *Letters from the Lake Poets: Samuel Taylor Coleridge, William Wordsworth and Robert Southey, to Daniel Stuart* (London: printed for private circulation by West, Newman, 1889).
[45] 'Christ's Hospital Five and Thirty Years Ago', in *Elia.*
[46] His notes on them can be found in *CN* I, 634.
[47] *CL* II, 681.   [48] *Ibid.*, 695.

backward to find the road again – like a sick man he recoils after every affection. The Serpent by which the ancients emblem'd the Inventive faculty appears to me, in its mode of motion most exactly to emblem a writer of Genius. He varies his course yet still glides onwards – all lines of motion are his – all beautiful, & all propulsive . . .[49]

This was a more radical and searching critique, embodying the view that true mental genius would express itself in a more organic fashion than Mackintosh's mechanical mode, so that the hearer would enjoy a sense of animation. There had been not only a further sight of Mackintosh in the lecture room – the occasion of the slight to Godwin – but a development in his sense of what he believed Mackintosh to be lacking (and himself – at least by implication – to possess when at his best). In addition, knowledge of his turncoat actions led to a long notebook entry in which he analysed how such a change might have found acceptability in Mackintosh's own mind:

Did Mackintosh change his opinions with a cold clear predetermination, formed at one moment, to make 5000£ a year by that change? I neither know nor care. Probably not. But this I know, that to be thought a man of consequence by his contemporaries, to exercise power, to excite admiration, & to make a fortune are his habitual objects of wish & pursuit.[50]

He went on to maintain that once such fundamental aims had established themselves, the honesty of such a man might die away until 'he turns hypocrite so gradually & by such little tiny atoms, that by the time he has arrived at a given point he forgets his own hypocrisy in his conversion'. Indignation had been replaced by an impulse to interpret psychologically the processes involved.

Although little attention has been given to the fact, there was further contact between the two men shortly after the London lectures, including a visit by James and Catherine associated with their Scottish tour of 1801.[51] During their return in the summer, they paused for two days and dined with Coleridge, who a year later recorded his recollection:

---

[49] *CN* I, 609.
[50] *Ibid.*, 947. The entry was later used, with Mackintosh's name changed, for the 1812 *Omniana*: see *CSWF* I, 311 and n.
[51] *CN* I, 947n, citing *Memoirs of the Life of The Right Honourable Sir James Mackintosh*, edited by his son Robert James Mackintosh. 2 vols. (London: Edward Moxon, 1835), I, 169. The date is further supported by a note by Mackintosh in his copy of Kant's *Anthropologie* (Königsberg: F. Nicolovius, 1798): 'Given to me by Coleridge I think at the Lakes in 1801.' *CM* III, 236.

Mackintosh, (who is a large tall man) spent two days with me at Keswick, & was very entertaining & pleasant. He is every inch the being, I had conceived him to be, from what I saw of him at Cote House. We talked of all & every thing – on some very affecting subjects in which he represented himself by words as affected; on some subjects that called forth his verbal indignation – or exultation: but in no one moment did any particle of his face from the top of his forehead to the half of his neck, move. His face has no lines like that of a man – no softness, like that of a woman – it is smooth, hard, motionless – a flesh-mask! – As to his conversation, it was all uncommonly well-worded: but not a thought in it worthy of having been worded at all – He was however entertaining to me always; & to all around him then chiefly, when he talked of Parr, Fox, Addington, &c &c. When I asked him concerning Davy – he answered Oh! – little Davy – Dr Beddoes' Eleve, you mean? – This was an exquisite trait of character.[52]

Coleridge was returning to his sense of a lack in Mackintosh and tracing a lifelessness – this time in his facial behaviour rather than his verbal expression. His comments indeed suggest a reaction resembling that of D. H. Lawrence to Bertrand Russell a century later. As is generally recognized, Lawrence's portrait of Sir Joshua Malleson in *Women in Love* is a thinly disguised rendering of Russell; he appears first in the chapter entitled 'Breadalby', 'a learned, dry Baronet of fifty, who was always making witticisms and laughing at them heartily in a harsh, horse-laugh'. When this 'elderly sociologist' comments 'Knowledge is, of course, liberty', he receives a sharp reply:

'In compressed tabloids,' said Birkin, looking at the dry, stiff little body of the Baronet. Immediately Gudrun saw the famous sociologist as a flat bottle, containing tabloids of compressed liberty. That pleased her. Sir Joshua was labelled and placed forever in her mind.[53]

A later comment expands Birkin's sense of Malleson as

always talking in his harsh, yet rather mincing voice, endlessly endlessly, always with a strong mentality working, always interesting, and yet always known, everything he said known beforehand, however novel it was, and clever.[54]

Birkin's response (presumably endorsed by Lawrence) was projected as the reaction of a man who regarded thinking not just as a rational process but as an activity that must be intimately related to the whole of one's human nature. Coleridge, who was, at the time of his early encounters with

[52] Letter of 31 October 1801: *CL* II, 770.
[53] D. H. Lawrence, *Women in Love,* ed. David Farmer, Lindeth Vasey and John Worthen (Cambridge University Press, 1987), p. 86.
[54] *Ibid.*, p. 98.

Mackintosh, creating his philosophy of the 'one Life', evidently sensed something similarly incomplete about his inflexibility of facial expression and accompanying rigidity of mind. It would have been all the more galling to find such a 'thinker' being apparently listened to by his patrons more readily than himself.

If one turns back to the letter to Godwin of September 1800[55] already quoted from, the word that is evidently key to his speculations of his own that he regarded as more important than Mackintosh's shallow felicities is 'living'. How far might one be able to take the speculation that words should be regarded as organisms? This attractive idea may have been nursed ever since 1792, when he borrowed Tooke's volume Ἔπεα Πτεροεντα from his college library. At that time, Tooke was particularly attractive to young men on account of his radical opinions: Coleridge's guarded approbation has already been mentioned. But he also had a lasting reason for interest. In a lecture of 1811–12, he said that Tooke's book might more properly have been called 'Verba Viventia', 'for words are the living products of the living mind & could not be a due medium between the thing and the mind unless they partook of both'.[56]

By the time he came to write *Aids to Reflection* a decade later, he had developed his terminology further; there he wrote:

Horne Tooke entitled his celebrated work, Ἔπεα πτερόεντα, Winged Words: or Language, not only the *Vehicle* of Thought but the *Wheels*. With my convictions and views, for Ἔπεα I should substitute λόγοι, that is, Words *select* and *determinate*, and for Πτερόεντα ζῶοντες, that is, *living* Words. The *Wheels* of the intellect I admit them to be; but such as Ezekiel beheld in 'the visions of God' as he sate among the Captives by the river of Chebar. 'Whithersoever the Spirit was to go, the Wheels went, and thither was their Spirit to go; *for the Spirit of the living creature was in the wheels also.*'[57]

The shift from 'επεα' to 'λογοι' indicates an important development in his thinking. Already, by the February of 1801, writing to Humphry Davy, he had been able to lay out his long-term project more clearly. While hoping to devote himself to the study of chemistry, following Davy's leads, what his heart burned to do once he was free, he claimed, was to

concenter my free mind to the affinities of the Feelings with Words & Ideas under the title of 'Concerning Poetry & the nature of the Pleasures derived from it.'

[55] *CL* I, 625–6.   [56] *CLects* (1808–19) I, 273.   [57] *CAR*, p. 7.

– I have faith, that I do understand this subject / and I am sure, that if I write what I ought to do on it, the Work would supersede all the Books of Metaphysics hitherto written / and all the Books of Morals too. – To whom shall a young man utter *his Pride*, if not to a young man whom he loves?[58]

Another aspect of his thinking stands out from this summarizing. If not only the books of metaphysics but the books of morals were to be superseded, there are implications for his religious thinking also. There too, he appears to be setting up his thought as original. And indeed during this period he was becoming more and more convinced that the Unitarianism that he had embraced during the 1790s provided an insufficient basis for his philosophy. The psychology involved was not, he thought, sufficiently subtle.

This was the element in his thinking which would in the end seem most innovative: it led him to produce the term 'desynonymization' by which he characterized the process of development in language, assuming that in their evolution words constantly became more refined, and that as they did so they split into dualities, by which a purity would be preserved in the one, while the other indicated a necessary ambiguity. A favourite example was the pair 'property' and 'propriety'; he took over meanwhile from Horne Tooke the supposition of a similar relationship between 'give' and 'if'. Yet even as he developed new ideas and freer expressions, another side of his experience was admonitory. When he asserted the desire to 'utter *his Pride*', the very words must act as a reminder of the need for human beings to exercise proper humility – which must in turn draw him back towards traditional religious attitudes.

The exact trajectory of his subsequent thought is not easy to trace, but by the time that he went to Malta he had evidently come to feel increasingly the need to reconsider biblical values. In 1798 he had preached on the episode in St John's Gospel where Jesus resisted the pressure to make him a king by force and departed into a mountain, 'himself alone',[59] as if it licensed the need for every human being to nurse individual prophetic vision; now he would devote more of his time to the opening words of that gospel, 'In the beginning was the Word, and the Word was with God and the Word was God', and their communal implications.

The main Greek expression for 'Word' was, of course, 'Λογος'. One of the first occasions when the word assumed its advanced significance for

---

[58] *CL* II, 671. He had already told Davy that his 'Essay on Poetry' would in reality be 'a disguised System of Morals & Politics': *ibid.* I, 632.

[59] John vi: 15.

Coleridge came in April 1805, when he mused how natural phenomena might correspond so closely to the inner needs of human beings as to become true symbols:

In looking at objects of Nature while I am thinking, as at yonder moon dim-glimmering thro' the dewy window-pane, I seem rather to be seeking, as it were asking, a symbolical language for something within me that already and for ever exists, than observing any thing new. Even when that latter is the case, yet still I have always an obscure feeling, as if that new phaenomenon were the dim Awaking of a forgotten or hidden Truth of my inner Nature. / It is still interesting as a Word, a Symbol! It is Λογος, the Creator! and the Evolver!

What is the right, the virtuous Feeling and consequent action, when a man having long meditated and perceived a certain truth finds another, a foreign Writer, who has handled the same with an approximation to the Truth, as he had previously conceived it? Joy! Let Truth make her Voice audible! While I was preparing the pen to write this remark, I lost the train of Thought which had led me to it. I meant to have asked something else, now forgotten: for the above answers itself – it needed no new answer, I trust, in my Heart.[60]

This new stress on the word Λογος signals a development that was to be increasingly important during the years immediately succeeding. It reached a point of definition in a letter to John May in 1815, where he wrote of the work to which he was now devoting himself, claiming that his current work on a drama for Drury Lane was designed with the aim of giving himself the necessary time and leisure to complete it. This work would itself be entitled a 'Logosophia', or, alternatively, 'on the Logos, divine and human, in six Treatises'. These six would consist, first of a 'History of Philosophy and it's Revolutions from Pythagoras to Plato and Aristotle', then a 'logos koinos', which would be a system of practical logic – 'not so much a Novum Organum as an Organum vere Organum' – to be followed by 'Logos Architectonicus' on the 'Dynamic or constructive Philosophy', which would lead into a detailed commentary on the Gospel of St John, 'collating the Word of the Evangelist with the Christ crucified of St Paul', with a fifth Treatise, 'Logos agonistes' – on Pantheists and Mystics such as Bruno, Boehme, Fox and Spinoza – to be followed by a sixth and last Treatise, 'Logos alogos', devoted to the causes and consequences of modern Unitarianism.[61]

For the remainder of his life this would be a key word (and key concept) in Coleridge's thinking. In her study *Coleridge's Philosophy:*

---

[60] Note of 15 April 1805: *CN* II, 2546.   [61] *CL* IV, 501.

The Logos as Unifying Principle,[62] Mary Anne Perkins has explored its extent and pervasiveness. It could still be argued, nevertheless, that the 'real' Coleridge was to be traced in the uncertainty that ends the notebook entry quoted above, with its final rueful confession, 'While I was preparing the pen to write this remark, I lost the train of Thought which had led me to it.' Such uncertainties of mind were preferable to the rigidities that he had experienced from some of his contemporaries, or the overdependence on words as logical entities epitomized in Mackintosh.

The upshot of all these currents of thought in Coleridge's mind was to transform it into a sea of contraries. It was a sea lacking a rock to which he could cling; nor could he even look to a sure ark on which to survive. If he turned to the Anglican Church, it was not as an object of detailed faith: his days in Highgate would not be notable for church-going. The Anglican Church was a model not for any doctrines or practices, but rather for its refusal to align itself with any one position, offering instead a framework of reconciliation, not to be associated with a form of words or a dictionary, but rather to be a site where the Word could live, its best model being the living cell itself, with its power to reach out into the infinite or contract to the permanent, but never stopping its own process. Hence the extraordinary complexity of the later Coleridge and his thinking.

To those (and they were many) who had not followed his (often tortuous-seeming) intellectual path and who could not therefore work on from that state, the way forward was less clear, more likely to involve some deconstruction of words into their component energies and illuminations. That was a task for the future, however. In the meantime there was still scope for writers who found the task of dealing with words less fraught than he had done and who still wanted to explore some of the implications of the world that he, and they, had inherited. For them, Coleridge was truly a seminal mind, but never himself to be treated as a model.

---

[62] Mary Anne Perkins, *Coleridge's. Philosophy: The Logos as Unifying Principle* (Oxford: Clarendon Press, 1994).

CHAPTER 8

The Nature of Hazlitt's taste

After the years of uncertainty surrounding the struggle for superiority between England and France, the élan produced by final victory at Waterloo was accompanied by restlessness. It was not easy to see how development might now take place: one could not think of returning to the *status quo ante*; there was no obvious way forward. Yet younger writers were encouraged by the emergence of new voices: Keats expressed his feelings in a poem of 1816 beginning 'Great spirits now on earth are sojourning . . .' – the spirits he had in mind being Wordsworth, Leigh Hunt and Benjamin Haydon; while one of the most striking statements of the time is in his letter to the last-named of January 1818 that concluded, 'every day older I get – the greater is my idea of your atchievements in Art: and I am convinced that there are three things to rejoice at in this Age – The Excursion Your Pictures and Hazlitt's depth of Taste'.

To think of someone finding Hazlitt's 'depth of taste' a cause for rejoicing is strange, to say the least – not to mention Keats's linking of it with Wordsworth's *Excursion* and Haydon's own pictures. Some light has been thrown on the matter, however, by David Bromwich, who pointed out that Hazlitt had in fact written one of the most interesting critiques of Wordsworth's poem at the time, and that in order to appreciate it fully one should turn, not to the version in his *Round Table* collection but to the original review as it appeared in *The Examiner* between August and October 1814. This review differed from the notorious one by Jeffrey in the *Edinburgh Review*. Afterwards, Hazlitt was particularly delighted to learn how pleased Wordsworth had been by some of its phrases when read to him, and to hear of his 'outrageous incredulity' when he was told the identity of its author.

It is not difficult to make sense of Hazlitt's enthusiasm for Wordsworth's poem once one recalls his preference for solitude, and the well-known opening to an essay:

One of the pleasantest things in the world is going a journey; but I like to go by myself. I can enjoy society in a room; but out of doors, nature is company enough for me.

The sentiment is one that he shared with Wordsworth, and which permeates *The Excursion,* a poem which thrives in accounts of the lonely by the lonely. The poem is also notable for its occasional groupings – most notably perhaps in the rather casual one to be found in the last book, when the Wanderer's discourse rises virtually to a prophetic strain, the note of despair at the state of persons whose promise is shut up by lack of proper development being coupled with hope for a more enlightened state of things if such human beings are enabled to realize their potential.

At its most favourable, however, Hazlitt's praise of Wordsworth was directed to the quality of the imagination sensed behind this poem, which he described as if it were truly God-like. When he writes that Wordsworth's 'imagination broods over that which is "without form and void", and "makes it pregnant"', the juxtaposing of quotations from the Bible and from *Paradise Lost* indicates a belief that in this poem he was rivalling Milton in creative reach – though, as Bromwich points out, his praise is modified by an assertion that the effect of the poem is often diminished by a reliance on detail, reducing it to the point where it should really be 'considered as a philosophical pastoral poem – as a scholastic romance . . .' This is not exclusively disabling, however: 'It is not so much a description of natural objects, as of the feelings associated with them, not an account of the manners of rural life, but the result of the Poet's reflections on it.'[1] Any criticism, in consequence, must accept this limitation:

If the skill with which the poet had chosen his materials had been equal to the power which he has undeniably exerted over them, if the Objects (whether persons or things) which he makes use of as the vehicle of his sentiments, had been such as to convey them in all their depth and force, then the production before us might indeed 'have proved a monument' as he himself wishes it, worthy of the author, and of his country.[2]

The limited admiration expressed in this review brings out something often remarked concerning eighteenth-century writing – that Milton's achievement cast its shadow everywhere. Inasmuch as Hazlitt found Wordsworth a true innovator, he was appreciating his respect for the true 'hardness' of the English character at its best. But if one is looking for a

---

[1] *HW* XIX, 10.   [2] *Ibid.*, IV, 124–5.

true response to the crisis of language as it was being experienced at this time in the revolt against stiffness of form, one should turn back to Coleridge, who, in an essay on Pitt much admired by Hazlitt and reprinted by him in a collection of political essays, listed what he believed most lacking in the man: he had had

no feelings connected with man or nature, no spontaneous impulses, no unbiassed and desultory studies, no genuine science, nothing that constitutes individuality in intellect, nothing that teaches brotherhood in affection![3]

What was missing from Pitt's personality, in other words, was a sense of the human beings who were responding to the new demands of the times, and in whom new kinds of language were being forged – natural, spontaneous, individual and brotherly.

Hazlitt's acquaintance with Coleridge, and his sense of new things happening, had begun when, living in his father's house in Wem in Shropshire a few years before, he had heard that the ministry of the Unitarian chapel at nearby Shrewsbury was about to be offered to the poet – until then known mainly for his writing, lecturing and preaching in the West of England. The account of his expedition to hear the sermon Coleridge had been asked to preach is one of the great set pieces of his writing: he rose before daybreak and walked 'ten miles in the mud' to attend the chapel, where he heard with pleasure the pacifist element in the preacher's message – one reason for his delight being that Coleridge's message spoke so directly to the dilemma facing people like himself. As mentioned earlier, his father was a Unitarian minister, having given his allegiance to a sect that denied the divinity of Christ and so was thought of as offering the unrespectable face of Nonconformity. The offence that caused his father most trouble during his early career, however, was not this but his open criticism of the ill treatment of some American prisoners of war by the officers of a regiment at Kinsale in the south of Ireland. A fiercely independent man, always announcing firmly that he would die in a ditch rather than submit to anyone's authority in matters of faith, he had already alienated some people in England by his support for the Americans' struggle for independence; after the trouble now created by his outspokenness on what he saw as acts of inhumanity, he decided that his main hope was to emigrate with his family to what he thought of as the land of liberty where, he must have felt, he could speak and act in full freedom.

[3] *CET* I, 221; quoted in *HW* VII, 328.

He was to find, however, that it was not so. Instead, he would encounter a condition that recurs again and again in the history of the time: even in America advocates of freedom could find themselves battling against an equally powerful pressure in favour of compliance with existing authority. In the case of religion, also, a Unitarian congregation could still contain advocates of Calvinism opposed to unlimited freedom of thought. So William Hazlitt Senior, suffering in any case from illnesses contracted as a result of contact with the New World, found his efforts to earn a living as a minister thwarted by doctrinal opponents. In the end his only course was to return to England, where he settled in the small Shropshire town already mentioned.

It was one of his dearest hopes that his young son, growing up there, should follow him as a minister; to this end he sought to arrange for his training. As is well known, however, older universities such as Oxford and Cambridge were then closed to Dissenters, who as a result had been forced to set up institutions of their own. These 'Dissenting Academies', numbering over one hundred, of which perhaps the best known was at Warrington in Lancashire, included others at Daventry and Carmarthen. Their teaching was often better than that available in their older compeers – particularly in terms of the useful arts. Joseph Priestley, who had thus acquired a 'modern' education in philosophy, science and history, himself became a tutor at Warrington.

At the time, as it happened, a new educational establishment set up in London represented an important advance. At the New College – deliberately called College rather than Academy – in Hackney, the avowed aim of its founders was to promote the aims of a liberal Unitarianism, the education being 'comprehensive and liberal, and adapted to youth in general, whether they are intended for civil and commercial life, or for any one of the learned professions'. This would evidently have appealed to Hazlitt's father, who, with his independent spirit and unwillingness to accept the authority of others, would have been happy for his son to be brought up in exactly the same way.

The time of young William's arrival, however, was more fraught than might have been expected. The College was set up in 1786; within two or three years events in France had made liberal thinking more dangerous. It was a sermon preached to the 'friends of the Revolution' in 1789 by a former lecturer, Dr Price, that prompted Edmund Burke to reply with his famous *Reflections*; shortly afterwards a sermon from Joseph Priestley caused some to consider calling him to account. A student of the College circulated a pamphlet in Birmingham that led to the riots there, including the notorious destruction of Priestley's own library and laboratory. In spite of Priestley's urgings of caution in political matters, the young men of the College at Hackney, eager for political change, were rebellious against 'kings, priests and aristocrats'. When the Habeas Corpus Act was suspended in 1794, Jeremiah Joyce, an ex-student of the College, was one of the first to be arrested, remaining in prison until the famous acquittals in October; while in January 1796 a member of the College Committee was tried on a charge of treacherous conspiracy. Again the result was an acquittal, but the notoriety of the College cooled the enthusiasm of its supporters. Its finances dried up, and at midsummer 1796 its doors finally closed.

The young William Hazlitt, having arrived in the midst of this turmoil in September 1793 with an exhibition from the Presbyterian Fund, stayed until midsummer two years later, when, in the words of the Secretary of the fund, he 'declined pursuing his studies for the ministry'. Apart from a few letters to his father, we know little of his reaction to life in the College; his later opinions, however, suggest a young man not untouched by the radical opinions of those around him but too independent to go along with any general movement, working out instead a position of his own – even if that proved in many respects more extreme than the surrounding fashionable radicalism. Since his future could not lie in the ministry, he resolved instead to spend his life primarily as a thinker, attempting to solve some of the foremost philosophical questions left by the work of men such as Locke and Hartley. His main desire, apparently, was to find a way past the problems presented by contemporary necessitarianism to those who, like his father, firmly accepted the principle of liberty, yet needed to grapple with the Hartleian assumption that the associating of ideas must ultimately be controlled by necessity. The fact that Coleridge's *Religious Musings*, published in 1796, concerned itself with a similar problem may have helped explain his desire to hear him in action.

Another intellectual figure dominating the scene in those years was that of William Godwin. 'No work in our time', Hazlitt wrote many years later, 'gave such a blow to the philosophical mind of the country as the celebrated *Enquiry concerning Political Justice*. Tom Paine was considered for the time as a Tom Fool to him, Paley an old woman, Edmund Burke a flashy sophist. Truth, moral truth, it was supposed, had here taken up its abode; and these were the oracles of thought.'[4]

---

[4] Essay 'Mr Godwin', in *The Spirit of the Age* [1825]: *HW* XI, 17.

By 1798, however, Godwin's attraction had palled, inviting criticism of his overweening confidence:

The fault, then, of Mr. Godwin's philosophy, in one word, was too much ambition – 'by that sin fell the angels!' He conceived too nobly of his fellows (the most unpardonable crime against them, for there is nothing that annoys our self-love so much as being complimented on imaginary achievements, to which we are wholly unequal) – he raised the standard of morality above the reach of humanity, and by directing virtue to the most airy and romantic heights, made her path dangerous, solitary, and impracticable. The author of the *Political Justice* took abstract reason for the rule of conduct and abstract good for its end. He places the human mind on an elevation, from which it commands a view of the whole line of moral consequences, and requires it to conform its acts to the larger and more enlightened conscience which it has thus acquired. He absolves man from the gross and narrow ties of sense, custom, authority, private and local attachment, in order that he may devote himself to the boundless pursuit of universal benevolence.[5]

In Hazlitt's later, chastened view such an arrogant attitude could not be sustained; yet it was equally impossible to abandon the cultivation of 'universal benevolence'. For this reason the enthusiasm of Wordsworth and Coleridge for the potential powers of imagination and the human heart seized his attention.

Meanwhile, whatever his hopes for humanity's future, Hazlitt needed to make a living. In spite of the impact of Coleridge, his first resort was not to literature, but to visual art: he resolved to train as a painter, and spent some time in London working towards this end. His most forceful experience was at the Orléans Gallery, hosting in December 1798 an exhibition of Italian pictures from the Orleans collection in Paris, where he was bowled over by the work of Raphael, Guido and, especially, Titian – though over the coming years the supreme master for him would remain Rembrandt. A year or two later, when the Peace of Amiens opened up Europe again, Hazlitt was able to go and live in Paris, enjoying masterpieces that Napoleon had brought back from galleries in the various places he had conquered.

Returning to the Lake District, he made a scanty living from portraits, including some with members of the Coleridge family as subjects, but was then driven out of the district as the result of an obscure incident involving a local girl. When Coleridge on one occasion criticised his capacity there for rage and hatred, however, it was in the context of a 'most unpleasant dispute' with both him and Wordsworth concerning Ray, Durham and Paley.[6]

---

[5] *Ibid.*, 18–19.   [6] *CN* I, 1616.

Hazlitt valued in Wordsworth the simplicity of a figure appreciating the beauties of nature and what the poet himself might have regarded as his chief gift – an ability to promote a sense of 'joy in widest commonalty spread'. But however strong his earlier enthusiasm for the virtues of village life, renewed acquaintance had caused it to fade. Chastened by the experience, he contended in his poem 'Home at Grasmere' that his neighbours' behaviour sometimes left much to be desired.

Hazlitt was meanwhile exercising himself in political reflection. From the middle of the 1790s his own sympathies were divided: as Catherine Maclean put it:

He responded to the personality of Fox (indeed his character-sketch of Fox has a note of personal affection absent from any of the others), and the personality of Burke was alien to his sympathies; he felt that the consequences of Burke's writing on the French Revolution 'as instruments of political power' had been almost fatal to the well-being of mankind, while Fox had been from the beginning its warm apologist; yet he did not hesitate to describe Burke as 'a profound commentator on that apocalyptical chapter in the history of human nature', and to say that to him Fox had never seemed such. They had both of them 'tried their strength in the Ulysses' bow of politicians, the French Revolution', and they had both been foiled, but 'Burke was to Fox what the geometrician is to the mechanic'.

Yet if the truth in him compelled him to concede to the one whom he regarded as having been the enemy of mankind in its hour of crisis that vision which he denied to the one who had wished to be the friend of mankind, the truth in him enabled him also to do ample justice to the statesmanship, the humanity and the passionate oratory of Fox, again enacted in vivid words:

'Every thing showed the agitation of his mind. His tongue faltered, his voice became almost suffocated, and his face was bathed in tears. He was lost in the magnitude of his subject. He reeled and staggered under the load of feeling which oppressed him. He rolled like the sea beaten by a tempest'.[7]

If Fox's mind could not match that of Burke, Hazlitt was clear about his superiority to his chief contemporary, the younger Pitt:

Whoever, having the feelings of a man, compared him at these times with his boasted rival, his stiff, straight, upright figure, his gradual contortions, turning round as if moved by a pivot, his solemn pauses, his deep tones, 'whose sound

---

[7] C. M. Maclean, *Born under Saturn* (London: Collins, 1943), pp. 221–2.

reverbed their own hollowness', must needs have said, This is a man; that is an automaton.[8]

Hazlitt's feeling for Burke's eloquence – a feeling nursed in spite of other natural instincts – was of long standing, dating from the time when he first came across his prose. In 'My First Acquaintance with Poets', he recalls how at dinner in 1798, after the discussion of Burke and Mackintosh mentioned earlier, he had ventured the observation that 'the speaking of Burke with contempt might be made the test of a vulgar democratic mind' – which Coleridge thought 'very just and striking'. Maclean also draws attention to the manner in which the apparent conflict between his warmth of sympathy for Fox and his admiration for the superior mental powers of Burke was in a sense resolved by his whole-hearted appreciation of their forerunner, Pitt the elder:

in the mind of Chatham, the great substantial truths of common sense, the leading maxims of the Constitution, the real interests and general feelings of mankind, were in a manner embodied. He comprehended the whole of his subject at a single glance – every thing was firmly rivetted to its place; there was no feebleness, no forgetfulness, no pause, no distraction; the ardour of his mind overcame every obstacle . . .[9]

While Hazlitt was steering his way through the hazards of British political thinking, views of his that touched on the larger European scene were greeted unsympathetically. It would be unfair, nevertheless, to ignore the strain of patriotism that ran though his writing, echoing the current suspicion of French intentions, and including both a scare of invasion towards the end of the decade, and a still more real fear a year or two later when it became clear that Napoleon was actually planning to invade England from across the Channel. He described the stir of preparation which was visible everywhere:

Not a fishing-boat but seemed to have new life put into it, and to prepare for the conflict. Upwards of five hundred ships of war, of various descriptions and sizes, scoured the ocean in different directions. English squadrons blockaded every port in the Channel or Mediterranean; and our cruisers were either seen scudding over the waters, like seagulls dallying with their native element and hovering near their prey, or stood in and insulted the enemy on his own shores, cutting out his vessels or dismantling their forts. By land, the hubbub and consternation was not less. Britain armed from one end to the other to repel the threatened invasion.

---

[8] *Ibid.*   [9] *Ibid.*, p. 224, quoting from *HW* VII, 297–8.

An army of volunteers sprang up like grasshoppers. Every hill had its horseman: every bush or brake its sharpshooter. The preparations were not the least active at the greatest distance from the scene of danger. Petitions were put into our liturgy to deliver us from an insolent and merciless foe who 'was about to swallow us up quick'; nor was there a church door in the remotest corner of Great Britain on which was not posted a call on high and low, rich and poor, to bestir themselves in the common defence, proceeding from Mr. Cobbett's powerful pen, which roused the hopes and fears of the meanest rustic into a flame of martial enthusiasm.[10]

In so far as it supported the need to defend the country against attack, he shared the common mood. 'There could be only one opinion on the necessity of defence in such a moment, and he promised Buonaparte a sharp welcome if ever he landed in England.'[11] But while he felt all this (continues Maclean) he never ceased to regret a renewal of the war into which it seemed to him that Buonaparte had been forced, and to regard it as the crown of all the calamities in which the country had been involved by the narrow and selfish policy pursued by the government since the outbreak of hostilities with France in 1793:

Where others felt only the élan of patriotic endeavour and even the anticipatory joy of battle, he could only feel the tragedy of this game of cross-purposes played by men and nations, and the piteous futility of the vast human agony which he foresaw.[12]

Maclean's explanation is complex:

He realised that Buonaparte had two aspects, and that he was being gradually led or forced in one of these aspects into some measure of betrayal towards the Cause of which he had originally been the champion and the main prop, of which he still, despite the alteration in himself, was the best hope. The Buonaparte who said frankly, 'I am for the white man against the black, because I am white,' and 'I am for the French because I am French,' and 'if it had been necessary to let all Italy perish or sacrifice two of my army, I would have let all Italy perish, because before all things I am of my army and for my army,' who was ready to crush any other people for the benefit of France, was betraying the Cause of Man in the interests of Country and enunciating a patriotism that was pernicious because 'exclusive' and therefore to be opposed. Hazlitt's attitude to this 'exclusive' patriotism can best be defined by his own words: 'True patriotism warrants no conclusion contrary to liberty or humanity . . .' It will be evident that in his conception of national and international values he was far ahead of his day.[13]

---

[10] *Ibid.*, p. 190, quoting from *HW* XIV, 207–8.
[11] *Ibid.*, p. 192.   [12] *Ibid.*   [13] *Ibid.*, pp. 193–4.

Surrounded by the contemporary mood of patriotism, in other words, Hazlitt refused to give up his passion for the spread of liberty. If Napoleon was seeming to become a tyrannical dictator, his few supporters in England could still argue that restoration of the Bourbon monarchy, involving a more obvious loss of liberty, would lead to greater evils.

By 1814, therefore, his sense that Wordsworth was following current fashion by abandoning the cause of freedom began to turn into more open hostility. It was then that, in the course of his rather favourable review of *The Excursion*, he deplored the narrowness of life in the Lake District, claiming that in consequence the inhabitants had nothing to distract them from 'mischief-making and backbiting' and listing the amusements from which they were debarred:

There are no shops, no taverns, no theatres, no opera, no concerts, no pictures, neither courtiers nor courtesans, no literary parties, no fashionable routs, no society, no books, or knowledge of books. Vanity and luxury are the civilizers of the world.[14]

Mary Wordsworth, writing to Dorothy just afterwards, seized briskly on the word 'courtesans': 'A pretty comment upon these opinions would be to relate the story of the critic's departure [from] this unaccommodating country.'[15] At about the same time William evidently did just that, in view of Lamb's reply to a letter of his: 'The "scapes" of the great god Pan who appeared among your mountains some dozen years since, and his narrow chance of being submerged by the swains, afforded me much pleasure . . .'[16] On a visit to London, Wordsworth also gave Haydon an account of the incident which, his son said afterwards, 'combined such an union of the fiendish, the ludicrous, and the sublime as not to be surpassed by any story ever told of Hazlitt'.[17]

During this visit, Wordsworth let it be known that he did not wish to meet Hazlitt, a gesture for which Haydon rebuked him: 'Had you condescended to visit him when he praised your Excursion . . . his vanity would have been soothed and his violence softened – he was conscious from what an emergency you had helped to rescue him . . . and then your taking no notice of his praise, added to his acid feelings.'[18]

[14] *HW* XIX, 22.
[15] Letter to Dorothy Wordsworth, 29 October 1814, *Letters of Mary Wordsworth 1800–1815*, ed. M. E. Burton (Oxford: Clarendon Press, 1958), p. 24.
[16] Letter of 28 December 1814: *LL* (Marrs) II, 125.
[17] Haydon, *Correspondence and Table-talk: With a Memoir by his Son F. W. Haydon* (London, 1876), I, 110.
[18] MS Letter to Wordsworth, 15 April 1817, Dove Cottage Papers, quoted by M. Moorman, *William Wordsworth*, 2 vols. (Oxford: Clarendon Press, 1957–65), II, 281. (Haydon would hardly have

Early in 1816 Hazlitt also began a series of attacks on Coleridge in the *Examiner*. (He was at the time devastated by the defeat of Napoleon at Waterloo.) After reviewing Schlegel's *Lectures on Dramatic Literature* in February without any mention of Coleridge,[19] he turned in June to the 'Christabel' volume. There he chided Coleridge for confronting public taste with the term 'mastiff bitch', yet not following up that assault in any way, and pointed out that Coleridge had omitted from the description of Geraldine a line, 'Hideous, deformed and pale of hue', which, he said, would have made it clear that she was a witch; he also commented: 'There is something disgusting at the bottom of his subject, which is but ill glossed over by a veil of Della Cruscan sentiment and fine writing . . .'[20] In this review, however, there is always an undertow of praise; his full venom was reserved for Coleridge's political opinions. In September he wrote a mock review of *The Statesman's Manual*, which had not yet been published, accusing Coleridge of being a turncoat in politics ('He belongs to all parties and is of service to none').[21] Two attacks on the pamphlet when it did appear (in the *Examiner* and *Edinburgh Review* for December) have also been attributed to him.[22]

Hazlitt's hostile writing induced in Coleridge, meanwhile, the conviction of a strong malevolence. 'Malice prepense', 'pure malignity', 'frantic hatred': the extreme terms can be matched by later references to 'avowed hatred' and to the 'poisoned arrows' of his 'wanton enmity'. Whether or not he had spoken of Hazlitt's Keswick escapade in London before this, from 1816 he was giving highly coloured accounts. To Hugh J. Rose in September he wrote of him as one whom he and Southey 'saved from infamy and transportation'.[23] He referred to 'vices too disgusting to be named' in a December letter; and in June to 'the most unmanly vices, that almost threatened to communicate a portion of their own Infamy to my family, and Southey's and Wordsworth's', Hazlitt having been 'snatched from an infamous Punishment by Southey and myself (there were not less than 200 men on horse in search of him)'.[24]

---

written this, incidentally, if he had believed Hazlitt to have been guilty of grossly criminal behaviour.)

[19] *HW* XVI, 57–99. According to Coleridge, Hazlitt elsewhere acknowledged the priority of his theory of *Hamlet* over Schlegel's. See *CL* IV, 831 and *CShC* I, 19 and n.

[20] *HW* XIX, 33.

[21] *HW* VII, 118.

[22] *HW* VII, 118–28; XVI, 99–114.

[23] *CL* IV, 670.

[24] Letter to R. H. Brabant, 5 December 1816: *CL* IV, 693; to F. Wrangham, 5 June 1817, *ibid.*, 735.

The December number of the *Edinburgh Review* contained in addition a hostile review of 'Christabel' that Coleridge believed was also by Hazlitt. A reported remark inflamed him still further, and he wrote to R. H. Brabant, in the letter mentioned above:

The man who has so grossly calumniated me in the Examiner and the Ed. Review is a Wm Hazlitt, one who owes to me more than to his own parents – for at my own risk I saved perhaps his Life from the Gallows, most certainly his character from blasting Infamy – His reason I give in his own words – 'Damn him! I *hate him*. For I am under obligations to him.' – When he was reproached for writing against his own convictions, and reminded that he had repeatedly declared the Christabel the finest poem in the language of it's size – he replied – 'I grumbled part to myself, while I was writing – but nothing stings a man so much, as making people believe Lies of him.' – You would scarcely think it possible, that a monster could exist who boasted of guilt and avowed his predilection for it. – All good I had done him of every kind, and never ceased to do so, till he had done his best to bring down infamy on three families, in which he had been sheltered as a Brother, by vices too disgusting to be named – & since then the only *Wrong*, I have done him, has been to decline his acquaintance.[25]

If Hazlitt did indeed write the *Edinburgh* review of *Christabel*, he was guilty of a greater divergence from his early views than he had shown in the *Examiner*. The later review was absolute in condemnation.[26] Coleridge's attribution of it (based perhaps on the fact that the few lines singled out as exceptions to the general condemnation corresponded with those which Hazlitt, also, had lighted upon) may have been mistaken, however. When he repeated the accusation, without naming Hazlitt, in *Biographia Literaria*, Francis Jeffrey, editor of the *Edinburgh Review*, took it to refer to himself and inserted a puzzled disclaimer to having reviewed the book.[27] (If Hazlitt was the reviewer concerned, Jeffrey was guilty of some duplicity here.)[28]

[25] *CL* IV, 692–3.
[26] *Edinburgh Review* 27 (Sept. 1816), 58–67 (*Coleridge: The Critical Heritage*, ed. J. R. de J. Jackson (London: Routledge, 1970), pp. 226–36).
[27] *Edinburgh Review* 28 (Aug. 1817), 507–12 nn. (*Heritage*, pp. 295–322).
[28] Elisabeth Schneider argued forcefully some years ago that the real reviewer had been Tom Moore. See her piece, 'The Unknown Reviewer of *Christabel*', *PMLA* 70 (1955), 417–32, and her later reply, *PMLA* 77 (1962), 71–6; Hoover Jordan, in 'Thomas Moore and the Review of *Christabel*' (*Modern Philology* 54 (1956), 95–105, repr. in *The Evidence for Authorship: Essays on Problems of Attribution, with an Annotated Bibliography of Selected Readings*, ed. David V. Erdman and Ephim G. Fogel (Ithaca, N.Y.: Cornell University Press, 1966) argued even more forcefully that internal evidence could as easily be used to support the case for authorship by Hazlitt and Jeffrey, while W. S. Dowden, in 'Thomas Moore and the Review of *Christabel*' (*Modern Philology* 60 (1962), 47–50), argued against Moore's authorship, drawing attention to Moore's own denials. See also, however,

What has not, I think, been noticed is that Coleridge's letter almost certainly does involve a misunderstanding, this time of Hazlitt's reported words. His indignation at Hazlitt as one who 'boasted of guilt and avowed his predilection for it' must be based on an assumption that his words beginning 'nothing stings a man . . .' meant 'I have determined to sting Coleridge as much as possible and the best way of doing so is to make people believe lies about him.' It is far more likely, however, that what Hazlitt meant was 'the reason why I have been so fierce in my criticism of Coleridge is that he has stung me by his lies about me'. The sentence can bear either interpretation, but the second squares much better with what we know of Hazlitt, and would be very natural if Hazlitt thought Coleridge had been exaggerating his part in the Keswick affair to his friends in London.

If my account is correct, it illustrates once again the vulnerability of the verbal: it is not enough to have the exact text unless one can be sure of the recipient's preconceptions. Coleridge's reading was based ultimately on his own interpretation.

Hazlitt himself was in a cleft stick. Since the stories had been circulating in private, he could not reply to them publicly without drawing more attention to the affair than it would otherwise have received. Nor could he tell the true story without running the further risk that he might become a laughing-stock. When in 1818 he was asked a series of questions in *Blackwood's*, including whether it was true that he once owed his personal safety and perhaps existence to the 'humane and firm interference' of the Wordsworth whom he had recently been attacking, he responded by bringing an action against the magazine.[29] Mrs Coleridge commented privately that if he persisted he would 'cut a very ridiculous figure'. 'I think I told you the ridiculous story of Hazlitt's behaviour to a Peasant Girl when he was here 12 or 14 years ago', she went on: 'some person has taken up this tale . . .'[30]

These apparently minor affairs could also take on a political colouring, as 'right-thinking Englishmen' such as Wordsworth and Coleridge condemned Napoleon's excesses, while rebellious spirits such as Hazlitt not only took Napoleon's part but believed that his early good fortunes foreshadowed

Kathleen Coburn, 'Who Killed *Christabel?*', *TLS*, 20 May 1965, p. 397, citing a notebook of 1829 in which Coleridge assumes Moore's authorship.

[29] For a good account, see Maclean, *Saturn*, pp. 363–6.

[30] Letter to Poole, September 1818, *Minnow among Tritons*, ed. S. Potter (London: Nonesuch Press, 1934), p. 64.

still more sweeping successes, towards a universal triumph of the liberty promised by the American and French revolutions. Having lived in North America during his childhood and spent some years of the new century in Paris, Hazlitt embraced the internationalist viewpoint mentioned earlier, regarding English patriotism as a temporary phenomenon that must give way to a broader view. In the 1790s his attitude had been much influenced by reading Napoleon's work. As Tom Holmberg has put it:

His dialogue published in 1793, Le Souper de Beaucaire, championed the Jacobins over the federalist Girondins. What Napoleon admired was the Jacobins' strong centralized government, their determination to deal decisively with the problems facing the fledgling republic, and their attempt to forge a strong stable France while winning the war against its enemies.

Napoleon, he continues, clearly felt, like the Jacobins, that an energetic centralized state was essential in order to consolidate the advances achieved by the Revolution; at the same time, he wished to bring about the stability for which he sensed many French people to be longing, after the upheavals of the previous decade:

In his eyes this meant the need for a strong executive. From 1799 until his death on the South Atlantic island of St. Helena, Napoleon spoke of himself as the man who had completed the Revolution. By this he meant that the basic goals enumerated above had been obtained and that now it was time to consolidate and institutionalize those goals.[31]

Hazlitt clung firmly to his support, believing that Napoleon's success in overcoming feudalism greatly outweighed his nationalist stance and imperialist ambitions.

The turning of the military tide, culminating in the victory at Waterloo, left him, as a result, utterly devastated. Benjamin Haydon wrote:

it is not to be believed how the destruction of Napoleon affected him: he seemed prostrated in mind and body, he walked about, unwashed, unshaved, hardly sober by day, and always intoxicated by night, literally, without exaggeration, for weeks; until at length, wakening as it were from a stupor, he at once left off all intoxicating liquors, and never touched them after.[32]

---

[31] Tom Holmberg, entry 'Napoleon Bonaparte', 1988, in the Internet Guide (www. napoleonbonaparte.nl).
[32] Quoted from Haydon's *Autobiography* by Ralph M. Wardle, *Hazlitt* (Lincoln: University of Nebraska Press, 1971), chapter vii, p. 157.

Thomas Noon Talford gave a similar account:

When I first met Hazlitt; in the year 1815, he was staggering under the blow of Waterloo. The reappearance of his imperial idol on the coast of France, and his triumphal march to Paris, like a fairy vision, had excited his admiration and sympathy to the utmost pitch; and though in many respects sturdily English in feeling, he could scarcely forgive the valour of the conquerors; and bitterly resented the captivity of the Emperor in St. Helena, which followed it, as if he had sustained a personal wrong. On this subject only, he was 'eaten up with passion'; on all others he was the fairest, the most candid of reasoners . . .[33]

This was by no means the end of Hazlitt's career as a radical protester, nevertheless, as Catherine Maclean points out:

To a political opponent who wished him better principles and a better temper, he replied: 'I despair of either. For my temper is so bad as to be ruffled almost as much by the roasting of a Protestant as by the spoiling of my dinner: nor have I better hopes of mending my principles, for they have never changed hitherto.' He might have added that the fight against parliamentary corruption, the fight against inertia with regard to the distress of the poor in years of unprecedented hardship, the fight against the gag and the scourge, the fight against the ill-treatment of political prisoners, the fight against the decimation of English villages by game preserving landlords who showed an almost complete disregard of human suffering, the fight against the creation in the great towns of a helot class in what had hitherto been a free country – had little in it to sweeten any man's temper. Nor had loss of hope, and Hazlitt fought, believing that he fought on the losing side. 'The chain in which they hung up the murdered corse of human Liberty is all that remains of it,' he wrote in the summer of 1816, 'and my Lord Shallow keeps the key of it.'[34]

Political questions were now being complemented by issues of culture. In the post-war years, Hazlitt came up against new people, contributors to the advanced journals of the time. These included Thomas Wainewright, a young man regarded by some as an insufferable fop who, with his exquisite clothes, had the reputation of being a dandy, but whose intelligent conversation Lamb and others relished. Later, accused of being a poisoner, he was brought to trial and sentenced to transportation – though condemned not for murder but for forgery. It was no doubt the suspicion of his having committed murder that drove the charges against him, nevertheless, and he went to Van Diemens Land, where, after serving a sentence of penal servitude, he died in 1847.

[33] Quoted by Maclean, *Saturn*, p. 326.
[34] Maclean, *Saturn*, p. 333.

An apparent strain of misanthropy in Wainewright from his early childhood (which might possibly be associated with a later readiness to be profligate of human life) emerges in his controversies with Hazlitt in the *London Magazine*. Though superficially trivial in content, these light-hearted disagreements seem to mask, at a lower level, significant divergences. In the *London Magazine* for March 1820, Hazlitt advised his readers where theatres worthy of their attention might be found: they should not frequent the fashionable ones, but 'hover over the Surrey Theatre; or snatch a grace beyond the reach of art from the Miss Dennetts at the Adelphi; or take peep (like the Devil on Two Sticks) at Mr Booth at the Cobourg – and one peep is sufficient'. In the June number Wainewright ('Janus Weathercock') denounced Hazlitt's vulgarity:

By what strange obliquity . . . does Mr Drama persevere with unabated constancy in his patronage of three little unformed girls – notable favourites with the Gallery and the *Whitechapel orders?* . . . He profaneth Spenser to rhapsodize Miss E. Dennett, Harlequin's wife!

Wainewright went on to castigate Hazlitt for his hearty praise of bread, cheese and porter – all very well in the country, perhaps –

But surely, in the centre of fashion, we might be now and then indulged with more elegant fare, – something that would suit better with the diamond rings on our fingers, the antique cameos in our breast-pins, our cambric handkerchief breathing forth Attargul, our pale lemon-coloured kid gloves! some chicken fricaseed white for instance; a bottle of Hock or Moselle, and a glass of Maraschino.[35]

The banter and needling continued back and forth for several months; as a result the core of the contention between the two men became steadily clearer: Wainewright was faulting Hazlitt for his indifference to fashion, while in reply the more famous critic was declaring his intention to praise excellence wherever it was to be found – whether or not the fashionable approved.

Hazlitt's unashamed humanity, deriving partly from Wordsworth, was his ultimate response to the French Revolution. *Lyrical Ballads* had shown him how one might write poetry under the guidance of a 'levelling muse' – a Muse who could take her stance from the recognition that human beings shared a common nature. All had access to a common imagination, and a universal heart: what part could exquisite clothes or

---

[35] T. G. Wainewright, *Essays and Criticisms*, ed. W. C. Hazlitt (London, 1880), pp. 74–5.

refined food and drink play in the culture of such a dispensation? Human beings must be taken in their wholeness: urban knowledge should be set against that of the village-dweller.

At the same time, Hazlitt's generalized benevolence, his feeling for humanity as a whole, was accompanied by a counterpointing contraction, a love of solitude which he shared with Wordsworth, and an obsessional intensity, a feeling for the aesthetic moment and a desire for exclusive love, that linked him to Coleridge.

As with Coleridge, and partly as a result of political disappointment, this became narrowed to a single obsessive individual love affair – in his case starting in 1820 and involving his landlady's daughter, Sarah Walker. Whereas Coleridge's love of Sara Hutchinson was always a private matter, known only to one or two intimate friends, Hazlitt made his love a matter of common knowledge, dwelt on at large to casual acquaintances, and written about obsessively. His behaviour indeed, as recorded at this time, was compellingly like that of Coleridge's Ancient Mariner, button-holing any person likely to listen. Yet the driving force was the same as Coleridge's: a belief that love from the heart must in itself be omnipotent and all-justifying. The feelings of the woman on whom his passion was bestowed must therefore take a secondary place. For Sarah Walker to say, as she did, that she had and could have no lasting affection for him might make sense in her world but could not in his. Yet the affair set in stark contention his desire to embrace all mankind and his passionate desire for a single exclusive love.

The account which he produced in his *Liber Amoris* shocked his literary friends, unused as they were to such works, by its leap ahead into a new form of expression without regard for conventional decorum. (A twenty-first-century reader, in contrast, might be less disturbed by his behaviour than by his few divagations from presentation of a precise record.) The open frankness was typical of Hazlitt's attitude – at least at one end of its spectrum. He no doubt believed one of the qualities lacking from Wordsworth's writing to be present in his own: a characteristic of humanity that he himself would have referred to – using a term that would be gratefully taken up by his admirers – as *gusto*. It is the quality that makes for the attractiveness of essays such as 'The Indian Jugglers', or 'The Fight'. Not easily able to say just what he means by this quality, Hazlitt is reduced to the necessity of producing illustrative examples – of which the first and most essential is *The Beggar's Opera*. One scarcely comes closer to an understanding of the content of the term when, in his essay 'The Indian Jugglers', he praises Joshua Reynolds, 'with his grace, his grandeur, his blandness of *gusto*'. That piece does, however, give a good sense of his larger thinking. In its central discussion Hazlitt distinguishes between the kind of skill displayed by the jugglers and truly significant achievement. The former, he maintains, is not to be despised: anyone who tries to emulate it will soon discover its difficulty. Yet for every hundred people that might achieve some such rare skill, in painting, say, it is unlikely that even one will display the quality of a Reynolds. The difference now involved is that between skill and true power: 'This power is indifferently called genius, imagination, feeling, taste; but the manner in which it acts upon the mind can neither be defined by abstract rules, as is the case in science, nor verified by continual unvarying experiments, as is the case in mechanical performances.'[36] The distinction no doubt derived from his intercourse with Coleridge.

It could be argued, however, that this is not the extreme point of his assertion here, which is reserved rather for approval of the noted fives player John Cavanagh. What Hazlitt clearly finds to admire so highly in this man is his total fitting to his setting: 'He had equal power and skill, quickness and judgment. He could either outwit his antagonist by finesse, or beat him by main strength.' His achievement was not simply, moreover, that he could utilize every gift while knowing just when each was appropriate, but that he could at the same time shut out every other consideration, feeling 'neither the past nor the future "in the instant"'. An achievement like his marked the utmost in authenticity.

In such a dispensation, language was either everything or nothing – a dilemma Hazlitt attempted to solve by relying on the beneficence of mobility. As with Wordsworth, meanwhile, his attacks on Coleridge were accompanied by eloquent sadness not only at the failure of his former hero to live up to the political hopes he had once inspired but at his shortcomings as a human being. Yet if one looks for convincing sources of the accompanying vitriol, one combs the records of his life in vain. Instead, one is struck by the *bravura* quality of the longest account, his essay on Coleridge in *The Spirit of the Age*, which carries on the melancholy note of nostalgia from the previous essay, on Godwin, as he traces the course of his subject's successive enthusiasms, ranging from Greek tragedy to Jean-Jacques Rousseau, with incidental tributes to thinkers such as Hartley and Berkeley, along with more exotic figures such as Plato, Boehme, Spinoza and Giotto. The binding image for Coleridge's

---

[36] 'The Indian Jugglers': *HW* VII, 82, 83.

quest is Satan's heroic journeying through Chaos – though overshadowed by recall of Milton's admonitory comment that in their metaphysicizing discussions, the devils 'found no end, in wandering mazes lost'[37] – a point echoed in Hazlitt's subsequent comment:

Alas! 'Frailty, thy name is Genius!' What is become of all this mighty heap of hope, of thought, of learning and humanity? It has ended in swallowing doses of oblivion and in writing paragraphs in the Courier. Such and so little is the mind of man!

No particular intellectual thread is traced in the long account of Coleridge's intellectual wanderings, and there is certainly no attempt to suggest chronological development. Indeed the chief impression left by Hazlitt is that of a new Satan trying to make his way; though the heroic implications are not altogether lost on a writer for whom Coleridge was, like the Miltonic Satan, 'not less than arch-angel ruined'. In 1818 that note predominated again: Coleridge was 'the only person I ever knew who answered to the idea of a man of genius . . . the only person from whom I ever learnt any thing'.[38] In 1822 Hazlitt appealed again from the serpentine to the angelic: 'But oh thou! who didst lend me speech when I was dumb, to whom I owe it that I have not crept on my belly all the days of my life like the serpent . . . wake thou out of thy mid-day slumbers . . . and shake the pillared rottenness of the world!'[39] Such cries were far from the accents of a wanton malice.

They also suggest a genuine puzzlement as to how Coleridge could have been transformed from the former poet, committed to human vitality, into a moralizing teacher. The process can be seen in action even in his poetic composition. In the period after his return from Germany, he had amused himself with a number of epigrams, or epigrammatic verses, in one of his notebooks. They included the address to the author of *The Ancient Mariner* discussed earlier, and two lines comparing consciousnesses of life and of death:

> He lived like one who never thought to die
> He died, like one who never thinks to live –

Taken on their own, these lines read like a continuation of the meditations on the difference between life and death that had preoccupied him

---

[37] Milton, *Paradise Lost*, ii. 561.   [38] *HW* VII, 18; V, 167.
[39] *Ibid.* XVIII, 251. (See also XVII, 312 and 378.)

and Wordsworth during their time in Somerset, directed now towards the paradoxical fact about the consciousnesses involved, that they were mutually exclusive. Surrounded by living beings, it was impossible to think of them as dead, or even as fated to die; in the experience of death, equally, the fact of life could seem totally inexplicable. In his essay 'New Year's Eve', Lamb had mused on one aspect: the impossibility of imagining the expansiveness of summer in the contractions of winter, or the shrivelling of winter in the height of summer.

Hazlitt had been made aware of this preoccupation during his first Somerset meeting, when Coleridge had criticized Godwin for attempting to establish future human immortality without 'knowing what Death was or what Life was', noting that 'the tone in which he pronounced these two words seemed to convey a complete image of both'.[40]

When Coleridge prepared his lines for publication in the *Morning Post* on 22 September 1801 he expanded them into a four-line stanza, and entitled it 'Epitaph on a Bad Man':

> Of him, that in this gorgeous tomb doth lie,
>   This sad brief tale is all that Truth can give –
> He liv'd, like one who never thought to die,
>   He died, like one who dar'd not hope to live![41]

The subject is now specifically a 'bad man', introducing a moralizing note which may recollect similar lines in a poem by Fulke Greville:

> Whenas man's life, the light of human lust,
>   In socket of his earthly lanthorn burns,
> That all his glory unto ashes must,
>   And generation to corruption turns,
> Then fond desires that only fear their end,
>   Do vainly wish for life, but to amend.
> But when this life is from the body fled,
>   To see itself in that eternal glass,
> Where time doth end, and thoughts accuse the dead,
>   Where all to come is one with all that was;
> Then living men ask how he left his breath,
> That while he livèd never thought of death.

When he heard of Hazlitt's death many years later, the *Morning Post* version came back into his mind, as he wrote in a notebook

---

[40] 'My First Acquaintance with Poets': *HW* XVII, 112n.
[41] *CPW* (CC) I(2), 576. See also *CN* I, 625 f 120v.

Obit Saturday, Septr 18, 1830
W. H. Eheu !
Beneath this stone does William Hazlitt lie,
Thankless for all that God or man could give,
He lived like one who never thought to die,
He died like one who dared not hope to live.[42]

In so transcribing his old published poem, he was automatically con-
signing Hazlitt to the rank of an evil man; yet some residue of the former,
less moralizing, context in which the original epigram had been formulated may have survived. Despite the bitterness still felt at Hazlitt's
apparent hostility, he still found his character puzzling, and seems to have
played with the idea that some impersonal principle of evil might be at
work, over which Hazlitt had been powerless to exercise control – something,
possibly, akin to the 'motiveless malignity' that he diagnosed in the
personality of Iago. From the time when he first described him as 'brow-
hanging, shoe-contemplative, strange',[43] he had been struck by such an
alien element. Remembering how he had reacted on first encountering
him as a young man, he wrote:

what I then found Hazlitt, encourages me to hope, that his almost savage
butting against & goring all, who from an anticipative faith in his mental powers,
were anxious to befriend him, & who perseveringly did befriend him, had it's
ground in some constitutional warp, for which he is not institutionally
responsible.[44]

Shortly afterwards a prose paragraph, a kind of afterthought, conveyed
a similar attempt to convey his puzzlement:

With a sadness at heart, and an earnest hope, grounded on his misanthropic
strangeness when I first knew him, in his 20 or 21st year, that a something existed
in his bodily organism that in the sight of the All-merciful lessened his responsibility – and the moral imputation of his acts & feelings . . .[45]

In the end, nature was being invoked to redress the moral judgment
otherwise felt necessary: and the life–death antithesis was evidently still
active in his mind, as it would be when he composed the epitaph-wish for
himself a short time later,

---

[42] *CN* V, 6467.
[43] Letter of 16 September 1803: *CL* II, 990.
[44] *CN* V, 6429.   [45] *Ibid.*, 6468.

> That he who many a year with toil of Breath
> Found Death in Life, may here find Life in Death.[46]

In the second generation of Romantic writing, the impossibility of finding a proper language for what needed to be said weighed on writers more and more. It is as if the need for action seemed greater: imitators of Byron found it more appropriate to join a war of independence than to write in support. If one relied on language alone, one must be struck by the loss of sublimity, savouring as it did of the artificial; the urge must be in the opposite direction, embracing abhorrence of falsity. Wordsworth's exemplary achievement, in Hazlitt's view, was to have expressed the ordinary, but to make it extraordinary, as with the haunting sound of the cuckoo, the nest of a linnet or even the lichens on the rock: 'He has described all these objects in a way and with an intensity of feeling that no one else had done before him, and has given a new view or aspect of nature.'[47] But by the same token, the language was not in itself enough: as Hazlitt also remarked of Wordsworth's poetry, it could not be sufficiently appreciated unless one had heard the poet himself:

His manner of reading his own poetry is particularly imposing . . . Perhaps the comment of his face and voice is necessary to convey a full idea of his poetry.[48]

But if poetry owed so much to the presence of the poet, was there no other way that intensity of feeling could be conveyed? Keats, evidently believing that it could, declared in a letter of 1817 to George and Georgiana Keats,

The excellence of every Art is its intensity, capable of making all disagreeables evaporate, from their being in close relationship with Beauty and Truth.[49]

'Intensity' was indeed the keyword and key concept, culminating in his supreme poetic tribute:

> Verse, Fame, and Beauty are intense indeed,
> But Death intenser – Death is Life's high meed.[50]

In this way Keats tried to give reality to Hazlitt's dream that nature might find true fulfilment in an individual human being. Hazlitt himself, in turn, seeing immediately the magnitude of Keats's poetic gift, and the grievous short-sightedness of current attacks on him, yet questioned

---

[46] *CPW* (CC) I, (2), 1145.
[47] 'Mr Wordsworth', in *The Spirit of the Age* [1825]: *HW* XI, 86–95.
[48] *Ibid.*
[49] Letter of 21 December 1817: *KL* I, 192.
[50] 'Why did I laugh tonight?' *KP*, pp. 488–9.

whether intensity could be conveyed *simply* through being expressed – leaving future generations of readers to be bemused by the problem.

At another level, nevertheless, Keats was proving himself to be actually more intelligent than his champion. To illustrate this, one need only set side by side two accounts of Coleridge, the first being the range of his interests, ranging from Plato to Rousseau, listed by Hazlitt. Despite its magnificence it contains no coherent thread, suggesting instead the winning ramblings of an incorrigible enthusiast, leaping from one topic to another. Against it can be set Keats's own account of Coleridge's conversation as he heard it one day in a lane near Highgate:

I walked with him at his alderman-after dinner pace for near two miles I suppose. In those two Miles he broached a thousand things – let me see if I can give you a list – Nightingales, Poetry – on Poetical sensation – Metaphysics – Different genera and species of dreams – Nightmare – a Dream accompanied by a sense of touch – single and double touch – A dream related – First and second consciousness – the difference explained between will and Volition – so many metaphysicians from a want of smoking the second consciousness – Monsters – the Kraken – Mermaids – southey believes in them – southeys belief too much diluted – A Ghost story – Good morning – I heard his voice as he came towards me – I heard it as he moved away – I had heard it all the interval – if it may be called so.[51]

If at first sight this list strikes one as very like the one constructed by Hazlitt, closer inspection reveals a major difference. Keats's summary is bound into firmer coherence: everything that Coleridge is running together has in common its theme of doubleness. What Keats evidently picked up from Coleridge's discourse was evidently the sense of different levels of consciousness that underlay distinctions such as that between talent and genius, between the verbal and the sub-verbal. Hazlitt may have registered this, but if so was not equipped, whether by training or inclination, to explore it further. When he returned to the matter of taste, it would always be to rejoice, as in Cavanagh's case, in the quality of human power when physically and precisely organized. At this point the polarities of mechanical and organic, of talent and genius, would be lost, overpowered by the sheer intensity of that which was self-reinforcingly actual.

If it was Hazlitt's peculiar gift to be so peculiarly focused on what could be deepened into a truly humane taste, it also meant that he turned his back on what was most pregnant in Coleridge's speculation. Earlier it was

[51] *KL* II, 88–9.

suggested that an understanding of the *Lyrical Ballads* called for a kind of double reading that would be responsive both to their outward and material quality and to the poetic imagination behind what is being said; this does not presuppose the existence of any magical template for the reading of Romantic literature, but rather the need for readers to recognize the existence of a similar duality in themselves. Those who do so may also be encouraged to develop a flexibility of the reading mind: so far from relying on cut and dried meanings, they will expose their reading of texts to the accessibility of more than one approach. In such a reading verbal stability may be lost, but if so it is exchanged for hermeneutic fecundity, sustained by an essentially humane gusto akin to Hazlitt's.

CHAPTER 9

Jane Austen's progress

At the end of the eighteenth century, the fashion for cultivation of sensibility that had emerged could be thought of as a middle way, mediating between the competing rationalisms of writers such as Burke and Paine. Even at the time, however, the movement was viewed with uneasiness and even suspicion. Johnson, for example, deprecated the cult when it seemed to pass into glorification of feeling:

BOSWELL.   'I have often blamed myself, Sir, for not feeling for others as sensibly as many say they do.'

JOHNSON.   'Sir, don't be duped by them any more. You will find these very feeling people are not very ready to do you good. They pay you by feeling.'[1]

Some years later a striking example of the interplay between reason and sensibility was offered by the relationship between Mary Wollstonecraft and William Godwin. In her early days Wollstonecraft was a strong advocate of rationality. When she wrote her *Thoughts on the Education of Daughters*, the need that they should be taught to use their minds was uppermost. Yet Godwin regarded her as the very embodiment of sensibility, so that in his *Memoir* he invited contrast with his own cast of mind – about which he was explicit:

Mary and myself perhaps each carried farther than to its common extent the characteristic of the sexes to which we belonged. I have been stimulated, as long as I can remember, by the love of intellectual distinction; but, as long as I can remember, I have been discouraged, when casting the sum of my intellectual value, by finding that I did not possess, in the degree of some other persons, an intuitive sense of the pleasures of the imagination. Perhaps I feel them as vividly as most men; but it is often rather by an attentive consideration, than an instantaneous survey. They have been liable to fail of their effect in the first

---

[1] Boswell's *Life of Johnson*, 19 October 1769.

experiment; and my scepticism has often led me anxiously to call in the approved decisions of taste, as a guide to my judgment, or a countenance to my enthusiasm. One of the leading passions of my mind has been an anxious desire not to be deceived. This has led me to view the topics of my reflection on all sides, and to examine and re-examine without end the questions that interest me. Endless disquisition however is not always the parent of certainty.

What I wanted in this respect, Mary possessed in a degree superior to any other person I ever knew. Her feelings had a character of peculiar strength and decision; and the discovery of them, whether in matters of taste or of moral virtue, she found herself unable to control . . . The warmth of her heart defended her from artificial rules of judgment; and it is therefore surprising what a degree of soundness pervaded her sentiments.[2]

Mary Wollstonecraft herself, meanwhile, put the case against sensibility bluntly: 'Misery demands more than tears.' Her statements resembled some by Coleridge, who in a lecture of the 1790s attacked the 'false and bastard sensibility' of the typical polite woman who 'sips a beverage sweetened with human blood, even while she is weeping over the refined sorrows of Werter or of Clementina'.[3] When he returned to the theme years later, he insisted even more urgently on the difference between 'sensibility' and 'Principle':

Sensibility, that is a constitutional quickness of sympathy with pain and pleasure, [is not to be confounded with] the Moral Principle . . . Sensibility is not even a sure pledge of a GOOD HEART . . . How many are there in this over-stimulated age . . . whose sensibility prompts them to remove those evils alone, which by hideous spectacle or clamorous outcry are present to their senses and disturb their selfish enjoyments. Provided the dunghill is not before their parlour window, they are well contented to know that it exists, and perhaps is the hotbed on which their own luxuries are reared. Sensibility is not necessarily Benevolence . . .

All the evil . . . of Materialists will appear inconsiderable, if it be compared with the mischief effected and occasioned by the sentimental Philosophy of STERNE and his numerous Imitators. The vilest appetites and the most remorseless inconstancy towards their objects, acquired the titles of the Heart, the irresistible Feelings, the too-tender Sensibility; and if the Frosts of Prudence, the icy chains of human Law, thawed and vanished at the genial warmth of human Nature, who could help it? It was an amiable Weakness!

. . . I know not how the Annals of Guilt could be better forced into the service of Virtue than by such a Comment on the present paragraph as would be afforded by a selection from the sentimental correspondence produced in Courts

[2] William Godwin, *Memoirs of the Author of 'The Rights of Woman'*, ed. Richard Holmes (London: Harper Perennial, 2005), pp. 96–7.
[3] Revised version in *CWatchman*, 25 March 1796, p. 139.

of Justice . . . fairly translated into the true meaning of the words, and the actual Object and Purpose of the infamous Writers.[4]

Consideration of Jane Austen's resemblance to such contemporaries has to be balanced against awareness of the state of England at the end of the eighteenth century: a country in which four-fifths of the population still lived in a countryside sprinkled with villages, each with its own church and beneficed clergyman. Many of the inhabitants were illiterate, moreover, limiting the possible reading public. In the circumstances it is interesting that much dissenting opinion, whether in religion or politics, was able to flourish, even if news of what was happening across the Channel did not spread swiftly. The urge to know of newly discovered scientific facts and techniques must have been very strong in some areas, particularly the industrialized.

Had Austen been born a man, she would no doubt have been destined, like her brothers, for a professional career. Instead, she was deprived of an academic education, a fact that she seems to have accepted with some equanimity – though her disclaimer of being deeply read ('I think I may boast myself to be . . . the most unlearned and uninformed female who ever dared to be an authoress'[5]) must be taken with a pinch of salt. It may be that, as she said, she 'knew nothing' of science and philosophy in the sense of not having devoted herself to standard works on those subjects, but as an avid reader and as a member of a family with wide-ranging interests, she could not avoid knowing a great deal about the issues involved.

This was true also of politics. Some years ago a book was published, entitled *Jane Austen and the French Revolution*, which caused amusement to some readers by the fact that the author had to admit on an early page that Austen never once referred to the French Revolution directly, whether in her fiction or her letters. (There was in fact a literary competition at the time to suggest further possible non-topics.) Nevertheless, the book achieved a reasonable (or as Austen herself might have said, a tolerable) success; publishers do not usually accept books on non-topics, so that if a book is published with an unpromising title, the author must be arguing for an unexpected resonance. A writer does not have to mention events to be deeply influenced by them: without being referred to directly, they may nevertheless be leaving an indelible mark on the minds of contemporaries.

[4] *CAR*, pp. 60–3.   [5] *AL*, p. 448.

There were also factors within the culture which encouraged reticence – particularly the convention that in polite society women should not discuss politics or religion. Awareness of such constraints helps modify reception of the well-known story concerning the Prince Regent. An admirer of her fiction, he made it known to her in 1816 that he would like her to write a historical romance on a larger scale, whereupon she replied:

You are very kind in your hints as to the sort of composition which might recommend me at present, and I am fully sensible that an historical romance, founded on the House of Saxe Cobourg, might be much more to the purpose of profit or popularity than such pictures of domestic life in country villages as I deal in. But I could no more write a romance than an epic poem. I could not sit seriously down to write a serious romance under any other motive than to save my life; and if it were indispensable for me to keep it up and never relax into laughing at myself or at other people, I am sure I should be hung before I had finished the first chapter. No, I must keep to my own style and go on in my own way; and though I may never succeed again in that, I am convinced that I should totally fail in any other.

> I remain, my dear Sir,
> Your very much obliged, and sincere friend,
> J. AUSTEN[6]

In a letter of the same year, Austen sympathized with her brother Edward for the loss of two chapters of his own work but pointed out that she could not be suspected of having purloined it herself, since 'How could I possibly join them on to the little bit (two Inches wide) of Ivory on which I work with so fine a Brush, as produces little effect after much labour?'[7] The request from the Prince Regent is thought to provide a good example of his obtuseness, and to support the view of her subject matter as having been social comedy, restricted to the activities of a group of small families and their limited concerns; but there is no need to accept all the possible implications that go with such an assumption. As the member of a large family in which wider issues were commonly discussed, she evidently shared and participated in them, offering, in fact, a prime example of the phenomenon examined above, whereby English writers who knew what was happening across the Channel might not succeed in commenting directly but nevertheless produce work demonstrably affected by their awareness.

---

[6] *AL*, pp. 452–3.   [7] Letter of 16 December 1816: *AL*, pp. 468–9.

The fact remains, nevertheless, that her main equipment for responding to the events in France consisted in the literary tradition that had been available to her as she grew up: the novels she had read, and the writers regarded as central. On occasion her father read to the family the work of William Cowper, whom she saw as one of the major poles of her literary universe, along with Dr Johnson ('my dear Dr Johnson', as she once called him[8]) at the other. She recorded in 1798 that they had Boswell's 'Tour to the Hebrides' and were to have his 'Life of Johnson' and planned to lay out further money on the purchase of Cowper's works.[9] In the case of Johnson, it was probably Boswell's record of him that she recalled best; when, having written in 1813 'I am glad William's going is voluntary, & on no worse grounds', she continued:

An inclination for the Country is a venial fault. He has more of Cowper than of Johnson in him, fonder of Tame Hares & Blank verse than of the full tide of human Existence at Charing Cross.[10]

Although Austen no doubt felt that a marriage of Johnsonian sense with Cowperesque sensibility would constitute her human ideal, it is doubtful whether Johnson's work as a lexicographer appealed to her. Precise spelling was not something that greatly bothered her, always cavalier with the order of her i's and e's.

This lack of patience with literary detail went along with a sense that other matters were more important: recent scholarship has demonstrated the breadth of her wider concerns. Her reading of fiction had made her aware not only of the current fashion for Gothic tales, to be satirized in *Northanger Abbey*, but of the strain that had developed from the female conduct books of the time. In this sphere, it is true, her enterprise was limited to pricking the bubble of inflated self-importance and to questioning those gestures towards wider knowledge that simply displayed the ignorance of the speaker – often at the expense of more accurate local knowledge. Even at this level, however, an important mental questioning can be glimpsed, probing the relationship between appearance and reality. Among her first novels, *Pride and Prejudice* was first planned with the title 'First Impressions', while the comedy in *Northanger Abbey* is based on the difference between the world as it might be viewed by a mind steeped in interpretations based on reading romantic novels and one that attends to

---

[8] *AL*, p. 181 (and later note), citing Johnson's letter to Boswell of 4 July 1774.
[9] *Ibid.*, pp. 32–3.
[10] *Ibid.*, p. 368. The Johnsonian reference is of course to Boswell's record of 2 April 1775.

direct presentations of the world. But it should not be supposed that she felt it her mission simply to restore her readers from illusion to everyday reality: she not only delighted in what fiction had to offer, but even accepted the desirability of fairy-tale endings.

The chronology of the novels has gradually been established through careful work on the surviving documents; it is also possible to trace characteristics of her developing attitudes at particular periods. Looking for signs of such development throughout her career enables one also to validate her consistency. When she first worked on her novels in the 1790s, the comic spirit was evidently uppermost, but she could not totally ignore the political events around her. As mentioned earlier, many of Austen's contemporaries evinced at first a somewhat complacent response, which she perhaps to some extent shared. Like Wordsworth, for instance, Richard Payne Knight viewed the outbreak of revolution in natural terms, a necessary outburst of passion that would soon be satisfied. In his poem of 1794, 'The Landscape', he wrote how the breaking of a dam could result in its stagnant waters settling into alluvial wasters that might turn back into rich and fertile soil:

> So when rebellion breaks the despot's chain,
> First wasteful ruin marks the rabble's reign . . .
> Then temperate order from confusion springs.[11]

Within a few years, however, when the despotism of the actions of those in control in France was becoming clearer, additions for his second edition expressed pity for the imprisoned Marie Antoinette and sympathy with participants in the La Vendée rising.

It was not only questions of possible political reform that preoccupied her contemporaries. At the time, as Knight's poem shows, questions of landscape were also controversial. Recent scholarship has shown the further extent of her interests – which does not mean that she took all her opinions from elsewhere. Some years ago, Marilyn Butler, in an important assault on the view of Austen as a cosy parochial novelist, drew attention to the growth of anti-Jacobin writing, enlisting her as a chief spokeswoman.

That view has been challenged by various writers, among whom Peter Knox-Shaw has argued that she should not be seen primarily as an anti-Jacobin or, still less, as a dyed-in-the-wool Tory, but associated

---

[11] R. P. Knight, *The Landscape: A Didactic Poem. In Three Books. Addressed to Uvedale Price, Esq.* (London: G. Nicol, 1794).

rather with the sceptical element in the Enlightenment, as cultivated by Anglo-Scottish philosophers.[12]

Yet Austen was not simply a sceptic. She was too good an Anglican not to appreciate the force of moral language, particularly in so far as it was the language of fidelity. Yet fidelity was not to be unreservedly supported either, since in itself it was all too ready a resource for hypocrisies and falsities of every kind. Her own position might best be described rather as a 'critical fidelity'.

Mr Collins is an excellent touchstone, since although the reader has every reason to suspect that the professions of allegiance sustaining his calling as a clergyman are hypocritical, the sincerity of his commitment to his calling is never undermined in the novel by any statement regarding his beliefs. His priorities are more revealing. He believes the first call on a busy clergyman's time must be for the administration of his tithes, with the preparation of his sermons – two of which he hopes may be published – taking second place.[13]

Knox-Shaw's persuasive figuring of the shape of Austen's career suggests a gradual intensification of the complex tension created by the contemporary exploration of the relation between 'sensibility' and moral concern, reaching a climax in the struggle presupposed in the title of *Sense and Sensibility*. As he notes, the twin terms existed in an acutely complex relationship, so that while the general reader might make the obvious connection that identifies Elinor with sense and Marianne with sensibility, even a contemporary reviewer could suggest that it was Elinor who was sensibility's true protagonist.

This searching account of Austen's relation to her novels not only resists the temptation to read her in polarizing terms but makes it possible to conceive the kind of consciousness that underlay her writing self. It also suggests something of her relationship to Coleridge, whose background was not dissimilar. Both were gifted writers and thinkers from clerical homes where the members of the family were encouraged to take up professional posts of some kind. Just as Coleridge's brothers divided themselves between the Church, the Army and the Law, so Jane Austen's brothers were clergymen or naval officers, two of them becoming admirals.

The matter of contemporary concerns raises itself again. Despite her gift for social comedy and her disclaimers of being deeply read, it is not

---

[12] Peter Knox-Shaw, *Jane Austen and the Enlightenment* (Cambridge University Press, 2004). See also below, p. 168.

[13] *Pride and Prejudice*, chapter xviii: *AN* II, 101.

necessary to assume that she was so fully preoccupied by questions concerning fiction as to be blind to all else. She was, after all, constantly reminded of events in the world around by her more active relations – notably the brothers serving as naval officers during a period of extreme danger. She was also bound to be aware of the intellectual issues agitating her contemporaries, ranging from the ferment of politics following the Revolution to the hard-fought debates in religious circles.

Each of these areas of concern left its own mark on her fiction; meanwhile, she was happy that if present, their role should be unemphasized. Thus, when she wrote *Mansfield Park*, she took care to make the local colour accurate and adopt a timescale for her plot fitting known events exactly – yet so unobtrusively that unless they happened to investigate it for themselves, later readers might miss the extent of her accuracy.

Austen's underlying concerns revealed their presence more as time went by, however. *Pride and Prejudice*, which according to her sister Cassandra was first planned in October 1796,[14] worked mainly as social comedy, as did *Sense and Sensibility* shortly afterwards. The underlying themes in *Northanger Abbey*, drafted first of all but published much later, were stronger, given the naïve behaviour of its heroine and the underlying questions of landscape, but it was not until *Mansfield Park* that the intellectual issues became more overt.

About the turn of the century, however, a more mordant note in her writing, particularly in her letters, was accompanied by a shift of tone. Warren Roberts, who has gathered some of the relevant evidence, points to possible personal factors. In 1800 she reached her twenty-fifth birthday, a benchmark traditionally indicating the conclusion of the period when young women might best hope to marry. She must have been increasingly aware that eligible suitors were now thin on the ground. Public affairs were meanwhile darkened by current events. The violent effects of the Revolution had taken their toll; the growing influence of Anti-Jacobinism now prevailed over hopes for renovation in society. Reading Austen's letters makes one increasingly aware of the obverse to her acute social observation, a camera-like truth to fact and a merciless accuracy devoid of concessions to kindly forbearance. This quality, an essential accompaniment to Christian efforts at truth-telling, would eventually be a goad also to conscience, as notably lacking in love. Austen's moments of harsh observation provoke uneasy awareness of a spring that has failed – venial

---

[14] See the introduction by R. W. Chapman to his edition of *Sense and Sensibility* (*AN*, I), p. xiii: cited by Marilyn Butler, *Jane Austen and the War of Ideas* (Oxford: Clarendon Press, 1975), p. 86n.

enough in a twenty-year-old who was having to face her own disgust at the behaviour of her own contemporaries, but now suggesting a troubling lack of human warmth.

In those years, however, the emerging clear-eyed matter-of-factness was complemented by a devotion to the issue of 'principle'. The search for lasting principles to be set in place of the ones dominating the French Revolution had preoccupied Coleridge in his year at Malta and just after, and had been notably prominent in the gestation and production of *The Friend*. Coleridge's daughter Sara later recalled vividly the current mood:

How gravely & earnestly used STC and WW, & my Uncle Southey also, to discuss the affairs of the nation, as if all came home to their business & bosoms – as if it were their private concern. Men do not canvass these matters now-a-days, I think, quite in the same tone. Domestic concerns absorb their deeper feelings – national ones are treated more as things aloof, the speculative rather than the practical.[15]

The new mood of seriousness corresponded to anxiety about recent political developments. In the autumn of 1808, Wordsworth and Coleridge were concerned by the sense of betrayal felt throughout the country at the concluding of the Convention of Cintra. Wordsworth wrote out his misgivings at length in the long pamphlet produced on the occasion, and his deploring of the lack of principle displayed by English statesmen, taken up by Coleridge, furnished a dominant theme for *The Friend*. A favourite saying, shared by them in both texts, was that 'formerly men were worse than their principles, but that at present the principles were worse than the men'.[16] In his pamphlet Wordsworth quoted it as the observation of 'an enlightened friend' and made 'in conversation';[17] it may well have been set off originally by a remark made by Charles William Pasley in August 1805 to Coleridge and recorded by him in his notebook: 'Pasley remarked last night . . . that men themselves in the present Age were not so much degraded, as their sentiments / This is most true – almost all men nowadays act and feel more nobly than they think.'[18] Pasley was probably introduced by Coleridge to Wordsworth, who went on to correspond with him. Whether Jane Austen could have come across *The Friend* in

---

[15] Appendix, 'The Autobiography of Sara Coleridge': Bradford Keyes Mudge, *Sara Coleridge: A Victorian Daughter: Her Life and Essays* (New Haven: Yale University Press 1989), pp. 261–2.
[16] *CFriend* (1809) II, 28. The point had probably originated from a remark by Cicero, who, in the course of his reply to Torquatus, had spoken of people who were worse than their principles.
[17] *WPrW* I, 317. [18] *CN* II, 2627.

its 1809 version is doubtful, though by no means impossible;[19] but as it happens she echoed their admiration for Pasley, reading his *Essay on the Military Policy and Institutions of the British Empire* of 1810 and writing to Cassandra that it was a book she had protested against at first, 'but which upon trial I find delightfully written & highly entertaining'. Indeed, she went so far as to confess herself 'in love with the author . . . the first soldier I ever sighed for – but he does write with extraordinary force & spirit'.[20]

Austen was sufficiently responsive to the spirit of the time to allow her predilection for the navy to give way here, at least temporarily, to concerns for the military. And in so far as this was part of the larger political and philosophical demand of the moment, she herself became more serious, sharing the desire of men such as Coleridge, Wordsworth and Southey for a stronger grasp of principle. Among other things, this may account in the subsequent period for her greater focus on religion. We might take one well-known example, her response when Fanny Knight consulted her about her situation, having originally encouraged her suitor John Plumptre, but now realizing that she was not in love with him. On the one hand Austen felt that if there was not enough affection, and particularly if his 'deficiencies of Manner &c &c' outweighed his positive qualities, she should not allow the relationship to continue, yet she was unwilling to press that point if it was simply a matter of Fanny's being apprehensive that it was his moral qualities that were superior:

And as to there being any objection from his Goodness, from the danger of his becoming even Evangelical. I cannot admit that. I am by no means convinced that we ought not all to be Evangelicals, & am at least persuaded that they who are so from Reason and Feeling, must be happiest & safest.[21]

Read in conjunction with her attitude in writing *Mansfield Park*, it is tempting to take the middle sentence straightforwardly, and claim that she was adopting – at least provisionally – a religious commitment. Many accounts of the novel have indeed worked from such an assumption. But it does not really square with other references by her to evangelicalism that suggest a more critical attitude – as, indeed, do certain elements

---

[19] Conceivable channels of communication are obviously rare, yet can be unexpected: Southey's brother Lieutenant Herbert Southey, who was then serving at Plymouth, was a subscriber to *The Friend*; his ship the 'Dreadnought' was commanded by Admiral Sotheby, brother of William Sotheby, Coleridge's friend. See *CFriend* (1809) II, 459.

[20] Letter of 24 January 1813, *AL*, p. 292 (see also pp. 294, 304). Knox-Shaw (*Enlightenment*, p. 156) associates her approval of Southey's attack on contemporary France in his *Poet's Pilgrimage to Waterloo* (*AL*, p. 476 and n.) with her praise of Pasley's views.

[21] Letter of 18 November 1814, *AL*, p. 410.

in the book itself. One need only read her reaction when Cassandra recommended Hannah More's novel, *Coelebs in Search of a Wife*:

My disinclination for it before was affected, but now it is real; I do not like the Evangelicals. – Of course I shall be delighted when I read it, like other people, but till I do I dislike it.[22]

It is equally easy, moreover, to read the statement itself as involving a deliberate drawing back, a suggestion that her attraction towards such a commitment is immediately checked by an inability to accept all its probable implications. This is the drift of Knox-Shaw's account of her attitude in writing the novel, in which he insists that while there may be some sympathy towards the religious views of Fanny Price and Edmund Bertram, the main concern is always with matters of conduct – in which Austen was likely to submit the characters of her 'religious' people to a critical examination as searching as those directed towards other personages. To quote his own summarizing account, he believes that 'the whole thrust of the novel's commentary is profoundly secular, that its concern with religion centres in conduct, and that human happiness is integral to its morality'.[23] Certainly the very liveliness of her intellect means that she is not always easily to be pinned down to endorsing a particular point of view. Some statements, however, can be thought of as central. Assuming that she was serious in her religious asseverations, her prayers must be given that kind of status; and in that context phrases from the prayer composed at the end of her life earn the respect that Marilyn Butler affords them:

Incline us oh God! to think humbly of ourselves, to be severe only in the examination of our own conduct, to consider our fellow-creatures with kindness, and to judge of all they say and do with that charity which we would desire from them ourselves.[24]

The wording of this prayer corresponds to sentiments to be traced in some of the Gothic novels to which she bore such an ambiguous relation.

The increasing intensity of the Napoleonic Wars had a further effect, again betraying links with Coleridge's views. His writings came to include a strong nationalistic element, contrasting with the relaxed attitude towards France and things French commoner in his earlier writings. Warren Roberts draws attention to a similar 'francophobic' element in

[22] Letter of 24 January 1809, *ibid.*, p. 256.
[23] Knox-Shaw, *Enlightenment*, p. 173.
[24] Jane Austen, *Minor Works*, ed. R. W. Chapman (Oxford: Clarendon Press, 1954), AN VI, 456.

Austen's writings, and particularly her portrayal in *Mansfield Park* of Mary Crawford, in whom he detects a constant resort to the kind of persiflage that Hannah More strongly reprehended in the French, claiming that their 'cold compound of irony, irreligion, selfishness and sneer' blasted the opening buds of piety.[25] (Twenty years later she was still of the same mind, contrasting 'French polish, urbanity, wit, and irreverence' with the 'more sober and plain virtues of the English'.[26]) On such a view Mary Crawford's levity and frequent failures of reverence betray 'French' failings.

Austen's 'francophobia', however, in so far as it existed, was a cultural, rather than a literary, phenomenon. Whereas Coleridge, for instance, after a certain point in his development, consistently abhorred everything French, including not only the ideas but even the literature of the country, she constantly and effortlessly introduced French phrases into her writing: her letters contain almost twenty examples. This is not surprising when one considers that Cassandra, to whom most were addressed, spoke French readily, knowledge of that language being a recognized 'accomplishment'. Austen is so commonly regarded as thoroughly English, however, that the possible indebtedness of her novel 'Lady Susan' to Laclos' *Les Liaisons Dangereuses* was hardly noticed until pointed out by Warren Roberts.[27]

Roberts also drew attention to the fact that however powerful her opposition to the French during the early years of the nineteenth century, her knowledge of their life and culture must have been strongly influenced by the Frenchwoman Eliza de Feuillade. Eliza was married to the Comte de Feuillade, a Royalist who after various intrigues was guillotined in 1794; she subsequently married Jane's brother Henry in 1797, eventually dying in 1813. With such histories in the background, it was impossible for Jane not to be acquainted with the Revolution and its violence; indeed, it was probably through Eliza that she came to know some French writers. Roberts is probably right also to follow Hannah More's line and infer a connection between Eliza's levity and the behaviour of Mary Crawford in *Mansfield Park*. As a young girl Jane had seen Eliza flirting with Henry while she was still married to the count, during the private theatricals at

---

[25] *Strictures on the Modern System of French Education* (1799), p. 318; quoted in Warren Roberts, *Jane Austen and the French Revolution* (London: Macmillan 1979), p. 34.

[26] Roberts, *Revolution*, citing her *Moral Sketches of Prevailing Opinions and Manners, Foreign and Domestic: With Reflections on Prayer* [1819], in her *Works*, 2 vols. in 1, (New York: Harper & Brothers, 1839), p. 435.

[27] Roberts, *Revolution*, pp. 128–9.

Steventon, and was also aware that she had been opposed to Henry's taking orders (a course delayed until after her death). Her influence on Jane's blend of buoyancy and uprightness should not be underestimated.

Austen would thus seem to have been particularly true to the period in which she was writing. Underlying the strong religious revival, and urging it on, was a sense of crisis, following the French Revolution, and an accompanying fear that the whole of civilization was under threat. The underlying anxiety haunts her tale *Catharine*, where the heroine's guardian Mrs Percival offers her a copy of *Coelebs in Search of a Wife*, meanwhile voicing her complaint that 'everything is going to sixes & sevens and all order will soon be at an end throughout the Kingdom'.[28] Such anxieties rendered Mansfield Park a haven of peace and order and made Fanny Price's instinctive appeal to principle heroic.

At the same time, a reader in the twenty-first century is more likely to be struck by Austen's apparently unquestioning acceptance of the material elements in the Anglican establishment: in her novels livings are distributed by patrons in country areas without raising the question of inequitability, or of the differing spiritual qualities of those in receipt of them. Jane Austen evidently takes them for granted, a part of the everyday economic life that in her time could not be foreseen as likely ever to be change. But this did not mean that criticism was entirely ruled out. As Knox-Shaw puts it, she

not only reacted against rationalism and related idealisms, but sought to find a logic in the real world, in the hope of changing it for the better.[29]

Knox-Shaw also discusses further awarenesses that she shows, and which are often missed by critics who do not pay sufficient attention to points of detail, since the main thrust of the novels is undoubtedly weaving of plot, together with incidental social comments. The reader naturally reads first for the working out of the plot and the weaver's ingenuity; from attention to her evident enjoyment in developing the details of the little world she has created, it is all too easy to restrict her knowledge to that of the minutiae of everyday life in a Georgian community. Knox-Shaw is an excellent guide to the range of her wider knowledge indicated earlier. It has often been observed, for instance, that Sir Thomas Bertram owes his wealth to his West Indian plantations (for which his absence during the

---

[28] *Catharine and Other Writings*, ed. Margaret Anne Doody and Douglas Murray, World's Classics edition (Oxford University Press, 1993).
[29] Knox-Shaw, *Enlightenment*, p. 242.

crucial early sequence is responsible) and that the decline of those estates was the reason for Fanny Price's need to go and live with her aunt Norris; but Knox-Shaw also shows how the whole question of slavery is a constant presence in the novel, actually set at the time of emancipation. The latter was intimately linked to questions of human rights and independence dear to religious campaigners such as the Quakers; it also had an immediately contemporary political relevance, one of the strong arguments in the abolitionists' case being Napoleon's unwillingness to do anything about slavery in the areas he was taking under his sway – citable as an example of the tyranny against which his foes, including the English, were fighting.

Yet in spite of the laudable resistance to Napoleon generally aroused, there was a sense in which most writers must have felt a covert pleasure in the way that, under his distasteful tyranny, they might still sense (as Hazlitt, evidently, did) the ghost of the spirit that had burned brightly in the first years of the Revolution. This quality is still to be traced even in a late novel such as *Persuasion*, where Wentworth's character displays a quality persistently ambiguous in Austen's evaluation. In *Sense and Sensibility* it had been a mark against Colonel Brandon in Marianne's eyes that his understanding had 'no brilliancy', his feelings 'no ardour' and his voice 'no expression'.[30] Willoughby, by contrast, gained her favour as 'a young man of good abilities, quick imagination, lively spirits and open affectionate manners. He was exactly formed to engage Marianne's heart, for with all this, he joined not only a captivating person, but a natural ardour of mind which was now roused and increased by the example of her own.'[31]

Willoughby lacks principle: his lively personality can easily be subverted and displays its evanescent quality when the whim takes him. It is a point to be made even more emphatically concerning Henry Crawford in *Mansfield Park*. Yet it would be wrong to assume that this is her last word on the subject; for when we reach *Persuasion* it is to discover that just this quality of ardour, which Anne Elliot distrusted, Lady Russell even more, also lay at the core of his success. When he first knew Anne, he 'was confident that he should soon be rich: full of life and ardour, he knew that he should soon have a ship, and soon be on a station that would lead to everything he wanted. He had always been lucky; he knew he should be so still.'[32]

---

[30] *Sense and Sensibility*, chapter x: *AN* I, 51.   [31] *Ibid.*, 48.
[32] *Persuasion*, chapter iv: *AN* V, 27.

Distrusting his estimate of his own future, she was later forced to change her mind on realizing that his qualities had, in the event, 'bestowed earlier prosperity than could be reasonably calculated on':

All his sanguine expectations, all his confidence had been justified. His genius and ardour had seemed to foresee and to command his prosperous path. He had, very soon after their engagement ceased, got employ: and all that he had told her would follow, had taken place.[33]

In view of this it is not surprising that Anne Elliot 'at seven and twenty thought very differently from what she had been made to think at nineteen':

She was persuaded that under every disadvantage of disapprobation at home, and every anxiety attending his profession, all their probable fears, delays, and disappointments, she should yet have been a happier woman in maintaining the engagement, than she had been in the sacrifice of it.[34]

The use of the title word is particularly telling here. Originally it had been Lady Russell who did the persuading: 'She was persuaded to believe the engagement a wrong thing – indiscreet, improper, hardly capable of success, and not deserving it.' Through the somewhat archaic sense of the word to indicate a sense of conviction, however, the alert reader is made aware that any persuading in the matter must now be the work of Anne herself. If the action is to be considered as endorsed by the author, the implication is that while a young woman may be right to accept the persuadings of an older person when relatively inexperienced, she must eventually be prepared to do her own self-persuading.

This in turn suggests that along with her call for adherence to fixed principles Austen was increasingly inclined to accept the desirability of development. The writing of *Persuasion* might have provoked some second thoughts on the subject of ardour, for example, as she made Wentworth's triumphant against Anne's misgivings.

The new economic world, based on credit, that was opening up as a result of the Napoleonic Wars was certainly one of development, not to say 'Speculation'. As Knox-Shaw's use of it for his chapter title suggests, the word provides a key for making sense of the novel-fragment known as *Sanditon* (not a title given it by Austen herself), which concerns the venture of transforming a seaside village into a fashionable watering-place.

---

[33] *Ibid.*, 29.   [34] *Ibid.*

Although at first sight there may seem to be no direct reference to the recent war there, a clear and obvious one emerges in the garrulous patter of Mr P as they approach Sanditon and his new house:

You will not think I have made a bad exchange when we reach Trafalgar House which by the bye, I almost wish I had not named Trafalgar for Waterloo is more the thing now. However, Waterloo is in reserve; and if we have encouragement enough this year for a little crescent to be ventured on (as I trust we shall) then we shall be able to call it Waterloo Crescent and the name joined to the form of the building, which always takes, will give us the command of lodgers. In a good season we should have more applications than we could attend to.[35]

Whatever her distaste, Austen could not altogether despise the energy inherent in such enterprises. Did she then view the quality of ardour more kindly now than when Willoughby exhibited it so questionably in her earlier novel? If so, she hid her change of view when Edward Denham in *Sanditon* laid on his voice of justification extravagantly in attempted exculpation of Robert Burns:

'His Genius & his Susceptibilities might lead him into some Aberrations – But who is perfect? – It were Hyper-criticism, it were Pseudo-philosophy to expect from the soul of high toned Genius, the grovellings of a common mind. – The Coruscations of Talent, elicited by impassioned feeling in the breast of Man, are perhaps incompatible with some of the prosaic Decencies of Life; – nor can you, loveliest Miss Heywood' – (speaking with an air of deep sentiment) – 'nor can any Woman be a fair Judge of what a Man may be propelled to say, write, or do, by the sovereign impulses of illimitable Ardour.' This was very fine; – but if Charlotte understood it at all, not very moral . . .[36]

Charlotte's misgivings are justified, since, as the reader is about to be made aware, Denham's taste in novels, all of a piece with his praises in poetry, licenses indulgence in unrestrained energy:

Such are the Works which I peruse with delight, & I hope I may say, with Amelioration. They hold forth the most splendid Portraitures of high Conceptions, Unbounded Views, illimitable Ardour, indomptible Decision – and even when the Event is mainly anti-prosperous to the high-toned Machinations of the prime Character, the potent, pervading Hero of the Story, it leaves us full of Generous Emotions for him; – our Hearts are paralized –.[37]

---

[35] Austen, *Minor Works*, *AN* VI, 380. Jane Austen may have known that Ramsgate had Nelson and Wellington Crescents, as well as 'the Plains of Waterloo'. Coleridge, who regularly took holidays in Ramsgate, usually stayed in Wellington Crescent.
[36] *Ibid.*, pp. 397–8.   [37] *Ibid.*, pp. 403–4.

The word 'illimitable', thus repeated, suggests what is faulty with such an effusion – a point brought out further on the next page when the narrator makes clear that Sir Edward's intention to seduce Clare is already determined upon. His happy endorsement of the condition when 'our hearts are paralized' sufficiently indicates his moral state.

Since the novel breaks off shortly afterwards, it is idle to suppose how it might have continued, though Sir Edward's aim of seducing Clara and her own firm determination not to be seduced would no doubt have been resolved, probably to his discomfiture, with the moral code of Austen's world left neatly intact. Before settling for such a squared- off neatness, however, it is worth discussing some signs picked up in recent criticism that her art itself was still in process of development. Knox-Shaw notices, for instance, the favour accorded to the virtue of visiting the sea, which in the first draft is seen dancing 'under a Sun-shiny Breeze',[38] and the qualities of which as a source of renewal are never really questioned. Certainly Charlotte, who appears always as a sane and healthy young woman, and whose impatience at the valetudinarianism in elements of the Parker family can readily be sensed (she 'could perceive no symptoms of illness which she, in the boldness of her own good health, w^d not have undertaken to cure by putting out the fire, opening the Window and disposing of the Drops & the salts by means of one or the other'[39]), is nevertheless forced to hear Arthur Parker's apologies for the presence of a fire:

'We sh^d not have had one at home,' said he, 'but the Sea air is always damp. I am not afraid of anything so much as Damp.' 'I am so fortunate,' said Charlotte, 'as never to know whether the air is damp or dry. It has always some property that is wholesome & invigorating to me –'[40]

Her response to a first sight of the resort is equally indicative of her spirits as she surveys 'the miscellaneous foreground of unfinished Buildings, waving Linen, & tops of Houses, to the Sea, dancing & sparkling in Sunshine & Freshness. –'[41]

It is hard to imagine that the author of such a sentence remained purely the detached ironist, that she was not actively enjoying the liveliness of the projected scene. If so, Austen might be viewed as having passed beyond celebration of the status quo. In the post-war world of England, it might be suggested, she perceived some virtue in the restless energy of the speculators that was producing the craze for travel, and the urge to set up lodgings as resting-places for those who had thus been set in motion.

---

[38] Knox-Shaw, *Enlightenment*, p. 50, citing R. W. Chapman's work.
[39] Austen, *Minor Works*, p. 413.
[40] *Ibid.*, p. 415.   [41] *Ibid.*, p. 384.

To rely on a moving energy of some kind was, after all, only natural to an artist. It furnished the dilemma for any reader who was tempted to prefer the energy of a Lovelace to the stillness of a Clarissa, As Blake argued in a famous apophthegm, the problem was age-old:

Note. The reason Milton wrote in fetters when he wrote of Angels & God, and at liberty when of Devils & Hell, is because he was a true Poet and of the Devil's party without knowing it.[42]

Was something of the same sort true of Jane Austen? An approach to an answer can be looked for in her private writing, where, addressing her niece Fanny Knight, she found herself wondering at the strange complexities of her personality:

I cannot express to you what I have felt in reading your history of yourself, how full of Pity & Concern & Admiration & Amusement I have been. You are the Paragon of all that is Silly & Sensible, common-place & eccentric, Sad & Lively, Provoking & Interesting. – Who can keep pace with the fluctuations of your Fancy, the Capprizios of your Taste, the Contradictions of your Feelings? – You are so odd! – & all the time, so perfectly natural – so peculiar in yourself, & yet so like everybody else! It is very, very gratifying to me to know you so intimately.[43]

In her next letter we may assume that Fanny had questioned this analysis in some way, since Austen returned to the matter:

how could it possibly be any new idea to you that you have a great deal of Imagination? You are all over Imagination. – The most astonishing part of your Character is, that with so much Imagination, so much flight of Mind, such unbounded Fancies, you should have such excellent Judgement in what you do! – Religious Principle I fancy must explain it . . .[44]

Imagination and Religious Principle; these were the poles between which Austen's admiration seemed to swing; though perhaps Warren Roberts is right to point to Austen's account of Mrs Smith in *Persuasion* as providing an even more subtle encapsulation of the qualities she valued most:

In the course of a second visit she talked with great openness, and Anne's astonishment increased. She could scarcely imagine a more cheerless situation in itself than Mrs Smith's. She had been very fond of her husband: she had buried him. She had been used to affluence: it was gone. She had no child to connect her with life and happiness again, no relations to assist in the arrangement of perplexed affairs, no health to make all the rest supportable. Her accommodations were limited to a noisy parlour, and a dark bedroom behind, with no

---

[42] William Blake, *The Marriage of Heaven and Hell*, Plate 6.
[43] Letter of 20 February 1817, *AL*, p. 478.   [44] Letter of 13 March 1817, *AL*, pp. 485–6.

possibility of moving from one to the other without assistance, which there was only one servant in the house to afford, and she never quitted the house but to be conveyed into the warm bath. Yet, in spite of all this, Anne had reason to believe that she had moments only of languor and depression to hours of occupation and enjoyment. How could it be? She watched, observed, reflected, and finally determined that this was not a case of fortitude or of resignation only. A submissive spirit might be patient, a strong understanding would supply resolution, but here was something more; here was that elasticity of mind, that disposition to be comforted, that power of turning readily from evil to good, and of finding employment which carried her out of herself, which was from nature alone. It was the choicest gift of Heaven; and Anne viewed her friend as one of those instances in which, by a merciful appointment, it seems designed to counterbalance almost every other want.[45]

On the movement between the opening of the last sentence, and the close of the one before, swings the precarious balance between the two moral positions that claimed Austen's allegiance. How far can something that springs from 'nature alone' be regarded as 'the choicest gift of Heaven'? Only, if ever, it might be argued, in a most extraordinary providential dispensation.

Yet in combining the two, Austen brings together the twin impulses of creativity that give shape to her words: 'elasticity of mind', and the power of 'finding employment which carried her out of herself'. The 'crisis of the word' was for her, even more than for other writers of her time, the crisis involved in any language that is doubly charged. Inasmuch as human words must necessarily be at one and the same time the expression of nature alone and yet acknowledge the demands of fidelity, they must remain the seat of an unending conflict. As a moralizing figure Austen remained always of the Anglican persuasion, taking her linguistic cues from Dr Johnson, but as the creator of fictions she could never afford to lose her capacity for being fascinated, and even delighted, by the intricate ways, good and bad, through which human beings are forever persuading one another. She must remain a sympathetic protagonist of disciplined ardour, also, for when such activities succeeded in reconciling the natural and the moral, her own creative gifts would become most evident.

[45] *Persuasion*, chapter XVII: *AN* V, 153–4.

Languages of memory and passion: Tennyson, Gaskell and the Brontës

Some years ago, when I was invited to contribute to the *Cambridge Guide to the Arts in Britain* by providing the literary section of the volume relating to the years 1785 to 1851, I was made to realize once again how compartmentalized our treatment of literature has tended to be. We think of the Romantic period as falling between 1785 and 1830, and then of subsequent developments as 'Victorian'. Yet, as Kathleen Tillotson pointed out many years ago, it can be a mistake to fence off the late 1830s and the 1840s in this way. If those years are regarded as prudish, for instance, it has to be remembered that Bowdler's edition of Shakespeare had been made some years earlier and was not very representative of current assumptions, while the strong interest in fashionable subjects such as aristocratic manners, reflected in many novels of the period, was only slowly challenged and subordinated to the more middle-class ethos of the central 'Victorian' period.

It was also becoming evident to the inhabitants of the years in question that they had passed a crucial turning-point, and that the phenomenon that had made it so was above all the meteoric rise of the railways – the period of 'railway mania' falling particularly in the years 1846–8, when the opening of about 2,500 miles of new track virtually doubled the amount available until then. As Thackeray was to put it in his *Roundabout Papers* of 1860–3:

Then was the old world. Stage-coaches, more or less swift, riding-horses, pack-horses, highwaymen, knights in armor, Norman invaders, Roman legions, Druids, Ancient Britons painted blue, and so forth – all these belong to the old period. I will concede a halt in the midst of it, and allow that gunpowder and printing tended to modernize the world. But your railroad starts the new era, and we of a certain age belong to the new time and the old one.

. . . We elderly people have lived in that prae-railroad world, which has passed into limbo and vanished from under us. I tell you it was firm under our feet once, and not long ago. They have raised those railroad embankments up, and shut off the old world that was behind them. Climb up that bank on which the irons are laid, and look to the other side – it is gone. There is no other side.[1]

In spite of such a sense of irreparable loss, however, there was also a growing interest in memory, coupled with a belief that the early Romantic poets had opened up new poetic territory by concentrating on the significance of the human heart. Coleridge's distinctive contribution to this awareness came from his extraordinary ability to link such experiences to an awakening of the imagination, while Wordsworth's was associated with his belief that human beings learned most from those experiences when suffering opened out their spirit to a sense of infinity that at times of action might be blocked or inhibited.

Their contemporaries and successors developed particular elements of this 'heart-lore'. Lamb's self-awareness led him to argue (in his essay of that title) that one must allow for 'imperfect sympathies'. Yet even as he was acknowledging prejudices frankly, what he was evidently demanding from those he failed to sympathize with was some sign on their part of an equivalent sympathy and play of mind. The strictures sometimes levelled against him are more properly to be directed against those who take over his attitudes and mannerisms as the model for a comfortable conservatism. Doing that misses what is hidden behind Lamb's reserve – a reserve half broken in his 'Confessions of a Drunkard', where he speaks of his own weakness in a more moralizing and self-condemnatory tone than customarily, yet masks all indication of the self-sacrifices that his devotion to his sister had led him to make, with the resulting losses and benefits. In his intertwining of love and reticence, an uprightness beneath whimsicality that is also crossed by sharpness of perception, one may trace a direct link back to Cowper, along with an advance – a distinctive combination of affection and imagination recognized by Coleridge:

he has an affectionate heart, a mind sui generis, his taste acts so as to appear like the unmechanic simplicity of an Instinct . . . Lamb every now & then *eradiates*, & the beam, tho' single & fine as a hair, yet is rich with colours, & I both see & feel it.[2]

Another early admirer of Coleridge and Wordsworth, Thomas de Quincey, read *Lyrical Ballads* while still at school and, on running away, even thought of going to the Lake District. The Coleridge he actually met in 1807, however, was a man whose eloquence now seemed more that of a

---

[1] Thackeray, 'De Juventute', in *Roundabout Papers* (London: Smith, Elder, 1882), pp. 56–7.
[2] Letter to Godwin, 21 May 1800: *CL* I, 588.

somnambulist. Nevertheless, he took up residence near Grasmere for a few years and was one of the first to be permitted to read *The Prelude*.

Before meeting Coleridge, he had already become addicted to opium, and the acquaintance did nothing to lessen his interest in its effects. While Coleridge allowed himself to mention the drug only rarely in his published works and tried repeatedly to rid himself of the habit, de Quincey's fascination often triumphed over self-loathing. When in 1822 he published anonymous reminiscences under the title *Confessions of an English Opium-Eater*, the identity of the author was soon an open secret. The *Confessions* were followed by further autobiographical accounts of his earlier life, including reminiscences of Wordsworth and Coleridge which made it clear that his attitude to both had become, like Hazlitt's, deeply ambiguous. He could not escape the sense of a debt to their poetry (traceable in many verbal reminiscences), but he also felt in some sense betrayed. Wordsworth, despite his affirmation that 'we have all of us one human heart', had not been willing to acknowledge the Grasmere girl whom de Quincey courted and married; nor could he be sure whether Coleridge's intellectual legacy, which had included an idiosyncratic reading of Kant, had been a blessing or a disaster. His greatest achievement lay in the production of prose dream-visions which were memorable for faithfully rendering the circularity, repetition and unexpected emphases characteristic of dream experience.

For his deepest mode, however, de Quincey looked to Wordsworth's belief that human beings learned most from experiences of suffering. By the time he came to know him personally, Wordsworth had passed into the penumbra of his long reaction to the death of his brother John. The kind of insight produced by his human sorrow corresponded to states of mind which de Quincey recognized from his own experiences under laudanum, and which he personified in 'The Dark Interpreter': 'The machinery for dreaming planted in the human brain was not planted for nothing. That faculty, in alliance with the mystery of darkness, is the one great tube through which man communicates with the shadowy.'[3] The Interpreter was the dark symbolic mirror for reflection to the daylight of what else must be hidden forever;[4] what he showed de Quincey could be of extraordinary beauty, as in his vision of Savannah-la-Mar, the city that had been removed to the bottom of the ocean. Feeling for such scenes

[3] From *Suspiria de Profundis*, in de Quincey, *Confessions of an English Opium-Eater and other Writings*, World's Classics edition, ed. Grevil Lindop (Oxford University Press, 1985), p. 88.
[4] *Ibid.*, p. 156.

of timeless immobility was matched by delight in energy. De Quincey's was a different delight from the 'railway mania' of his contemporaries, one of his most impassioned essays, 'The English Mail-Coach', being an elegy[5] over the animal spirits powering the form of transport that had dominated earlier years.

De Quincey's writing could move naturally between energy and stasis, between consciousness and the unconscious; a modern – even more a post-modern – mind finds much material for exploration in his labyrinthine processes. In his own time, however, a final question lurked for him, that of a providence whose motives and purposes were riddling (a riddling actualised during de Quincey's own infancy in the behaviour of a mother whose love for her children could never be demonstrated by any gesture more physical than the sprinkling of lavender-water and milk of roses over them at their stern morning parades). During de Quincey's lifetime this question pressed hard, as writers turned from affirmation of God's law to stress, rather, his love.

Methodism, the founding experience of which had been John Wesley's moment of 'heart-warming' during a Moravian gathering, had contributed strongly to this new emphasis on heart rather than head, on the New Testament as opposed to the Old. But for some this affirmation made the workings of divine providence only more mysterious. Blake put the point vigorously:

I cannot help saying 'the Son, how unlike the Father!' First God Almighty comes with a thump on the Head. Then Jesus Christ comes with a balm to heal it.[6]

One of the attractions of de Quincey's writing, then as now, was the sense it gave of a man questioning providence – and finding an answer, if anywhere, only in the strange fidelities of the human heart.

Another effect was to foster a literature of memory. There began to emerge that looking back into the past in search of security that was to mark a good deal of later literature, music and art, with the result that even a major event such as the Great Exhibition of 1851, though dominating the press and conversation, was little reflected in the literature of the day, the currently popular works being more concerned with the past than with enthusiasm for British invention. It was accidental, perhaps, that Wordsworth's death the previous year released for publication *The Prelude*, his great autobiographical work. It was less fortuitous, on the other hand,

---

[5] [1849]: de Quincey, *Confessions*, pp. 184–233.   [6] *BK*, p. 617.

that Dickens should in that previous year have produced *David Copperfield*, where autobiographical structure combined with fictional exploration to induce a basic affection for the past. In 1850, also, Tennyson finally published poems concerning his grief over the loss, seventeen years earlier, of his friend Arthur Hallam.

At its most direct level a series of poems about grief and time, *In Memoriam* is a complex work. For Tennyson, pierced by the new sense of the past that the geologists were producing, the adage that time heals all wounds was less comforting than disturbing: 'O sorrow, then can sorrow wane? / O grief, can grief be changed to less?'[7] The pain felt at Hallam's death had been an earnest of the intellectual and emotional debts owed to him while alive. In the poem as a whole, however, he discovers that in time his grief is not destroyed but can rise up again just as sharply many years later.

That is perhaps the deepest note in the poem as a whole; it is certainly the most plangent. Yet it is equally important to Tennyson to learn that life can continue in its constant rhythmic movements of ebb and flow, systole and diastole; and this is reflected in the distinctive metre and form of the poem, where the last line of each stanza rhymes with the first, rounding it – while a rhythmic impulsion from the central couplet moves each stanza forward to the next. But there are also moments of stasis, producing unforgettable vignettes, as when the poet stands in the street where Hallam lived and finds in the knowledge of his loss a ready link with the impersonality and lack of significance in modern city life:

> He is not here; but far away
>   The noise of life begins again,
>   And ghastly thro' the drizzling rain
> On the bald street breaks the blank day.[8]

In happier periods, daybreak was the time of hope and promise that it had been for Coleridge and Shelley. But Tennyson, who knew that dawn itself might be to dying eyes the moment when 'the casement slowly grows a glimmering square', inducing a sense of the 'sad and strange', felt more at home with the twilight glimmerings of evening and morning, more appropriate settings for his alternations between elegy and tentative affirmation.

---

[7] Tennyson, *In Memoriam*, Section 78.   [8] *Ibid.*, Section 7.

A visit to Cambridge brought back memories of the time when he had attended meetings of the Apostles, the small group of idealistic young men who had met weekly to discuss ideas ranging from metaphysics to the play of market forces. Their ebullience came vividly to mind as he saw the door of the room

> Where once we held debate, a band
> Of youthful friends, on mind and art,
> And labour, and the changing mart,
> And all the framework of the land . . .[9]

It was again a moment of loss: another name was on the door.

In this poem the concern with public affairs that was to remain with Tennyson takes second place to the personality of Hallam, who had seemed not only to introduce a new note but even to be a new kind of man. At all times his memories take a darker tone from the intervention of that death, which has changed their colourings, yet the very activity of coming to terms with it is therapeutic.

One of the most memorable sections of the poem describes the Tennyson family's removal from the landscape that Hallam shared on his visits there: a countryside that they had always known and which had become saturated for them with the affection they bestowed on it. 'Unwatched', 'unloved', 'uncared for', these are the words that come to Tennyson's mind as he imagines the landscape without them:

> As year by year the labourer tills
> His wonted glebe, or lops the glades;
> And year by year our memory fades
> From all the circle of the hills.[10]

This idea of a landscape that had been in one sense sustained by loving perception witnesses also to the new consciousness fostered by geological investigations, rendering its thoughtful inhabitants more attentive to the local and particular landscape, even as they became increasingly aware of its temporary and passing nature.

In Memoriam is a central poem in the liberal tradition which, in the act of pursuing freedom, demanded that individuals prove their independence by coming to terms with a world granting no appeal to an external

---

[9] *Ibid.*, Section 87.   [10] *Ibid.*, Section 101.

moral authority. Tennyson tried to make the yearning and aspiration experienced in human love a test and earnest of relationship with the universe at large. In face of Hallam's senseless death, the main hope he could offer lay in the fact that there was no reason why such a man should exist only once. Perhaps he was 'a noble type / Appearing ere the times were ripe'.[11] A key word here is 'noble'; at the very moment when Tennyson is postulating a 'crowning race' that shall fulfil Hallam's promise, he looks back to older feudal and chivalric ideals in order to suggest what that race might be like. The past is invoked to make his redeeming concept of love an effective agent of progress.

Although *In Memoriam* was composed over many years, its publication in 1850 chimed with a strong elegiac mood. The year of European revolutions, 1848, had had its less violent British counterpart, the Chartist movement. Increasing awareness of what was happening across the Channel, on the other hand, made writers conscious of the fragility of the concordat between religion and science that had preserved a unity in English culture. The Alpine peaks of France and Switzerland, a severer challenge to human beings than the hills of Wordsworth's Lakeland, emblematized the point. In the autumn of 1849, Matthew Arnold wrote his 'Stanzas in Memory of the Author of "Obermann"', commemorating the life of Senancour – of all writers, in his opinion, 'the most perfectly isolated and the least attitudinizing'. Senancour's achievement focused Arnold's current problem – whether to follow him into isolation, or, if not, how to heed the demands of the world:

> Ah! two desires toss about
> The poet's feverish blood.
> One drives him to the world without,
> And one to solitude.[12]

Of the two great models that came naturally to his mind, Wordsworth, with his elected solitariness and eyes apparently averted from human fate, could not help, while Goethe's advantages of a peaceful youth were denied to those, like himself, 'reared in hours / Of change, alarm, surprise'.[13]

---

[11] Epilogue, lines 138–9, *ibid.*
[12] 'Stanzas in Memory of the Author of "Obermann"', lines 93–6, in *The Poems of Matthew Arnold*, ed. Kenneth Allott; 2nd edn, ed. Miriam Allott (London: Longman, 1979), p. 140.
[13] *Ibid.*, lines 69–70.

In the following year, Wordsworth's death prompted a continuation of this vein in his 'Memorial Verses', where another name was added to those who had inspired his generation: Goethe's diagnostic power and Wordsworth's supreme healing ability were now complemented by Byron's energy; among these endowments, however, it was Wordsworth's that seemed the least replaceable.[14] Arnold's sense of his own potentialities as a poet involved the development of a similar healing power, which must in turn be harmonizing. Aware of all that was happening in the European mind, including the growth of biblical criticism, he knew that the old order could not easily be sustained. He would now turn his thoughts increasingly to contemporary culture, seeking to educate and to animate those to whom it now belonged.

In this and other respects, 1850 is a surprisingly sensitive date, marking a shift to themes that were to dominate the second part of the century. In the 1840s Ruskin was confining himself mainly to writings such as the first two volumes of *Modern Painters*: the voice of Ruskin the social reformer belonged to the future. The dominant voice of that decade in fact was that of Thomas Carlyle, who, arriving in London in the 1820s, was already aware of the German literature now available. He might find fault with Goethe for his immorality but found in his writings, particularly *Wilhelm Meister* (which he himself translated), a power, a forthrightness and a vision of humanity missing from contemporary London. Coleridge, whose writings he had read with respect, seemed on a brief acquaintance vitiated by a damaging desire to have the best of all worlds, his philosophy to be summed up scornfully as 'the sublime secret of believing by "the reason" what "the understanding" had been obliged to fling out as incredible'.[15] John Stuart Mill's view of Coleridge, by contrast, was more embracing and far-seeing. Comparing his mind with that of Jeremy Bentham as the two most seminal intelligences of the age, he distinguished between their respective strengths:

By Bentham, beyond all others, men have been led to ask themselves, in regard to any ancient or received opinion, Is it true? and by Coleridge, What is the meaning of it?[16]

Carlyle, however, believed that the age demanded a more positive message. The devotion of the age to mechanism – in his view rightly denounced

---

[14] *Poems of Matthew Arnold*, pp. 239–43.
[15] Thomas Carlyle, *The Life of John Sterling* [1851] (London: Chapman and Hall, 1897), chapter 8.
[16] *Mill on Bentham and Coleridge*, with an introduction by F. R. Leavis (London: Chatto & Windus 1950), p. 99.

by Coleridge – needed to be attacked directly and vigorously – a purpose to which he brought his concept of 'The Eternal Powers', working out their way whether or not human beings chose to heed them. The turning-point for himself had come in a moment of conversion mirrored in the experience of his character Teufelsdrockh in *Sartor Resartus*.[17] From the sense of the world as a world of death, a 'huge, dead, immeasurable Steam-engine, rolling on, in its dead indifference', a world which had pervaded, as an 'Everlasting No', the whole of his being, Teufelsdrockh had found himself coming to recognize the alternative view which would prompt an 'Everlasting Yea'. Even while adeptly and ironically presenting his vision through the persona of an extravagant German thinker far from the commonsense scepticism of his English contemporaries, Carlyle was revolving the irony further: the vision of this strange figure was made to offer a true remedy for the age's problems.

Like others he turned to the past for the presentation and development of his vision, but it was a recent past, to be brought up to date still further by skilful appeal to the present. *The French Revolution* (1837) presented that portentous event in the grand style, his treatment offering a dramatic contrast to the cool, urbane, distancing approach of Gibbon. Against history appraised and considered rationally, this was a version in which the Eternal powers glimmered and glared immanently through a narrative working always in the present tense.

Carlyle's rhetoric – his 'lo!' and 'ah!', his 'dost thou' and 'art thou' – may look dated to modern eyes, but to many contemporaries it revived the tones of biblical prophecy. Abandoning the language of sensibility for the grander dialect of a time before the dominance of rationalism, he sought a diction adequate to modern needs. Even today he can still exert his original power, as when he tries to restore sublimity to a great industrial city:

Sooty Manchester, – it too is built on the infinite Abysses; overspanned by the skyey Firmaments; and there is birth in it, and death in it; – and it is every whit as wonderful, as fearful, unimaginable, as the oldest Salem or Prophetic City. Go or stand, in what time, in what place we will, are there not Immensities, Eternities over us, around us, in us . . .?[18]

Return to the past could not be simple, however; the changes in the world opened up by the development of science and technology meant

---

[17] Thomas Carlyle, *Sartor Resartus* (London: Chapman and Hall, 1831).
[18] Thomas Carlyle, *Past and Present* [1843], Centenary Edition (London: Chapman and Hall, 1899), III, chapter xiv, p. 228.

that impatience at the cult of sensibility must be met by a new kind of discourse, avoiding concessions to mechanism but more energetic than the pale velleities it replaced.

The recent world retained its attractiveness, however. Elizabeth Gaskell, for instance, her intelligence redolently aware of the challenge offered by this new world, was also absorbing contemporary literature. In 1836, already a wife and mother, she wrote of 'studying and writing about Coleridge, Wordsworth, Byron, Crabbe, Dryden and Pope'[19] and in May, of her pleasure in reading two of those poets at Sandlebridge, amidst an appropriate landscape:

I have brought Coleridge with me, & am *doing* him & Wordsworth – *fit place for the latter!* I sat in a shady corner of a field gay with bright spring flowers – daisies, primroses, wild anemones, & the 'lesser celandine' & with lambs all around me . . .[20]

The confusions of mind to which Wordsworth's nature lore offered a balm called also for shrewd perceptiveness: it is no accident that lines of Coleridge's are quoted as epigraph to a chapter of *Mary Barton*:

> Deeds to be hid which were not hid,
> Which, all confused, I could not know,
> Whether I suffered or I did,
> For all seemed guilt, remorse, or woe . . .[21]

Elsewhere in the same novel she takes it for granted that the reader will pick up a Coleridgean allusion: when Esther's attempt to talk to Jem Wilson is brushed off by him, she tries a more forceful approach:

'You must listen,' she said authoritatively, 'for Mary Barton's sake'.
    The spell of her name was as potent as that of the mariner's glittering eye. 'He listened like a three year child.'[22]

When Esther decides to go to Mary's house, there is a similar echo:

She had felt as if some holy spell would prevent her (even as the unholy Lady Geraldine was prevented in the abode of Christabel) from crossing the threshold of that home of her early innocence.[23]

---

[19] See Mary Kuhlman's article 'Education through Experience in *North and South*', in the *Gaskell Society Journal* 10 (1996), suggesting also the significance of works borrowed from the Portico Library by William Gaskell.
[20] *GL*, p. 7.
[21] 'The Pains of Sleep', lines 27–30: *CPW* (EHC) I, 390.
[22] *Mary Barton, and Other Tales*, chapter XIV: *GK* I, 184.
[23] *Ibid.*, chapter XXI: *GK* I, 275.

Gaskell had evidently read Coleridge's poetry and thought profitably about it, as is evidenced by the way in which some of his locutions are taken into her writing. *Ruth*, for instance, only a few years after *Mary Barton*, contains several examples: when Tristan sets out to appeal to his sister, she says that the situation called for a seraph – 'But there was no seraph at hand, only the soft running waters singing a quiet tune.' The only comparable use of a stream behaving like that is in Coleridge's *Ancient Mariner* (where the crew are to be seen eventually as a seraph-band):

> A noise like of a hidden brook
> In the leafy month of June,
> That to the sleeping woods all night
> Singeth a quiet tune.

Again, when Ruth senses her child's safety, 'this loosened the frozen springs, and they gushed forth in her heart . . .' – recalling directly the Mariner's

> A spring of love gushed from my heart
> And I blessed them unaware.

An even more evident presence, however, is that of Wordsworth, to whom she paid tribute at the close of a letter of 1836, having mentioned that her husband had been giving lectures on 'The Poets and Poetry of Humble Life' in the poorest part of Manchester:

As for the Poetry of Humble Life, that, even in a town, is met with on every hand. We have such a district, and we constantly meet with examples of the beautiful truth in that passage of 'The Cumberland Beggar':

> Man is dear to man: the poorest poor
> Long for some moments in a weary life
> When they can know and feel that they have been,
> Themselves, the fathers and the dealers out
> Of some small blessings; have been kind to such
> As needed kindness, for this simple cause,
> That we have all of us a human heart.

In short, the beauty and poetry of many of the common things and daily events of life in its humblest aspect does not seem to me sufficiently appreciated.[24]

Interestingly, she was not quoting meticulously from Wordsworth, writing 'simple' for his 'single' and 'a human heart' for his 'one human

---

[24] *GL*, p. 33.

heart'. That last line had entered her mind in its original wording, however, to become one of her favourite sayings[25]– according with Wordsworth's own belief that it lay at the heart of his message. In a letter to Crabb Robinson many years later, he argued that while 'dramatic writers' were naturally bound to emphasize the differences between characters, it was his own 'noble distinction' to focus on what human beings had in common:

> If my writings are to last, it will I myself believe, be mainly owing to this characteristic. They will please for the single cause, 'That we have all of us one human heart.'[26]

Gaskell's delight in Wordsworth's poetry extended well beyond her self-identification with his sense of the universal human heart, however: she was equally drawn to his fascination with individual human experiences as such. Her empathy with Ruth's passionate affection for her little son prompts her to quote in parenthesis[27] two lines from one of the 'Lucy' poems:

> O mercy! to myself I said,
> If Lucy should be dead!

The evocation of this momentary fear on Ruth's part as she hurries home to her child may also reflect something that A. W. Ward sensed – that Mrs Gaskell's extraordinary feeling for the bonding between Ruth and her child might be associated with the deep sense of loss experienced at the loss of her own child. In this context it is worth considering that a single line quoted elsewhere in the novel, again referring to Ruth's child,

> A child whom all that looked on, loved

is also a near-quotation from Wordsworth, taken from the verse which he inscribed on the grave of his own child, Thomas:

> A Child whom every eye that looked on loved . . .[28]

Her habit of allusion became increasingly subtle. When she wrote *North and South* two years later, there was little such literary reference, though

---

[25] Anna Unsworth points out other quotations of the phrase: *Elizabeth Gaskell: An Independent Woman* (London: Minerva Press, 1996), p. 52 and n.

[26] Letter of c. 27 April 1835: *WL* (1821–53) VI, 44.

[27] *Ruth, and Other Tales*, chapter xix: *GK* III, 208.

[28] 'Six months to six years added . . .' *WPW* IV, 254. Her use of the same misquotation in a letter to Harriet Anderson (*GL2*, p. 157), suggests the personal feeling attached to loss of her own child.

each chapter has its short poetic epigraph, taken from contemporary poets such as Landor, Hood and Elizabeth Barrett Browning. But towards the end, when Thornton is finally showing signs of change, it is signalled by the introduction of her favourite Wordsworthian phrase:

Once brought face to face, man to man, with an individual of the masses around him, and . . . out of the character of master and workman, in the first instance, they had each begun to recognise that 'we have all of us one human heart'.[29]

Although the source has not been lost on one or two scholars and editors,[30] one critic has branded the quotation 'a too easy invocation'. A reviewer challenged this, pointing out that, on the contrary, it is 'unstressed, unremarked on by the narrator, not perhaps noticed by many of her readers'.[31]

Allusions to Wordsworth persisted throughout her career, though from some novels they seem absent. A notable example is *Sylvia's Lovers*, set on the other side of England, where, despite a few Cumbrian connections, there are no straightforward Wordsworthian allusions. Yet in another sense it is a very Wordsworthian novel throughout, the crucial situation at its heart corresponding to a dilemma recognizably central to early Romanticism. For if the status of the human heart dogs every moral question, it must be recognized to be not exactly 'natural'. Sylvia Robson is presented throughout as basically a child of nature. She is never so happy as when out of doors and has no interest in book-learning, so that the linking of head and heart prescribed by Wordsworth and Coleridge for their culture has no appeal for her. When she encounters the harpooner, her response is immediate and passionate. The fact that he too is a creature of impulse means that despite his unexpected fidelity, he feels free to follow his impulse towards another woman, once he knows that Sylvia has agreed (however misguidedly) to marry Philip. The ultimate divide between him and the steady hero of the novel, Philip, is the divide between one who follows impulse and an adherent to principle, as the author recognizes in a brief comment on the relationship between Sylvia and Hester, whose fidelity to Philip took the form of not even mentioning her love to him:

What could ever bring these two together again? Could Hester herself – ignorant of the strange mystery of Sylvia's heart, as those who are guided solely by

---

[29] *North and South*, chapter 1: *GK* IV, 500.
[30] See, e.g., Stephen Gill, *Wordsworth and the Victorians* (Oxford: Clarendon Press, 1998), p. 121.
[31] *TLS*, 8 November 2006.

obedience to principle must ever be of the clue to the actions of those who are led by the passionate ebb and flow of impulse?[32]

In speaking thus of the 'mystery of Sylvia's heart', Elizabeth is aligning her, consciously or otherwise, with the figure of Wordsworth's 'Ruth', another 'child of nature' who gave herself to an attractive youth. Although he wooed her treacherously, his response to nature displayed something like nobility:

> Nor less to feed voluptuous thought
> The beauteous forms of nature wrought,
> Fair trees and lovely flowers;
> The breezes their own languor lent;
> The stars had feelings, which they sent
> Into those gorgeous bowers.
> Yet, in his worst pursuits, I ween,
> That sometimes there did intervene
> Pure hopes of high intent:
> For passions linked to forms so fair
> And stately, needs must have their share
> Of noble sentiment.

Ruth's desertion by the youth – a creature of impulse, therefore unstable and ruthless – leaves her without resource. Sylvia's own abandonment has no such tragic results, but the effect of her deception by Philip is to leave her totally unable to soften towards him: Hester finds it impossible to make any impression on her 'obdurate, unforgiving heart'.[33] This, as Wordsworth had stressed, is the ultimate dilemma facing any Rousseauist cult: the natural is also necessarily amoral. If there is a solution, it must lie in cultivating an outgoing nature and unconditional forgiveness – the unrelenting message drummed home in Blake's later Prophetic Books, and for him the essence of Christianity. How to attain that state remains the ultimate puzzle for Gaskell; the resolution of *Sylvia's Lovers* suggests that in such a case she believed the needed mutual forgiveness to be possible – but only, perhaps, in the moment of death.

If Gaskell appreciated the attractiveness of the Wordsworthian cultivation of the human heart more fully than most of her contemporaries, then, she remained troubled by the contradictions involved in the opposition between the nobility of the heart's affections and the amorality of being the servant of impulse. The subtlety of her musings on this matter, and of similar thoughts on the subject by the poet himself, is suggested by

---

[32] *Sylvia's Lovers*, chapter xliv: *GK* VI, 516.   [33] *Ibid.*

a strange little puzzle in Wordsworth's poetry and its correspondence with a passage in *Sylvia's Lovers*. Some of the most memorable lines in the Immortality Ode describe the interruption of his joy on a May morning:

> Now, while the birds thus sing a joyous song,
> And while the young lambs bound
> As to the tabor's sound,
> To me alone there came a thought of grief:
> A timely utterance gave that thought relief,
> And I again am strong . . .[34]

Despite the straightforward impact of these lines, editors and scholars alike have puzzled over one small point: what was that 'timely utterance'? Was it the writing of another poem, 'Resolution and Independence', say, which he might have thought expressed his intermitted grief adequately? Or was it something more open – a cry of anguish or a bursting into tears? The other part of that sentence, '. . . gave that thought relief', is also ambiguous: does he mean that the uttering relieved his spirit or that it actually sharpened it – throwing it as it were 'into relief'? If the first proposed meaning appeals more, Victorian 'heart-lore' is perhaps responsible. An age when there was such stress on the significance of the heart and its workings produced also extreme interest in anything that had to do with a 'hardening' of the heart, and in anything that might be seen as a means of softening, a 'change of heart'. In chapter xxxv of *Sylvia's Lovers*, entitled 'Things Unutterable', this issue is crucial in medical, physical terms. The doctor arrives to find Sylvia's mother dying:

> He did not ask many questions, and Phoebe replied more frequently to his inquiries than did Sylvia, who looked into his face with a blank, tearless, speechless despair, that gave him more pain than the sight of her dying mother.
> . . . the white, pinched face, the great dilated eye, the slow comprehension of the younger woman, struck him with alarm; and he went on asking for various particulars, more with a view of rousing Sylvia, even if it were to tears, than for any other purpose that the information thus obtained could answer.

The doctor is heartened to see her feeling for her baby, but Hester still has to report his anxiety over her condition:

> '. . . She were just stunned by finding her mother was dying in her very arms when she thought as she were only sleeping; yet she's never been able to cry a drop; so that t' sorrow's gone inwards on her brain, and from all I can hear, she

---

[34] *WP* IV, 279.

doesn't rightly understand as her husband is missing. T' doctor says if she could but cry, she'd come to a juster comprehension of things.'

Nevertheless Sylvia insists on going to the funeral, where she sees the servant Kester weeping at the graveside:

> His evident distress, the unexpected sight, suddenly loosed the fountain of Sylvia's tears, and her sobs grew so terrible that Hester feared she would not be able to remain until the end of the funeral . . .[35]

This is another example of utterance giving relief: an idea which seems to have entered medical lore as simply as it entered the 'heart-lore' of Wordsworth and Coleridge.

Allusions to Wordsworth persisted throughout her career, the supreme example coming in her last novel, *Wives and Daughters*. Here the growth of Molly Gibson's love for Roger is never for a moment acknowledged in the text; instead, she is shown as always accepting his infatuation with Cynthia as blinding him to any qualities of her own and resigning him to a future with her. Only when it seems that Roger is projecting an occasion for declaring his love to Cynthia while apparently planning to leave England without saying farewell to herself, does the strength of her reaction seem to give away her subconscious yearning for something from him more than brotherly:

> Molly did not hear these last words. She had escaped upstairs, and had shut her door. Instinctively she had carried her leaf full of blackberries – what would blackberries be to Cynthia now? She felt as if she could not understand it all; but as for that matter, what could she understand? Nothing. For a few minutes her brain seemed in too great a whirl to comprehend anything but that she was being carried on in earth's diurnal course, with rocks, and stones, and trees, with as little volition on her part as if she were dead.[36]

The final phrases here echo, of course, Wordsworth's well-known 'Lucy' poem:

> No motion has she now, no force;
>   She neither hears nor sees,
> Mov'd round in Earth's diurnal course
>   With rocks, & stones, and trees![37]

---

[35] *Sylvia's Lovers*, chapter xxxv: *GK* VI, 416–23.
[36] *Wives and Daughters*, chapter xxxiv: *GK* VIII, 432.
[37] *CL* I, 480 (cf. *WPW* II, 216).

The quotation is highly significant. The fact that Molly should feel so wholly deprived of her life-consciousness at this moment suggests that her feeling for Roger is not just the sisterly affection that she can openly acknowledge to herself, but something more profound, even more existential.

If one believed in the significance of the human heart, particularly as embodied in the feminine, certain difficulties arose. Despite his firm belief, Wordsworth was forced to recognize that village life did not show it very convincingly. Yet he could still maintain a faith that someone brought up in total solitude might produce a perfect philosophy of the heart. In his poem 'Lucy Gray, or Solitude' he made a specific point of this. When Lucy is urged by her father to take a lantern with her, she replies:

> 'That, Father! will I gladly do:
> 'Tis scarcely afternoon –
> The minster-clock has just struck two,
> And yonder is the moon!'[38]

According to a conversation recorded by Crabb Robinson in 1816, Wordsworth had intended in the poem 'to exhibit poetically entire solitude, and represented the child as observing the day-moon, which no town or village girl would ever notice'.[39] The implication was that an upbringing in such solitude might give such a girl unusual sensitiveness to the spirit of nature. (In my own work I have supposed that Wordsworth himself in his youth had known a girl who had had a similar sensitivity and who had later figured as the heroine of his 'Lucy' poems, so providing some of the assurance on which his nature philosophy was constructed.[40]) Gaskell was evidently fascinated by the idea of the benefits for a young girl of being brought up in such solitude, and indeed built on it a whole work of fiction, her novella *Cousin Phillis*, where she quoted Wordsworth himself directly. Shortly after having described her gathering wood-flowers and how she 'had the art of warbling, and replying to the notes of different birds, and knew their habits and ways, more accurately than any one else I ever knew', the narrator says:

My cousin Phillis was like a rose that had come to full bloom on the sunny side of a lonely house, sheltered from storms. I have read in some book of poetry –

---

[38] *WPW* I, 235.   [39] *Ibid.* 360.
[40] See chapter 2, 'Wordsworth's "Lucy", Fiction or Fact?' of my *Providence and Love* (Oxford: Clarendon Press, 1998).

'A maid whom there were none to praise,
And very few to love,'

And somehow these lines always reminded me of Phillis; yet they were not true of
her either. I never heard her praised; and out of her own household there were
very few to love her; but, though no one spoke out their approbation, she always
did right in her parents' eyes, out of her natural simple goodness and wisdom.[41]

There are indications everywhere of Gaskell's shrewd reflectiveness,
countering any tendency for her mastery of dialogue to beguile readers
into locating her achievement invariably at the level of immediate presentation. Along with her love of story-telling went an interest in the
language of ordinary speech, especially Lancashire speech, which she
shared with her husband. Recognition of the point needs, however, to
be balanced against broader effects such as that which (as Heather Glen
has pointed out) prompted Henry James to notice 'the gentle skill with
which the reader is slowly involved in the tissue of the story'. Kathleen
Tillotson also quotes James (writing this time on *Wives and Daughters*) in
support of her own view that even in her earliest fictions an 'almost
pedestrian truthfulness is already accompanied by something spacious:
her common flowers of human nature are rooted in earth, but over
them arches "the divine blue of the summer sky"'. Heather Glen has
commented also on the elements of gradual effect, of almost imperceptible growth, which make for her essential unobtrusiveness, producing
what she terms Gaskell's 'calm cumulative suggestiveness'.[42]

Such things point us further back, to the cleft that can be traced in the
consciousness out of which Gaskell's own art was made and which
affected the complexity of her language. It is evident from her biography
that from an early stage she inhabited conflicting worlds. From childhood
she, even more than most of her generation, had been forced into
awareness of change. Her early schooling in Barford had given her a
pastoral sense of the quiet enduring nature into which England had been
settling for centuries, and into which it was all too easy to locate oneself,
given the right circumstances. To take a simple instance cited by Glen, it
needed no more than a narrator reading aloud to two women darning
stockings in a farmhouse kitchen:

The tranquil monotony of that hour made me feel as if I had lived for ever, and
should live for ever droning out paragraphs in that warm sunny room, with my two

---

[41] *Cousin Phillis and Other Tales*: *GK* VII, 78.
[42] *TLS*, 8 November 2006.

quiet hearers, and the curled-up pussy cat sleeping on the hearth-rug, and the clock on the house-stairs perpetually clicking out the passage of the moments.[43]

This nostalgia for timelessness is recurrent in the novels: a backcloth, as it were, behind the varying events and dialogues. Another example can be found in Elizabeth Hale's experience of the southern countryside as she passes through it in the train, having lived for a time in the bustling north:

Broods of pigeons hovered around these peaked quaint gables, slowly settling here and there, and ruffling their soft, shiny feathers, as if exposing every fibre to the delicious warmth. There were few people about at the stations, it almost seemed as if they were too lazily content to wish to travel; none of the bustle and stir that Margaret had noticed in her two journeys on the London and North-Western line. Later on in the year, this line of railway should be stirring and alive with rich pleasure-seekers; but as to the constant going to and fro of busy trades-people it would always be widely different from the northern lines. Here a spectator or two stood lounging at nearly every station, with his hands in his pockets, so absorbed in the simple act of watching, that it made the travellers wonder what he could find to do when the train whirled away, and only the blank of a railway, some sheds, and a distant field or two were left for him to gaze upon. The hot air danced over the golden stillness of the land, farm after farm was left behind, each reminding Margaret of German Idyls – of Herman and Dorothea – of Evangeline.[44]

The pervasiveness of this sense as one presence in the country had also encouraged the growth of a corresponding sensibility in Tennyson's poetry, where, only a few years after its first publication, it provides an epigraph for one of her chapters, and so furnishes a tone for a whole episode:

> Unwatch'd, the garden bough shall sway,
>   The tender blossom flutter down,
>   Unloved, that beech will gather brown,
> This maple burn itself away;
>
> Unloved, the sun-flower, shining fair,
>   Ray round with flames her disk of seed,
>   And many a rose-carnation feed
> With summer spice the humming air;

Without quoting the remainder of this negative threnody, however, she cuts to the hope of imminent renewal:

> Till from the garden and the wild
>   A fresh association blow,

---

[43] *Cousin Phillis*: GK VII, 26.   [44] *North and South*, chapter vi: GK IV, 58.

> And year by year the landscape grow
> Familiar to the stranger's child;

After this she can reinvoke the sense that the decline of memory is nevertheless inexorable: 'And year by year our memory fades . . .'[45] Elizabeth Gaskell's relationship with the English language was unusually complex, even tortuous. On the one hand she was profoundly aware of the place occupied by the Authorized Version of the Bible, an authority shared by all the religious denominations of her time – including the Unitarians to whom she gave her allegiance. In that last respect a quite unusually careful heeding of the text was called for, a stress on the humane elements in the gospel discourses, with particular attention to the imaginative possibilities inherent in biblical language.

At the same time she was always aware of the disparities inherent in any writer's use of language in terms of their potential audience and her sense of the problems thus created. As she wrote to Charles Eliot Norton in 1858,

I can not (it is not will not) write at all if I ever think of my readers, and what impression I am making on them. 'If they don't like me they must lump me', to use a Lancashire proverb. It is from no despising my readers. I am sure I don't do that, but if I ever let the thought or consciousness of them come between me and my subject I could not write at all.[46]

Her Unitarian background, which had also encouraged her to marry a minister of the sect, would never be rooted out from her consciousness, just as the rectory home of his childhood and youth and the affections revolving around it played a continuing part in Tennyson's work; instead, she would develop some of the humane implications of their thought.

The risk inherent in such a diversity of possibilities was, of course, that it might expand infinitely. Wordsworth had seen something of this danger when he turned from his radical attitudes at the beginning of the new century and devoted himself to the pursuit of principle, the writings that he produced including the Victorian favourite 'Ode to Duty', with its recognition of those

> Who ask not if thine eye
> Be on them; who, in love and truth,

---

[45] Tennyson, *In Memoriam*, Section 101; cf. above, p. 180.

[46] *GL*, p. 503: quoted in Kathleen Tillotson, *Novels of the Eighteen-Forties*, (Oxford: Clarendon Press, 1954), pp. 222–3.

Where no misgiving is, rely
Upon the genial sense of youth.[47]

These lines are actually quoted in *Ruth*, to be followed by a passage which, as she describes the Bensons, embodies a Wordsworthian reconciliation between the moral law and the natural ('Thou dost preserve the stars from wrong . . .'[48]):

it seemed that their lives were pure and good, not merely from a lovely and beautiful nature, but from some law, the obedience to which was, of itself, harmonious peace, and which governed them almost implicitly, and with as little questioning on their part, as the glorious stars which haste not, rest not, in their eternal obedience.[49]

Gaskell's taking over of the 'Ode to Duty' and its values entailed apparent participation in the endorsement, implicit in Wordsworth's late attitude, of contemporary values – values to become commonplace in Victorian England. Her religious background also encouraged this Wordsworthian endorsement, giving rise to some tension with her belief in the universality of the human heart – particularly noticeable in *Ruth*, a novel which Stephen Gill has described as 'uncompromisingly severe'. However much later readers might sympathize with Ruth's situation, including her willingness as a young girl to walk in the country with Bellingham despite admonitions from her conscience, Gaskell cannot excuse any lapse from moral imperative, however venial. As Alan Shelston has put it, 'if Mrs Gaskell burdens her heroine with guilt it is because she, unlike Hardy, has absolutely no doubt that what she did, whatever the circumstances, was wrong'.[50] Even in her own time, however, as the mention of Hardy suggests, appeals to moral absolutes were beginning to meet doubts. If *Wives and Daughters*, like *Middlemarch* a few years later, is set many years before it was written, that must be partly because both Gaskell and Eliot saw the early years of the century as marked by a stability of assumptions that made it easier to work fictionally with them. This is true even of national assumptions, as with the

---

[47] *WPW* IV, 83–6.   [48] *Ibid.*
[49] *Ruth*, chapter xiii: *GK* III, 140–1. Compare Wordsworth's rebuke to the stationary gipsies (*WPW* II, 226–7) and the journeying moon and stars in Coleridge's gloss to *The Rime of the Ancient Mariner*.
[50] See his World's Classics edition of *Ruth* (Oxford University Press, 1983), p. xv. Nancy Henry, however, takes a twenty-first-century view in her Everyman edition: 'Ruth is implicitly absolved from guilt by her unconsciousness of Bellingham's designs on her' (London: J. M. Dent and Rutland, VT: Charles E. Tuttle, 2001), p. xxxvi.

Squire's response to any indication that an invitation from Lord Hollingford has to do with French interest in his son's intellectual pursuits:

'And what business has Roger – if it is Roger the man wants – to go currying favour with the French? In my day we were content to hate 'em and to lick 'em.'[51]

This throwback to attitudes from the Napoleonic Wars was redolent of an English stubbornness and rooted conservatism that had survived strongly in the following decades. Romantic liberals might look forward to an expansion of human values, but there remained a sense that the struggle between authoritarian firmness and critical openness had not been solved.

Further north, meanwhile, drama of a more intense kind was unfolding – again in a parsonage but one set against a bleaker landscape. At Haworth in Yorkshire, Charlotte, Emily and Anne Brontë, daughters of the perpetual curate there, having already, in their childhood, together with his son Branwell, produced the 'Chronicles' of Angria, an imaginary country they invented together, were exploring literary gifts that would achieve legendary status.

The current tension between the growth of independent, liberal instincts and the authoritarianism of traditional attitudes was internalized by them into a subterranean psychic struggle between their feeling for the passional life and a strongly held moral sense sustained by their association with the Church. Charlotte showed this tension throughout her career. As early as 1837 she was writing to a friend that her heart was 'a very hot-bed of sinful thoughts' and that she despaired of ever achieving true holiness – believing nevertheless that if she could spend more time with her friend, her spiritual state would be enhanced.[52] As the years passed, she partly solved the problem by regarding her imaginative faculty as a God-given gift, with her own novel-writing governed by her conscience,[53] yet was always disturbed by any suggestions that her work was 'wicked', as when the *Quarterly* reviewed *Jane Eyre* in scathing terms. Indeed, the struggle between a yielding to the conventional demands for female submissiveness and her restless creative urge led her at times into reprehensible prevarication. Reading Elizabeth Gaskell's *Life* of her, for instance, Harriet Martineau was put out to come across the instruction

---

[51] *Wives and Daughters*, chapter xxvii: *GK* VIII, 350.

[52] Elizabeth Gaskell, *The Life of Charlotte Brontë*, Everyman Library (London: J. M. Dent and New York: E. P. Dutton, 1908) (hereafter *GLife*), pp. 106–7.

[53] *Ibid.*, pp. 280, 285.

to a friend that if she was asked about the authorship of the novels she was to say that Miss Brontë 'repels and disowns every accusation of the kind', writing 'Fie!' and 'Bad!' in the margin.[54] The resolve of the three sisters to hide behind anonymity was, moreover, abruptly broken when a rumour claiming all three novels to be the work of one man reached their ears – at which point they threw caution to the winds, presenting themselves immediately to their publishers as an indisputable threesome.[55]

For Gaskell, Charlotte's anxiety about her reputation for uprightness must always have been a puzzle, given that her own moral sense extended well beyond the unorthodox beliefs she espoused – exhibited, for example, in the apparent warmth towards the philosophy of Immanuel Kant suggested when her Mr Farquhar found one side of his nature drawn to someone appreciative of the majesty of law:

He admired the inflexible integrity – and almost the pomp of principle – evinced by Mr. Bradshaw on every occasion; he wondered how it was that Jemima could not see how grand a life might be, whose every action was shaped in obedience to some eternal law; instead of which, he was afraid [Ruth] rebelled against every law, and was only guided by impulse. Mr. Farquhar had been taught to dread impulses as promptings of the devil.[56]

A fellow-feeling for the philosophy of Wordsworth and Coleridge was meanwhile suggested by Charlotte's approval of affection when it characterized her contemporaries: it was for her a strong redeeming point in Thomas Arnold's favour, or Harriet Martineau's.[57] Both writers drew back, however, from further exploration of the world of impulse, sometimes opening the door a little way before shutting it again in deference to the assumptions of their age. The possibility of combining head and heart remained an attractive third force, avoiding as it did the potential pitfalls of impulse, yet this was not easy of attainment. Of Mill, for instance, Charlotte could write, 'J. S. Mill's head is, I dare say, very good, but I feel disposed to scorn his heart',[58] and, of the Crystal Palace, that 'its wonders appeal too exclusively to the eye, and rarely touch the heart or head'.[59]

[54] Vera Wheatley, *The Life and Work of Harriet Martineau* (London: Secker and Warburg, 1957), pp. 329–30.
[55] *GLife*, pp. 247ff.   [56] *Ruth*, chapter xx: *GK* III, 213–14.
[57] *GLife*, pp. 323, 327.   [58] *GLife*, p. 344.   [59] *GLife*, pp. 337–8.

In trying to pursue this Romantic ideal of reconciling head and heart while remaining true to both, Charlotte Brontë exposed the tensions involved. She also turned away from the cultivated sentimentalities of contemporary literature, showing how the heart's truth might subsist most fully in people of a caustic disposition. The shrewdness of her observing eye led her to see clearly not only other people, but herself, and to appreciate the limitations of a life lived too prudently – however worthy one's moral character might be. William Crimsworth, the hero of her first novel *The Professor*, is a professor in more than one sense, the term being used at the time for someone who made his principles known and tried to act upon them. Crimsworth keeps a clear head and acts well at all times, and eventually wins a young woman whose rationality is countered by the workings of a heart more expressive than his own; yet the final chapters of the novel make the reader aware of limitations to which he himself is blind as he brings up his son to develop the same self-restraints that he has exercised.

Having escaped from the enclosure of her parsonage home by working as a governess in a Brussels still basking in the afterglow of Waterloo, Charlotte Brontë was drawing on her own experience of self-liberation: she was indeed to be condemned by some contemporaries (inexplicably as it might now seem) for outspokenness. Her essential moral seriousness is best seen in her concluding novel of 1853, *Villette*, where, in a subtle plot, the governess-heroine, never quite breaking the spell of the attractive male character with whom she first falls in love, is nevertheless drawn increasingly to the human profundity of the more sardonic Paul Emmanuel. Her fascination with the Byronic hero, natural enough in one of her generation, found its expression in the creation of other characters who refuse to fall neatly into the patterns offered them by society, her greatest creation in this mode being Mr Rochester in the 1847 *Jane Eyre*. Even Rochester, however, was thrown into the shade in the same year by her sister Emily's portrayal in *Wuthering Heights* of Heathcliff, the outsider rejected by the society in which he is brought up, who dominates the events of the novel by the power of his passion for his childhood love Catherine Earnshaw.

Both sisters were also concerned with the question of human identity and its establishment – particularly with the extent to which love might be impossible without a degree of identification between the lovers. When Paul Emmanuel begins to establish his claim on Lucy Snowe, it is by voicing his belief in their essential affinity:

Do you hear that you have some of my tones of voice? Do you know that you have many of my looks? I perceive all this, and believe that you were born under my star.[60]

It is a presumption of inescapable attachment that finds its apotheosis in Catherine's pronouncement in *Wuthering Heights*: 'I am Heathcliff' – in its turn an extreme version of the impulse towards self-identification with another being that had been an important presence among the Romantic writers and caused their fascination with the sisterly relationship, as in Shelley's poetry. This urge to identification with another, similar being had also characterized Tennyson's mourning over Hallam and would continue to cast its spell. But it also negated the virtues of dialogue, if that was based on the necessity of diversification between individuals. It seemed to call for some further innate quality that might underlie all the human resemblances and differences under investigation, and which might yet be free from traditional religious sanctioning. The need for such an overarching factor was acknowledged, but thwarted for the moment by the ability of passion to abolish the normal tendency towards diversification called for by linguistic development.

In the middle of the nineteenth century, in other words, the spell of traditional religion, and the need to mime the language of the Bible it had nurtured, were still too powerful to be broken by new young spirits, however strong their desire to break the conventional bonds of language. In such circumstances even the language of passion could be no more than a poor substitute. The need for full rational and emotional development remained, nevertheless, waiting for a more satisfactory fulfilment.

---

[60] Charlotte Brontë, *Villette*, ed. Herbert Rosengarten and Margaret Smith (Oxford: Clarendon Press, 1984), chapter xxxi, p. 532.

CHAPTER 11

George Eliot and the future of language

At first sight there might seem to be something supremely wrong-headed in making George Eliot an exemplar of 'the fate of the word', given her status as a practitioner of verbal artistry who, in her own words, saw that language could be 'the magic signs that conjure up a world'.[1] She was increasingly aware, however, that if words were to exercise the fullness of that magic, something more than simple text was needed.

Once the circumstances in which she began her intellectual writings are recalled, moreover, it becomes clear that throughout her career the status of the word was always for her uncertain. By the time she reached intellectual maturity, the temper of English culture had changed even from that prevailing at the time of the major Romantic poets. The varying impetus given to literature by the French Revolution, the revulsion against the Terror in France and the rise and fall of Napoleon, followed subsequently by the meteoric careers of Keats, Shelley and Byron, had been succeeded by a period of reappraisal and reflection, during which intelligent writers considered the problems left by the passing of the Napoleonic Wars.

As far as the Bible was concerned, George Eliot's views were even more advanced than those of Elizabeth Gaskell. The Unitarians of the time might be heretical in terms of doctrine, but they retained a reverence for the Word as such. For them it was not a matter of regarding the Bible as an authoritative text, but of interpreting the words of that text with emphasis on their simple human message.

Eliot, by contrast, was aware of intellectual currents that caught up in their sweep criticism of the assumptions behind the presented text. Already strands of questioning had arisen among biblical scholars, particularly in Germany, along with awareness that certain biblical texts

---

[1] George Eliot, *Romola*, ed. Andrew Brown (Oxford: Clarendon Press, 1993), chapter 38, p. 339.

were self-contradictory or confusing. Without being drawn into lengthy discussion of specific instances, moreover, Eliot accepted the existence of a case needing to be answered, being particularly drawn to the arguments of Strauss and Feuerbach (both of whom she translated) that the response called for must be philosophical.

At the same time, both the men in question, recognizing the difficulty of explaining such arguments clearly to ordinary people, wished to avoid possible imputations of hypocrisy; Eliot was also fully aware, moreover, of the almost supernatural magnetism which the physical text of a Bible could exercise. One need think only of Mr Tulliver, insisting that his son inscribe the words of his curse in the family Bible, or Silas Marner, invoking biblical authority for the practice of drawing lots.

In a letter of 1876 George Eliot wrote, 'My writing is simply a set of experiments in life – an endeavour to see what our thought and emotion may be capable of – what stores of motive . . . give promise of a better after which we may strive – what gains from past revelations and discipline we must strive to keep hold of as something more sure than shifting theory.'[2]

Taking her declaration at face value, Bernard Paris entitled his study *Experiments in Life*;[3] scholars have also been quick to trace the possible complement between her views and those of G. H. Lewes, who insisted on the need for scientists to cultivate imagination in their experimental work. But Paris was in time forced to recognize the existence of a difference between Eliot's kind of 'Experiments in Life' and those carried out by scientists: the latter began their work by trying to establish the nature of the world they were investigating as objectively as possible, whereas novelists created the universe which they then interpreted through fiction. It is true of course that scientists too exercise creative and imaginative powers in devising their accounts; but the possibility of self-interest being involved is not so blatant.

Eliot was fully alive to the dangers involved in creation generated by artists who might be criticized for having foreseen their conclusion from the very moment of conception. Her Mr Casaubon was certain that his work must ultimately end by justifying the account of creation in the Old Testament. She knew too that Casaubon's mind corresponded in certain respects to her own. This element of self-identification is easily overlooked

---

[2] Letter to Dr Parry: *GEL* VI, 216–17.
[3] Bernard J. Paris, *Experiments in Life: George Eliot's Quest for Values* (Detroit: Wayne State University Press, 1965).

in view of the hostility to him expressed at some places in the text, yet it was acknowledged by her on at least one occasion, as F. W. H. Myers recalled:

'But from whom then,' said a friend turning to Mrs Lewes, 'did you draw Casaubon?' With a humorous solemnity, which was quite in earnest, nevertheless, she pointed to her own heart.[4]

Her resort here to body language rather than words is significant; and it might be said that in one sense such willing self-criticism corresponded to a continuing correction of her early romanticism. Growing up in the 1820s and 1830s, she had been, like many young people, an early enthusiast for the poetry fashionable at the time. When many years later, in 1874, she received a copy of Keats's *Lamia* volume for publishing purposes, she wrote that it took her back to the days of her youth.[5] During the 1830s, however, with the movement for parliamentary reform, the efforts by members of the Oxford Movement to give a firmer basis for religious belief and growing awareness of the social problems created by industrialism, the taste for such poetry had already been superseded by a more mundane approach, the appropriate medium being prose. The greater attention to moral problems was accompanied by the growth of 'Victorian values', emphasizing family life and the domestic affections.

In these circumstances, Eliot, who while reading voraciously in her early years also looked to Evangelical Christianity for spiritual guidance, found her early enthusiasm for Keats, Shelley and Byron waning as she reflected on their moral behaviour. Later she wrote, concerning recent revelations of Byron's sexual life:

One trembles to think how easily that moral wealth may be lost which it has been the work of ages to produce, in the refinement and differencing of the affectionate relations. As to the high-flown stuff which is being reproduced about Byron and his poetry, I am utterly out of sympathy with it. He seems to me the most *vulgar-minded* genius that ever produced a great effect in literature.[6]

In these circumstances the one survivor of the younger Romantic poets to whom she could turn for reassurance was Wordsworth. Her discovery of his poetry when she was twenty had been, as she herself recognized,

---

[4] F. W. H. Myers, 'George Eliot', *Century Magazine* 23 (1881), 60. See also my *Providence and Love: Studies in Wordsworth, Channing, Myers, George Eliot, and Ruskin* (Oxford: Clarendon Press, 1998), pp. 201–2.
[5] *GEL* VI, 26, 28, 42, 57.
[6] Letter to Sara Hennell, 21 September 1869: *GEL* V, 56–7.

a major turning-point in her career: 'I never before met with so many of my own feelings expressed just as I could like them.'[7]

As she became more familiar with his work, she had been impressed by his refusal to pander to the contemporary taste for sensation, a refusal exemplified in some stanzas of 'Simon Lee':

> . . . My gentle reader, I perceive
> How patiently you've waited,
> And now I fear that you expect
> Some tale will be related.
> O Reader, had you in your mind
> Such stores as silent thought can bring,
> O gentle Reader! You would find
> A tale in every thing.[8]

When she wrote her first fiction, *Scenes of Clerical Life*, George Eliot dwelt on the same point. Describing the probable reaction from a typical reader to her character Amos Barton, who was 'in no respect an ideal or exceptional character', she wrote:

'An utterly uninteresting character!' I think I hear a lady reader exclaim – Mrs Farthingale, for example, who prefers the ideal in fiction; to whom tragedy means ermine tippets, adultery and murder; and comedy, the adventures of some personage who is 'quite a character'.

Her response to such a reader was that a majority of her fellow-countrymen were of an 'insignificant stamp':

They are simply men of complexions more or less muddy, whose conversation is more or less bald and disjointed. Yet these commonplace people – many of them – bear a conscience, and have felt the sublime prompting to do the painful right; they have their unspoken sorrows, and their sacred joys; their hearts have perhaps gone out towards their first-born, and they have mourned over the irreclaimable dead. Nay, is there not a pathos in their very insignificance – in our comparison of their dim and narrow existence with the glorious possibilities of that human nature which they share?[9]

The theme is taken up again in *Adam Bede* (in this sense her most Wordsworthian work) where she again insists on this part of her aim:

these fellow-mortals, every one, must be accepted as they are . . . these people . . . it is needful you should tolerate, pity and love: it is these more or less ugly,

---

[7] Letter of 22 November 1839: *GEL* I, 34.   [8] *WPW* IV, 63.
[9] George Eliot. *Scenes from Clerical Life*, ed. Thomas A. Noble (Oxford: Clarendon Press, 1985), chapter v, p. 42.

stupid, inconsistent people whose movements of goodness you should be able to admire . . .[10]

. . . the way in which I have come to the conclusion that human nature is lovable . . . its deep pathos, its sublime mysteries – has been by living a great deal among people more or less commonplace and vulgar . . .[11]

The point she valued most in Wordsworth was his willingness to take ordinary people seriously. The very elements of his poetry that other writers would find ridiculous or banal were for her tests of his worth. They also provided a touchstone by which other people might be judged, including the characters in her own novels. Arthur Donnithorne, for example, who found *Lyrical Ballads* 'twaddling stuff',[12] yet whose very name carries a possible allusion to Wordsworth's 'The Thorn', displays his shallow grasp of humanity by the manner in which he treats Hetty Sorrel. He is one with Mrs Transome in *Felix Holt*, who when young 'had been thought wonderfully clever and accomplished, and had been rather ambitious of intellectual superiority . . . had laughed at the Lyrical Ballads and admired Mr Southey's Thalaba'.[13]

Her feeling for ordinary people enabled Eliot to write about them with rare insight and at length. The most piercing yet fugitive allusion in this mode is her comment in *Middlemarch* that we do not expect people to be deeply moved by what is not unusual:

That element of tragedy which lies in the very fact of frequency, has not yet wrought itself into the coarse emotion of mankind; and perhaps our frames could hardly bear much of it. If we had a keen vision and feeling of all ordinary human life, it would be like hearing the grass grow and the squirrel's heart beat and we should die of that roar that lies on the other side of silence. As it is, the quickest of us walk about well wadded with stupidity.[14]

The one other point in major English literature where anyone talks about 'hearing the grass grow' is in Wordsworth's 'Idiot Boy', when Betty Foy has reached her point of desperation:

> The streams with softest sound are flowing,
> The grass you now can hear it growing,
> You hear it now, if e'er you can.[15]

[10] George Eliot, *Adam Bede*, ed. Carol A. Martin (Oxford: Clarendon Press, 2001), chapter xvii, p. 165.
[11] *Ibid.*, p. 172.
[12] *Ibid.*, chapter v, pp. 61–2.
[13] George Eliot, *Felix Holt, the Radical*, ed. Fred C. Thompson (Oxford: Clarendon Press, 1980), chapter 27.
[14] George Eliot, *Middlemarch*, ed. David Carroll (Oxford: Clarendon Press, 1986), chapter xx, p. 189.
[15] 'Idiot Boy', lines 284–6: *WPW* II, 76.

This can hardly be accidental; rather, it points to Wordsworth as one of the few who could walk about not 'wadded with stupidity' and invite readers to share appreciation of tender, apprehensive responses of the heart – taking one far into an understanding of human beings who might at first sight be dismissed as village idiots or doting mothers.

Her gift for immediate sympathy recalls Wordsworth's sister Dorothy, as described by de Quincey:

The pulses of light are not more quick or more inevitable in their flow and undulation, than were the answering and echoing movements of her sympathizing attention.[16]

Partly as a result of her guidance, this became a crucial element in her brother's thinking also. As he surveyed the world in the aftermath of the French Revolution, indeed, he came to believe that the two most important values worth clinging to were those of duty and affection. The domination of these two values in his thinking during the production of the poetry of his middle and late years has already been mentioned, as has his 'Ode to Duty', one of the great 'Victorian' statements which, along with poems such as 'Michael', eulogized the Stoic and domestic while accepting their tragic potential.

Like many of her contemporaries, however, she was still more moved by some of the central passages in the 'Lines Composed . . . above Tintern Abbey . . .' In the restlessness and anxiety characterizing the middle of the nineteenth century, it was a welcome balm to read of

> that blessed mood
> In which the burthen of the mystery,
> In which the heavy and the weary weight
> Of all this unintelligible world
> Is lightened: – that serene and blessed mood,
> In which the affections gently lead us on . . .'[17]

For minds oppressed by contemporary problems, particularly the intellectual ones, such lines were at once revealing and refreshing; this was even more clearly the case for Eliot herself, who twice in her letters spoke of 'the weight of all this unintelligible world' – a phrase which, employed to describe the feelings of Dorothea during her sterile Italian honeymoon

[16] Article 'William Wordsworth', in his *Recollections of the Lakes and the Lake Poets* [1839–40] (Harmondsworth: Penguin Books Ltd, 1970), p. 133.
[17] 'Lines Composed . . . above Tintern Abbey', lines 37–42: *WPW* II, 260.

in *Middlemarch*, became transposed into 'the weight of unintelligible Rome'.[18]

It was to Wordsworth, then, that she looked for a path of release from such problems. She was equally receptive to the sublime elements in his work, whether it was her 'sense of something far more deeply interfused' when she was contemplating a landscape painting[19] or the intuition of a possible sublimity in human nature itself that she traced in his poetry. At different times of her life she was fond of quoting to friends lines from an 1803 sonnet:[20]

> . . . every gift of noble origin
> Is breathed upon by hope's perpetual breath;

From *The Prelude*, similarly, she would quote

> There is
> One great society alone on earth:
> The noble living and the noble dead.[21]

During her first thirty years, the central values of duty and affection which informed the view of Wordsworth that had dominated the literary scene was one that he himself had taken pains to propagate: on such a reading his central poem was *The Excursion*, where these qualities were particularly celebrated. So ingrained was this assumption, that when a new and hitherto unknown long poem of his was published after his death, no one seems to have suggested that received perspectives might need to be questioned. Yet in 1850 *The Prelude* revealed a more introspective and self-questioning figure than had been visible before, foreshadowing a twentieth-century reputation when generations trained to read more closely and psychologically would find this the more exciting poem.

At the time, the traditional reading of Wordsworth's philosophy could come to the rescue of those who felt an increasing pressure from accounts of the universe that interpreted it in purely mechanist terms. Eliot led the dissatisfaction at attempts to give such readings the status of absolute truth by suggesting the flaw in arguments that regarded them as logically entailed by the processes of nature and their working. In a well-known judgment concerning Darwin and Huxley, she wrote, 'to me the Development

---

[18] *Middlemarch*, chapter xx, p. 188.   [19] *GEL* I, 248.
[20] 'These times strike moneyed worldlings with dismay . . .': see letters to John Sibree Jr, February 1848, and to Benjamin Jowett, 1879: *GEL* I, 251 and IX, 284.
[21] *WPrel* (1850) xi. 393–5.

theory and all other explanations of processes by which things came to be, produce a feeble impression compared with the mystery that lies under the processes'.[22]

This would have been for her related to what Wordsworth called 'the burthen of the mystery', which, during the Romantic period, was likely to be interpreted in one of two ways. The phenomena of the natural world could be viewed as part of a marvellous and intricate mechanism, fulfilling the processes of necessary law. In that case all science provided a deepening and furthering of the eighteenth-century world picture, with its God who had set laws in motion and left them to work in accordance with their own principles. At the other extreme, the universe could be approached from the quite different presupposition that its ultimate significance, beneath all the processes, was a mystery, the key to which lay in the depths of human nature. The argument in that case ran the opposite way: instead of seeing human capacities for benevolence and self-denial as amiable irrelevancies in a universe whose workings took no account of them, it was possible to start with the mystery that these qualities should exist at all, and to argue that, so far from being unnecessary excrescences in an indifferent mechanism, they might point to an underlying metaphysical reality, realizing itself more fully in human beings than in any other natural phenomena. So in the dawn of Romanticism, Coleridge had found a peculiar fascination in all those 'facts of mind', such as hypnotism, which suggested the subsistence of layers in the consciousness below those that aligned themselves with the natural world.[23] Blake, more sweepingly, had urged his readers to disregard those natural processes, as such, and to reawaken in themselves the eternal 'humanity' revealed in the workings of human imagination and human energy.[24]

Eliot did not experience directly the speculative power of Coleridge or Blake at their best, so that there was no opportunity for such ideas to work on her. Nor was she, living in a later time and place, exposed to any event so immediately disruptive of received opinions as had been the French Revolution. Her own background was comparatively peaceful, with roots, extending back into the eighteenth century, that had not been seriously

---

[22] Letter to Barbara Bodichon, 5 December 1859: *GEL* III, 227.
[23] See above, p. 115.
[24] See, e.g., my *Blake's Humanism* (Manchester University Press, 1968) and Morton Paley's *Energy and the Imagination: A Study of the Development of Blake's Thought* (Oxford: Clarendon Press, 1970).

disturbed by recent troubles. Her recognition of the sweeping changes that were taking place in the intellectual and social life of her time was more slow and drawn-out, therefore, involving such things as gradual contact with, and recognition of, the new social and scientific ideas raised by the Industrial Revolution and contemporary absorption of German thought. Yet the very thoroughness and honesty of this long reappraisal was such that in the end she succeeded – far better than Coleridge had done – in setting out the larger implications of what was happening to civilization in her time and in demonstrating the difficulty of reconciling acceptance of the demonstrable laws of nature with a belief in morality.

In one sense, clearly, she never finally lost contact with her forebears in English religious thought, particularly in the Evangelical movement. To the end there was a tone, a point of view in her writing, which affirmed the inexorability of the moral law. (This could give a peculiar quality – even a dark relish – to her portrayals of such workings within an actual event, the fall of Bulstrode, for example, in *Middlemarch*.) But in another sense she was broadening her mind to cover the whole range of intellectual life that had been addressed by thinkers such as Coleridge.

The limitations within which she worked may be shown by again tracing her devotion to Wordsworth. The citations of his work to be found throughout her career provide ample evidence that the terms of her reading were largely the stalwart assertions of duty and affection as twin virtues, referred to earlier, by which he himself had finally offered his works for approving acceptance. She was particularly struck by the sonnets of 1802–3 such as 'I grieved for Buonaparte', 'To Toussaint L'Ouverture' and 'O Friend! I know not which way . . .', with their tributes to 'plain living and high thinking' and to 'man's unconquerable mind'; 'The war is too much with me' she could write in 1871,[25] adapting another famous line. Wordsworth's sense of 'the burthen of the mystery' and its consequent weight on the individual consciousness spoke to her with the most force, however, in her intellectual struggles, when she could press their implications further. His feeling for the universality of the human heart gave a greater stress to some passages; when she remarked of *Silas Marner*, 'I should not have believed that anyone would have been interested in it but myself', she immediately added the parenthesis, '(since William Wordsworth is dead)'; and this, despite having adopted for that novel the Wordsworthian epigraph 'A child more than all other gifts . . .

[25] Letter of 2 January 1871: *GEL* V, 132.

Brings hope with it, and forward-looking thoughts'. In this respect an implicit rapport between her and Dorothy Wordsworth can again be sensed. Yet although she could respond to the immediacy of sympathy in William Wordsworth's text, she may also have been aware of Coleridgean themes. One has only to go to the next lines of 'These times strike moneyed worldlings . . .' to read 'That virtue and the faculties within / Are vital . . .' – which might recall Coleridge's exploration of the relationship between organic growth and vital energies.

The significance for her of Coleridge is evident from *Adam Bede*, where, as has already been mentioned, the insufficiencies of Arthur Donnithorne are indicated by the ill-disguised contempt with which he greets a copy of *Lyrical Ballads* that reaches him from London. He continues, however, 'the first is in a different style – "The Ancient Mariner" is the title. I can hardly make head or tail of it as a story, but it's a strange, striking thing.'[26] The suggestion is that Donnithorne, who has been simply moved to ridicule by Wordsworth's contributions, has at least found his curiosity aroused by *The Rime of the Ancient Mariner*. Eliot herself was evidently struck by elements in the poem. It seems, for example, that the 'glittering eye' of the Mariner made a permanent impression: in a letter of August 1868 to Emily Davies, she apologised for her overheated conversation the previous day by saying that this must have resulted in her being thought of as 'among the women of the "glittering eye" and excited demeanour'.[27] For the epigraph to one chapter of *Daniel Deronda*,[28] she chose the passage on the fixed curse in the eyes of the Mariner's shipmates.

In the 1840s, when Coleridge had been particularly celebrated for his religious thought, she had written to Francis Watts, 'I feel with Coleridge, that, the notion of Revelation abandoned, there is ever a tendency towards Pantheism, and the personality of the Deity is not to be maintained quite satisfactorily apart from Christianity.'[29] Just over a year later, she came into closer contact with his memory when she went to stay with Dr Brabant and his family at Devizes. Brabant had been friendly with Coleridge when he was in the district some twenty-five years before, and at his urging had learnt German, with the result that he had come to know the higher critics of the Bible at first hand. It is hardly conceivable,

[26] See above, p. 204.
[27] *GEL* IV, 467.
[28] George Eliot, *Daniel Deronda*, ed. Graham Handley (Oxford: Clarendon Press, 1984), chapter lvi.
[29] Letter of April 1842: *GEL* I, 136.

therefore, that while she was there, given the intimacy of their intellectual discussions, the two did not talk of the earlier friendship. The speculation may be taken further. It can be maintained that the knowledge of the Higher Criticism which she derived from Dr Brabant helped to form the critical position which she gradually assumed, in which sense of the sacred drained away from her view of the Bible, as from other texts. And this is of course precisely the view of the world that informs early novels such as *Scenes of Clerical Life*, where the narrator's prime aim seems to be to strip away fantasy.

This resort to the necessity of an illusionless view of human existence was to be strongly influential on those who admired her work, yet there are signs that, finding it unsatisfactory as an ultimate stance, she herself strove to move beyond it. The relationship with G. H. Lewes, and his demonstration of the need to appreciate the potentialities and the limitations of the scientific attitude, played an important part here.

From an early stage Lewes had shown a strong interest in the ability of a writer to portray the visual – indeed, he faulted Jane Austen for her lack of attention in this respect, claiming in an early piece on her that she was too much inclined to rely on her readers to construct their sense of characters by what they say and do, rather than to offer direct description:

It is impossible that Mr Collins should not have been endowed by nature with an appearance in some way heralding the delicious folly of the inward man. Yet all we hear of this fatuous curate is, that 'he was a tall heavy-looking young man of five-and-twenty. His air was grave and stately and his manners were very formal'.[30]

Balzac or Dickens, he goes on, would have made us *see* such a character, whereas Jane Austen is content that we should know him. There is room for considerable discussion here, obviously, but Lewes's view of the importance of visual description emerges clearly enough. It is of a piece with the conviction in his scheme of mental activities that the prevalence of concrete images distinguished the thought and language of artists from those of philosophers and scientists. Lewes used the term 'vision' as a metaphor for all thinking done primarily through images, arguing that mental vision, or 'seeing with the mind's eye', is as essential to perception, inference and reasoning as to imagination – by which he meant the mind's power to select, abstract and recombine images held in the memory, sometimes forming from them new images that correspond to

---

[30] G. H. Lewes, 'The Novels of Jane Austen', *Blackwood's Edinburgh Magazine* 87 (1859), 105.

no external reality. For this reason he valued the work of novelists such as Eliot, in whom he believed the work of such thinking was made manifest, while she, in turn, welcomed the assurance that the work of the novelist could in that sense be regarded as 'scientific'.

It also gave her a particular interest in Coleridge's similar enterprise – though reports of his state of mind during the later years of his life must have had a disturbing, even haunting, effect. In this regard the paragraph in Carlyle's account of him that she picked on in her review of his *Life of John Sterling* as one to which 'the emphasis of quotation cannot be too often given' is telling:

The truth is, I now see Coleridge's talk and speculation was the emblem of himself. In it, as in him, a ray of heavenly inspiration struggled, in a tragically ineffectual degree, with the weakness of flesh and blood.[31]

The paragraph also includes Carlyle's citation of Coleridge's description of himself as one who had 'skirted the howling deserts of infidelity',[32] and his comment that Coleridge had not had the courage to press resolutely across those deserts 'to the new firm lands of faith beyond'.[33] Since this was precisely the aim which she believed that she *had* followed, the indictment of Coleridge's failure in this respect could be seen as telling. But the statement that in him 'a ray of heavenly inspiration struggled' suggests that she could still discern elements of the kind of illumination to which she herself aspired.

Of further elements in Coleridge, the impetuous eagerness and ranging intelligence which had characterized him as a young man, for example, she had little direct knowledge. As mentioned earlier, she had not when she was young avoided some sense of the excitement that had character-ized the subsequent Romantic poets: there is evidence in her letters of an early devotion to the poems of Keats and Shelley, for example. Yet throughout her youth, when social questions were being urgently dis-cussed, the self-indulgence of their poetry had been under fire and that kind of censure would have been backed further by the Evangelical Christian principles which she at that time espoused. One result was that she found her own sense of Romanticism better characterized in versions to be found in Germany. She could not remain totally indifferent, for she

---

[31] From her review in the *Westminster Review* for January 1852; see Thomas Pinney (ed.), *Essays of George Eliot* (London: Routledge and Kegan Paul, 1963), p. 50.

[32] *CBL*, chapter ix, p. 152.

[33] Thomas Carlyle, *The Life of John Sterling* (London: Chapman and Hall, 1851), chapter 8.

was well aware of the dreariness and lifelessness to which eighteenth-century philosophy, if taken to its logical conclusions, led: the German version of Romanticism is indeed introduced into *Middlemarch* explicitly as the movement which had 'helped to fill some dull blanks with love and knowledge' but which in the 1830s had 'not yet penetrated the times with its leaven and entered into everybody's food'. In the period of the events described in that novel, it is described as having been 'fermenting still as a distinguishable vigorous enthusiasm in certain long-haired German artists at Rome'.[34] These, the Nazarenes, she later describes as having not only revived but expanded 'that grand conception of supreme events as mysteries at which the successive ages were spectators, and in relation to which the great souls of all periods became as it were contemporaries'. The vigour of such movements evidently impressed her as the most congenial form of Romanticism.

The point which needs to be stressed, however, is her apparent sense that although the attempt to live simply in Romantic feeling might to a certain point be innocent, and even admirable, human beings needed to be brought up against the ineluctable in nature, the limiting forces, the sense of what most individual human lives are actually like. There is also, in turn, the sense that a life lived totally under *that* vision would be almost unbearably bleak (as shown in 'The Lifted Veil') and that human hope lay therefore in the achievements of those who also manage to keep alive a sense of inner illumination. It is, in many ways, the vision which she found in Wordsworth, while reminding one how much Wordsworth himself owed to the invigorating power of Coleridge's early vision, the ability – which Coleridge's friends appreciated most in him – to be fully possessed by the enthusiasm of the moment.

The crucial point has, in fact, been made already, many chapters earlier in *Middlemarch*, in her ironic expression of sympathy with Mr Casaubon's condition, which is, she claims,

never to be fully possessed by the glory we behold, never to have our consciousness rapturously transformed into the vividness of a thought, the ardour of a passion, the energy of an action, but always to be scholarly and uninspired, ambitious and timid, scrupulous and dim-sighted . . .[35]

The further irony of Casaubon's position is, of course, that while he is pedantically pursuing the implications of solar myths in the Vatican

---

[34] *Middlemarch*, chapter xix, p. 183.   [35] *Ibid.*, chapter xxix, p. 274.

library, a realized solar myth is actually unfolding itself before Dorothea nearby in the form of Will Ladislaw, the illuminated young man of the novel. A similar element can be found in Coleridge's thinking also, emerging, for example, in his late drama *Zapolya*, where the imagery of nature constantly works in tune with the moral argument. The hero is advised by his mother, in Wordsworthian terms, to

> Leave then to Heaven
> The work of Heaven: and with a silent spirit
> Sympathize with the powers that work in silence!

while his mood of righteous anger is described by the most perceptive character, Glycine, in the words,

> So looks the statue, in our hall, o' the god,
> The shaft just flown that killed the serpent!

The statue of the Apollo Belvedere in the Vatican in Rome is, of course, the very model of handsomeness that Ladislaw has just been confronting when Dorothea encounters him there at the beginning of chapter 19 in *Middlemarch*.

Eliot's symbolism follows Coleridge's in a further respect. When in his drama Bethlen visits a cavern and asks by what name he should worship the hidden light, he is told:

> Patience! Truth! Obedience!
> Be thy soul transparent! So the Light,
> Thou seekest, may enshrine itself within thee!

Ladislaw may lack the superb manliness of the Apollo Belvedere, but he nevertheless has Apollonian characteristics, such as his abundant and curly hair. More importantly, he radiates an inner light which might be thought to fulfil the significance of the ancient myth. As the narrator puts it,

Will Ladislaw's smile was delightful, unless you were angry with him beforehand: it was a gush of inward light illuminating the transparent skin as well as the eyes, and playing about every curve and line as if some Ariel were touching them with a new charm, and banishing for ever the traces of moodiness.[36]

There is also an uncertainty about the effect he creates:

Surely, his very features changed their form; his jaw looked sometimes large and sometimes small; and the little ripple in his nose was a preparation for

---

[36] *Ibid.*, chapter xxi, p. 199.

metamorphosis. When he turned his head quickly his hair seemed to shake out light, and some persons thought they saw decided genius in this coruscation.

This illumination is matched by a visionary attitude to the world and to society that is reminiscent of no Romantic writer more than Shelley. The link is indeed made within the novel:

'He seems to me a kind of Shelley, you know,' Mr Brooke took an opportunity of saying . . . 'I don't mean as to anything objectionable – laxities or atheism, or anything of that kind, you know – Ladislaw's sentiments in every way I am sure are good . . .'[37]

Despite his garrulousness and intermittent foolishness, Mr Brooke's comments often show strong common sense. Here they pay their respects to an attitude that was common among those of Eliot's contemporaries who, while horrified by Shelley's treatment of his first wife and suspicious of his revolutionary politics, could hardly ignore his intellectual charm and evident good intentions.

Shelley's deepest beliefs reflected, like Coleridge's, an attempt to trace the divine in the depths of human consciousness. Such an enterprise, after the manner of Feuerbach, would be immeasurably strengthened if it could also be demonstrated that what was discovered there was also to be found in the depths of nature. In this respect Eliot's beliefs, though not rendered in explicit terms, several times emerge implicitly. A careful examination of them suggests the sense of a possible correspondence between the powers of genius and illumination in human beings and the energies and light of nature that surfaces from time to time in Coleridge's philosophy. The implication is that just as in nature energies which seem ambiguous may have at their heart a light that is purely beneficent, so the genial energies of man, often morally ambiguous in themselves, look back to a heart of light which prompts the kindliness of human actions.

Illumination is not sufficient, therefore. Throughout her fiction George Eliot betrays a constant feeling for the human manifestations of energy, to be aligned with a general mid-Victorian belief that the philosophy needed for the times must aim further. Matthew Arnold, feeling unease about his poem 'The Scholar Gipsy', wrote to Clough:

I am glad you like the Gipsy Scholar – but what does it do for you? Homer animates – Shakespeare animates – in its poor way I think Sohrab and Rustum

---

[37] *Ibid.*, chapter xxxvii, p. 350.

animates – the Gipsy Scholar at best awakens a pleasing melancholy. But this is not what we want.

> The complaining millions of men
> Darken in labour and pain –

What they want is something to animate and ennoble them – not merely to add zest to their melancholy or grace to their dreams. I believe a feeling of this kind is the basis of my nature – and of my poetics.[38]

Eliot would not have disagreed. The word is one, moreover, that covers many of her happiest effects – notably in the portrayal of characters such as Celia Brooke and Mrs Cadwallader in *Middlemarch*, where she evidently delights in the play of wit. The problem arises when animation, as the working of energy or passion, becomes morally ambiguous. Eliot charts her way towards a solution by the positive approval she evinces towards a purer and more human quality, that of ardour. The word is one that has slipped out of English usage in recent years, and would more often be found now in hostile or ironic contexts. For a person to be described as 'ardent' would suggest some lack of awareness. For Eliot, by contrast, the quality carried a stamp of approval; however critical she might be of a character, the presence of ardour would be a sign of grace, corresponding to its necessarily outgoing nature. From the beginning, ardour is frequently mentioned as a characteristic of Dorothea Brooke, who is introduced first as having a 'sweet, ardent nature' – shortly to be defined further as 'a nature altogether ardent, theoretic and intellectually consequent'.[39] When she reaches Rome the pressure of that 'ardent nature', which 'turned all her small allowance of knowledge into principles . . . and whose quick emotions gave the most abstract things the quality of a pleasure or a pain',[40] leads to depressive reaction in the face of 'unintelligible Rome' and the dry response of a husband whose taper-lit vision and close study of the solar deities had made him 'indifferent to the sunlight'.[41] When, as already mentioned, this is relieved by the encounter with Will Ladislaw, seen first standing near the Apollo Belvedere torso, his inner lighting strongly stressed, the contrast remains stark:

Mr Casaubon, on the contrary, stood rayless.[42]

---

[38] Letter of 30 November 1853, in *Letters of Matthew Arnold to Arthur Hugh Clough*, ed. H. F. Lowry (Oxford: Clarendon Press, 1932), p. 146.
[39] *Middlemarch*, chapter iii, pp. 24, 28. [40] *Ibid.*, chapter xx, p. 188.
[41] *Ibid.*, p. 192. [42] *Ibid.*, chapter xxi, p. 203.

Casaubon's lack of ardour is as pronounced as his lack of illumination, whether from within or without. He has only the self-enclosing energies fostered by an all-encompassing selfish concern. When we are told of his passionate egotism, we know that it is the second word that is the damning one, foreshadowing the further revelation of his limitations in the comment that 'his passionate longings, poor man, clung low and mist-like in very shady places'.[43]

Lydgate's 'intellectual ardour', by contrast, does not rank among his faults. Yet in spite of his characteristics as an idealistic young doctor, a limitation is present there too: 'He was an ardent fellow', we are told, 'but at present his ardour was absorbed in love of his work and in the ambition of making his life recognized as a factor in the better life of mankind'[44] – hence, we may assume, that larger human failure which causes him to fail so badly in his understanding of Rosamond Vincy. The quality of his intellectual ardour, on the other hand, is evident in the description of his scientific aspirations, which ignore the lower manifestations of scientific speculation for the higher workings of the scientific imagination

that reveals subtle actions inaccessible by any sort of lens, but tracked in that outer darkness through long pathways of necessary sequence by the inward light which is the last refinement of Energy, capable of bathing even the ethereal atoms in its ideally illuminated space.[45]

The idea that all energy, if sufficiently refined, will be apprehended as light, was evidently appealing and fascinating to Eliot – all the more so if related to the kind of thinking found in mystics such as Jacob Boehme, where human energies themselves look inwards to a lost heart of light. But when Lydgate's career is considered in this context, we are driven to ask whether the kinds of speculation he rejected do not also bear on the question:

reports of very poor talk going on in distant orbs; or portraits of Lucifer coming down on his bad errands as a large ugly man with bat's wings and spurts of phosphorescence . . .[46]

However vulgarly Lucifer is painted, he may still correspond to a principle actively at work in the universe; we are led to ask – particularly remembering the implication of Lucifer's name – whether Lydgate,

---

[43] *Ibid.*, chapter xlii, p. 415.   [44] *Ibid.*, chapter xvi, p. 162.
[45] *Ibid.*, p. 161.   [46] *Ibid.*

aspiring to refine his energies to the point of light, is not committing a Faustian error, opening himself to the fate that awaits over-reachers who take insufficient thought for the larger condition of humanity.

When considered against its Romantic themes, and stripped of all the other elements, *Middlemarch* may be seen to revolve around these qualities in its main characters. The person in the novel who best succeeds in combining illumination and ardour is, of course, Will Ladislaw, and in a sense the main point of the novel condenses in his attractiveness, an ultimate focus of the Middlemarchers' ideals.

Accordingly, when Eliot turned to write what was to be her last completed novel, the sense of the illuminated individual that she had explored in depicting Ladislaw figured less prominently – though it is notable that some of the chief scenes in the novel take place in a scene unusually illuminated, often by a sunset light. Ardour remains prominent, certainly, in the person of Daniel himself – indeed, it might be regarded as his chief characteristic. But the valuing of that quality is accompanied by a continuous probing of the implications of energy, which, like her Romantic predecessors, she was forced to regard as ambiguous. Yet in its highest form, poetic energy, it is to be seen as a force that enrols imagination without slipping into unreal fantasy. Instead, it can display an ability to extend well beyond what is normally termed the Romantic:

the fervour of sympathy with which we contemplate a grandiose martyrdom is feeble compared with the enthusiasm that keeps unslacked where there is no danger, no challenge – nothing but impartial midday falling on commonplace, perhaps half-repulsive, objects which are really the beloved ideas made flesh. Here undoubtedly lies the chief poetic energy: in the force of imagination that pierces or exalts the solid fact, instead of floating among cloud-pictures.[47]

This lesson is gradually brought home to Daniel, both by his growing appreciation of the Jewish surroundings in which his loved one lives, and by his encounters with Mordecai – a figure characterized less by illumination than by the piercingness of his eye, reminding one of the Ancient Mariner as he searches for a glimpse of the figure who may receive his own vision and carry it forward.

It may be significant, then, that Eliot's most searching discussion of Mordecai is also the occasion of a strong reference to Coleridge's poem. Daniel Deronda, trying to decide what he should make of this strange

---

[47] *Daniel Deronda*, chapter xxxiii, p. 352.

man, puts himself in Sir Hugo's place and imagines his comments, which his own reflections develop:

Scattered here and there in every direction you might find a terrible person, with more or less power of speech, and with an eye either glittering or preternaturally dull, on the look-out for the man who must hear him; and in most cases he had volumes which it was difficult to get printed, or if printed to get read.[48]

The ambiguity surrounding Mordecai is precisely that which attaches to Coleridge's Mariner: what was the likelihood that such a man's answer to the riddle of the world would be true, or correspond to the earnestness with which he seized the man to whom he must tell his tale?

Eliot had something of this doubt, we may assume, corresponding to the doubts that must have visited Coleridge equally – with the further problem that a novel was a less appropriate vehicle than a poem of the supernatural for rendering such a figure. Her instinct told her, nevertheless, that in order to convey her philosophy the novel must contain such a character, expressing a strain of totally committed energy, and that a respectful hearing should be accorded to it like that which Daniel was willing to give to what he saw (with some apprehension) as a strain of 'visionary excitement'. At one point he asks, concerning this element in Mordecai,

Was such a temper of mind likely to accompany that wise estimate of consequences which is the only safeguard from fatal error, even to ennobling motive? . . . perhaps his might be one of the natures where a wise estimate of consequences is fused in the fires of that passionate belief which determines the consequences it believes in. The inspirations of the world have come in that way too . . . And in relation to human motives and actions, passionate belief has a fuller efficacy. Here enthusiasm may have the validity of proof, and, happening in one soul, give the type of what will one day be general.[49]

Eliot adds one further factor: 'And if you like he was romantic':

That young energy and spirit of adventure . . . gave him a certain quivering interest in the bare possibility that he was entering on a like track – all the more because the track was one of thought as well as action.[50]

That the main qualities associated with Mordecai are those of vision and energy is conveyed by graphic phrases: 'his face . . . had something like a

---

[48] *Ibid.*, chapter xli, p. 474.   [49] *Ibid.*, p. 477.   [50] *Ibid.*, p. 479.

pale flame in it'; 'the hectic brilliancy of his gaze'.[51] The true role of such illumination and ardour, and the responsibility for carrying them forward into a new vision of society rest, however, with Daniel Deronda himself.

In such statements Eliot could show her continuity with some of the most important elements, and especially the aspirations, displayed in the Romantic tradition. But in this final achievement she went further, exploring something of the inquiry into the nature of human energies that is foreshadowed there also. One thinks of the imagery used to describe Gwendolen Harleth at the beginning, a strain recalling some earlier heroines – the Hetty in *Adam Bede* who was like 'waternixies and such lovely things without souls' and the Rosamond Vincy in *Middlemarch* who was a 'sylph caught young and educated at Mrs Lemon's'.[52] Gwendolen Harleth is first described as a 'problematic sylph' and then as a 'Nereid in sea-green robes and silver ornaments'.[53] But there is something more in this case, for immediately afterwards comes the comment that she 'has got herself up as a serpent now, all green and silver, and winds her neck about a little more than usual'.[54] That movement of the neck is rather like Rosamond's; and when it is followed by a remark about temptation by the serpent and reinforced in the following chapter by the author's observation that as she walked along the street her drapery fell 'in gentle curves attractive to all eyes except those which discerned in them too close a resemblance to the serpent, and objected to the revival of serpent-worship',[55] we may imagine that we are being tipped off concerning Gwendolen's insidious nature. Yet if so, the tip turns out to be not altogether reliable, since Gwendolen's behaviour is not really sinister. It is self-indulgent and shallow, or, as she herself later puts it, 'weak and ignorant', but little, if anything, in her actions is malignant. And another remark in the opening chapter – immediately after the serpent reference – is worthy of attention: 'She is certainly very graceful. But she wants a tinge of colour in her cheeks: it is a sort of Lamia beauty she has.'[56]

It is hard to believe that Eliot could have made such a point without having had Keats's poem in mind. For Gwendolen's fate in this chapter is to be, like his Lamia, quelled by a look. Keats's story is itself ambiguous, since the Apollonius who in reducing Lamia from beautiful woman to

---

[51] *Ibid.*, chapter xl, p. 466, chapter xlii, p. 494.   [52] *Middlemarch*, chapter xvi, p. 157.
[53] *Daniel Deronda*, chapter i, pp. 5, 7.   [54] *Ibid.*, chapter i, p. 8.
[55] *Ibid*, chapter ii, pp. 14–15.   [56] *Ibid.*, chapter i, p. 8.

serpent causes her to vanish in the process is a rational philosopher. The implication of his poem is that philosophy has robbed life of its magic – deprived the rainbow of its beauty and clipped angels' wings. Eliot, however, would probably have read the myth in the sterner terms of her belief that the need to accept the dulling glance of reality was an essential part of human maturing. It is the challenge that Gwendolen has had to face in meeting the look of Daniel Deronda, and to which she has not fully risen. And it might be argued that her inability to do so exposes her in time to the far more deadly gaze of Grandcourt, constantly surveying her throughout their married life with his withering gaze, and gradually arousing in her a murderous, serpent-like response.

There are echoes here not only of Keats but of Coleridge: the ambiguous beauty of Gwendolen, which is made an issue in the very first sentence of the novel, is reminiscent of Geraldine in *Christabel*, who can at times stand up 'Like a lady of a far countrée', but who can in other circumstances reveal herself in a snake-like glance.[57]

What is at issue here is not just a resemblance between authors but the whole area of human experience to be described as the daemonic. Both Keats and Coleridge felt that in some sense it was at the centre of human existence and to be extinguished only at the expense of life itself – at once both attractive and fearful. Neither heroine can quite resolve that dilemma. With Gwendolen, although the beauty which derives from her daemonic qualities is capable of being raised into a fuller power, the weight of the novel is against such an outcome: she seems in fact doomed from the start. (Indeed, one might have expected her to put up a better fight against Grandcourt; even within the constraints of Victorian England, a woman of her spirit would surely have given as good as she got.)

In her essay on *Middlemarch*, Gillian Beer has pointed out that the association of Will Ladislaw with the figure of the Apollo Belvedere gains in significance when looked at in the context of Mrs Jameson's reference to the Apollo Belvedere in relation to Christian angelic art and to the story of the bright boy who appears to St Dorothea in Mrs Jameson's telling. She sets in contrast Mr Casaubon, a 'Saturnian' character, and recalls his description of himself:

My mind is something like the ghost of an ancient, wandering about the world and trying mentally to construct it as it used to be, in spite of ruin and confusing changes.[58]

---

[57] See *Christabel*, lines 583–91; 600–6: *CPW* (EHC) I, 233–4.
[58] *Middlemarch*, chapter ii, p. 13.

This, she points out, encourages a reading of the two characters in terms of Keats's first *Hyperion*, where the young Apollo is destined to take over from a Saturn bound to the world of forms. We might add to this the mythology of Blake, where Urizen (like Tiriel and the Duke of Burgundy in his earlier prophetic books) seeks to establish permanence in a world where the energy necessary for dynamic change is sensed only as a threatening voice of destruction. In some ways Urizen is closer to Casaubon than is Saturn, since (as Gillian Beer also points out) Casaubon's mind has a quality in it that corresponds to a nightmare in George Eliot's own. This self-identification of hers has already been noted.[59]

We have also remarked that Blake, in similar fashion, would have recognized Urizen as a presence in his own mind, needing to be superseded through the energy of his own art. Eliot's solution, however, owes more to Shelley. It supposes that the Apollonian redemptive work will be achieved not through the godlike energy of Keats's Apollo (a conclusion which Keats himself seems to have faltered over, judging by his failure to complete the first *Hyperion*), but through recognition of the true achievement of Apollo as being to forgo language altogether. The Casaubons of the world may continue in their assurance of finding an ultimate verbal formulation to solve the universe, disregarding Coleridge's attestation that the only word truly capable of salvation is the logos of an energy that is also an illumination. What is needed, in other words, is not a sun that in the instant of its shining would also destroy, but a milder form of light, working subtly through the forms of life itself and issuing into generous love. Even if many readers find it understandably hard to find the associating of such a quiet spirit with gentleness, even a certain innocence, an apocalyptic revelation, it has some contact with the fact that most beneficent forces in human life (the activity of sunlight, the vitalizing energies of spring, the activity of smiling, and, Feuerbach's favourite, water) do in fact work in this unobtrusive manner. What Eliot is doing takes Shelley's ideal power, 'That Light whose smile kindles the universe', to render its action not in Shelleyan splendour but in the workings of ordinary human life.

The gradual emergence of this insight from her long novelistic enterprise suggests something of the difficulty that it had involved. Henry James, who reviewed *Middlemarch* quizzically but favourably, was impressed, despite what he saw as 'too often an echo of Messrs. Darwin

---

[59] See above, p. 202, and Gillian Beer's essay '*Middlemarch* and *The Lifted Veil*', in *This Particular Web: Essays on Middlemarch*, ed. Ian Adam (Toronto: University of Toronto Press. 1975).

and Huxley'.[60] But when he came to *Daniel Deronda*, his response was so complex that he needed to produce a 'Conversation' about it,[61] in which three possible attitudes were voiced, for and against, ranging from Pulcheria, the most hostile, finding fault with its lack of 'current' ('it is a series of lakes'), to Constantius, the most reflective, arguing (rather as would F. R. Leavis, many years later) that there are two distinct elements in Eliot, the 'natural' and the 'artificial'. The third member of the group, Theodora, a more uncritical admirer of the novel, takes issue with this, as implying that Eliot is 'too scientific'.

Right or wrong, Theodora points to the crux of Eliot's dilemma: her need to complement her humane grasp of the human condition by probing scientific analysis. James had evidently spotted in her something foreign to the traditional novelist's role and corresponding to the loss of authority in the word which has been increasingly the theme of this book. After Eliot, its status would continue to be debated and developed by writers who would experiment boldly and rewardingly – one need think only of James himself, D. H. Lawrence, James Joyce and the young T. S. Eliot – but never again with the old authority.

What had changed involved advances in scientific language during the century. In particular, it reflected the triumph of evolutionary theory, as championed by Charles Darwin and his associates. George Eliot claimed that what they were studying was process, whereas she was interested in the mystery that underlay all processes; however, hers was to remain for many years a minority view. More strident figures, following the lead of writers such as Hazlitt, wanted to replace the appeals to head and heart articulated by Wordsworth and Coleridge with a new language that would be clear, forceful and more broadly humane. Carlyle's impatience with what seemed to him obfuscation and pusillanimity made his the dominating voice of this new generation. When such an outlook was applied to the world of scientific investigation, however, and mainly to that, it ran the risk of becoming increasingly autocratic, bringing in its wake appeals to fascist authority, and even scientific programmes for the expunging of unfit human beings in the interests of racial improvement.

The hope nursed not only by Coleridge and Wordsworth, but also by Gaskell and Eliot, that a proper cultivation of head and heart might bring about the gradual elimination of baser human instincts was doomed to

---

[60] See his review, reprinted in *The Future of the Novel* (New York: Vintage Books, 1956), p. 89.
[61] 'Daniel Deronda: A Conversation', *Atlantic Monthly* 39 (December 1876), 684–94.

failure. Future development was not to take such an idealistic course. Yet their trust in the enduring wisdom implicit in the human traditions that they had learned to respect would not in the end prove to be without validity. While continued Romantic dealings with the word might include hopes for a revolutionary verbal apocalypse, true prophecy of the future of language turned out to involve recognizing that it could be developed only by transcending its very nature. In aligning herself with such perceptions, Eliot not only reverted to her long-maintained task of illuminating the diurnal by showing in a new way how the word might be made flesh and dwell among us, but affirmed, once again, her essential heritage from Coleridge – and even from the Wordsworth whose achievement remained her most enduring resource.

For Eliot, as for her Romantic predecessors, the very idea of language had split into constituent elements, so that from now on it would be hard to look to the force of words without invoking some sense of the need for them to be enlivened by the presence of some illumination or ardour in the human being who was speaking or writing. If such a decline was to be their fate, it would be by no means negative or fruitless; on the contrary the story of literature would be enriched by many new experiments and explorations of human sensibility. But the days of the word's undisputed authority had passed; and the growth of mechanical technology had opened the way for words themselves to be viewed as no more than dead things. As the century progressed, the triumph of the mechanical would become more and more absolute, until all its death-dealing propensities were unveiled in the mass destruction of the First World War. The world that remained would be, quite literally, a waste land, in which all was levelled to one dead level of reality. At the end of the tunnel lay the nightmare world revealed to Mrs Moore in Forster's Indian novel, where everything was reduced to the nullity of the Marabar Cave's sound, 'boum' – at which point the life of the human word virtually disappeared, to be replaced by the mantra 'Everything exists, nothing has value.' The words of religion – even of 'poor little talkative Christianity' – became utterly meaningless, since 'all its divine words from "Let there be light" to "It is finished" only amounted to "boum"'.[62] Those words, and the conclusion that they signified, did not mark the end of civilization, or, certainly, of significance itself; but they marked the end of that element in

---

[62] E. M. Forster, *A Passage to India* (London: Edward Arnold, 1924), end of chapter xiv.

the Romantic enterprise embodied in writers, ranging from Wordsworth and Coleridge to George Eliot and Forster himself, who had believed that cultivation of the heart might suffice to redress inequities produced by the dominance of the head. Henceforward, words would not cease to come alive and renew themselves eternally, but from now on other forms of human significance would also need to be honoured.

Index

JA Schwartz 'Worryfbbbt: Reacting Rancher, 'Minnesote 2012'.
Peter Otto, Multiplying Worlds, Romanticism, Modernity + the Emergence of Virtual Reality OUP 2011
A Regier, 'Fracture + Fragment in Br. Romaticism' CUP, 2012.

Lightning Source UK Ltd.
Milton Keynes UK
UKOW030411070213

205949UK00008B/222/P

9 781107 412620